effective
strategic leadership

John Adair is currently visiting professor in Leadership
Studies at the University of Exeter and an international
consultant to a wide variety of organizations in business,
government, the voluntary sector, education and health. He
has been named as one of the forty people worldwide who
have contributed most to the development of management
thought and practice.

Educated at St Paul's School, John Adair has enjoyed a
varied and colourful career. He served in the Arab Legion,
worked as a deckhand on an Arctic trawler and had a
spell as an orderly in a hospital operating theatre. After
Cambridge he became senior lecturer in Military History
and Leadership Training Adviser at the Royal Military
Academy, Sandhurst before becoming Director of Studies at
St George's House in Windsor Castle and then Assistant
Director of the Industrial Society. Later he became the
world's first professor in Leadership Studies at the
University of Surrey. He now writes extensively on
leadership, management and history, as well as working as
an international consultant.

John Adair is married with three children. He lives near
Guildford in Surrey.

Other titles in John Adair's
Effective Leadership and Management series:

effective time management
effective decision making
effective teambuilding
effective leadership
effective innovation
effective motivation
effective communication

All are available from Pan Books,
priced £6.99.

John Adair

effective
strategic leadership

PAN BOOKS

First published 2002 by Macmillan

This edition published 2003 by Pan Books
an imprint of Pan Macmillan Ltd
Pan Macmillan, 20 New Wharf Road, London N1 9RR
Basingstoke and Oxford
Associated companies throughout the world
www.panmacmillan.com

ISBN 0 330 48787 6

A CIP catalogue record for this book is available from
the British Library.

Printed and bound in Great Britain by
Mackays of Chatham plc, Chatham, Kent

CONTENTS

INTRODUCTION

There is a widespread sense that across the world – whether in industry and commerce, the public services, government or the voluntary sector – there are not enough really effective strategic leaders, at least not in the numbers required. This shortfall is actually a global phenomenon.

A strategic leader is essentially the leader of an organization. An *effective* strategic leader is one who delivers the goods in terms of what an organization naturally expects from its leadership in times of change.

This book is written primarily for those who aspire to become effective strategic leaders. You may already be head of an organization, or know that you are next in line for such a role, or you may simply be aware that the path of your vocation is leading you in that direction.

That doesn't exhaust the list of those who can read this book with profit! In large organizations there is – or should be – a strategic leadership team working under the conductor's baton of the head person. Obviously the more each member knows of the principles and practice of strategic leadership the better they can support and complement the contribution of their leader.

Do not assume, however, that this book only applies to those who work in large or medium-sized organizations. The body of knowledge and ideas, it contains, especially the parts relating to strategic thinking, is equally relevant to those in charge of small organizations, and indeed to those like myself who work in unstructured fields. As the Roman playwright Plautus said, '*Ergomet sum mihi imperator*' – 'I am myself my own commander.' Today each of us has to be our own strategic leader.

Leading the way – whether for an organization or for yourself – is never easy. I hope that this book equips you for the challenge and that you enjoy reading it too.

The book is largely self-explanatory. Part One maps and explores the sources and fundamentals of strategic leadership – as far as I can tell for the first time. Part Two moves on to what you have to do today to be effective in the role, focusing on five key themes. Since, as I have said, strategic leadership applies to us all, Part Three is much wider in scope. It tackles strategic thinking in your own life and career, examines what is important and long-term for your relations with others, and shows how to keep your inner fires of enthusiasm burning.

The idea that strategic leadership – *leading* your life – is a universal concept, one that is relevant to everyone, is so new that I doubt if this book will escape the fate of being classified, at least initially, as another management book. Yet there is material here for schools and universities as they gradually wake up to the challenge of helping young people to prepare for working life. 'To succeed in working life young people need to be equipped for lifelong learning and to be able to cope with change,' write the authors of *Preparation for Working Life* (1997), a report of the Qualifications and Curriculum Authority in the UK. They include *strategic thinking* and *integrity* on the new agenda.

As with other books in the *Effective* series, I have given as many case studies and practical examples as possible to illustrate the principles. You can skip the material in boxes if you like, or return to it on a second reading. The summary of Key Points at the end of each chapter is designed as a succinct *aide-mémoire*, but occasionally I throw in a new idea just to see if you are still awake! I have spared you checklists, but you can easily ask yourself questions as you go along in order to relate what I am saying to your own situation.

To get the best out of a book like this one, however, you do need to widen your span of relevance. By that I mean that we naturally look for examples or case studies in our own field, such as business or education, and deem these to be relevant. But to see relevance in the examples of say, an orchestral conductor or a Greek general to leading a company or a school does call for what I call a *wide span of relevance*. It is the same principle, incidentally, that lies behind creative thinking – the sparks of meaning jump between two or more apparently unconnected things to produce new ideas.

For my assumption is that there is an underlying unity in strategic leadership, whatever field you are in and however structured or unstructured your work in it may be. When you study effective strategic leaders in organizations or as individual contributors for yourself, encouraged I hope by these pages, you will be increasingly aware of how much they have in common. Therefore you can draw lessons and insights from many sources in order to grow as a strategic leader.

There are many paths to the top of the mountain
But the view is always the same.
Chinese proverb

PART ONE

UNDERSTANDING STRATEGIC LEADERSHIP

1

THE WORLD'S FIRST THOUGHTS

Those having torches will pass them on to others.
Plato

Words are sometimes like nuts: if you crack them open you discover the kernel of their meaning. *Strategy* is a case in point. It is made up of two ancient Greek words. The first part comes from *stratos*, which means an army spread out or a large body of people. The second part, *egy*, comes from the Greek verb to lead. There is a rough breathing mark in the Greek which explains the spelling of the English word *hegemony*, meaning the leadership one nation displays among others over others, which is derived from it.

It was Athens, rivalled only by Sparta, which claimed the hegemony of the Greek city states. Around 500 BC a senior commander in the Athenian army came to be called a *strategos*, leader of the army. The English word we use to translate this word is *general*. It literally means something (or someone) that is applicable to the whole. So a military *general* is accountable for the whole army as well as its parts.

In the Athenian citizen army during the fifth century BC, there were ten large units based on the old tribal strands in the city. Later in Athenian history these units were commanded by what we would call professional soldiers, but in the early days the ten *strategosi* were elected by their fellow citizens. To get elected a *strategos* was an important step on the political ladder for any ambitious young Athenian. Great leaders of the city state, such as Thermistocles and Pericles, had arisen by this very route. But the need for election acted as a hurdle: how could one get one's fellow citizens – the voters – to vote in one's favour? One man seems to have thought about this question – Socrates.

SOCRATES 'THE THINKER'

We tend to think of Socrates as an old man, but he was only about thirty-five years old when he began to be well known in Athens. By then he had served as a hoplite – a fully armed spearman – in at least three campaigns and carried himself with distinction. Indeed his courage and even heroism in battle became legendary. The gifted but wayward young general Alciabades tells us, for example, that during siege on the north Aegean coast Socrates saved his life when he was wounded and beset by enemies. He also remarked upon his friend's remarkable indifference to the bitter winter conditions, wearing his ordinary thin clothing and going barefoot in the snow.

The small group of young men who gathered around Socrates like moths at a lamp were drawn by both his remarkable intelligence and his personality. One of these 'Socratics' was Plato, who said of his master: 'Of all men whom we met at that time, he was the wisest, most just, and the best.' What sort of man did they see? In middle age Socrates presented an unusual appearance. He had a head like a satyr, it was said – snub-nosed, with wide nostrils, protruding eyes and thick lips – and a paunch. He wore simple threadbare clothes and still walked bare foot, but now with a peculiar limping gait. This was the man they nicknamed 'The Thinker'.

The son of a stonemason, Socrates constantly drew the analogy between the skills of artisans and craftsmen – the physician, the leather seller, the metal-worker – and the wider roles and responsibilities of a citizen's life, indeed that very life itself. All these practical skills can be learned by careful analysis, education and training and, where necessary, by experience, as everyone agreed. Socrates always professed himself unable to understand why the higher or more difficult arts – political leadership, statesmanship, the administration of justice – are not acknowledged to be susceptible of the same treatment. Instead, he observed, they are handed over to mere charlatans (like Thrasymachus the 'sophist' in Plato's *Republic* or demagogues like Cleon the leather seller and others of a similar kind described by Aristophanes and Thucydides).

Socrates himself wrote no books. Our principal sources of information about him are the writings of two of his inner circle: Plato and Xenophon. As they both wrote their various works in the form of Socratic dialogues it is not easy to determine whether the voice we hear is that of Socrates on the one hand or those of Plato and Xenophon on the other. But what is best called the situational theory of leadership – that in any situation people will tend to follow or obey the man or woman who knows what to do and how to do it – is found in both Plato and Xenophon and attributed to their master. It is a sound surmise that it goes back to Socrates himself. Both use the example of a ship's captain and his crew. Here is Plato's version from the *Republic*:

> The sailors are quarrelling over the control of the helm . . .
> they do not understand that the genuine navigator can only
> make himself fit to command a ship by studying the seasons
> of the year, sky, stars and winds, and all that belongs to his
> craft; and they have no idea that, along with the science of
> navigation, it is possible for him to gain, by instruction or
> practice, the skill to keep control of the helm whether some
> of them like it or not.

Encouraging others by confessing his own lack of knowledge, Socrates set out to think things through for himself
in discussion. Thereby he led his interlocutors on a journey
of the mind. Towards the end of it they began to see and
discover for themselves what knowledge or skill is required
in any human being. Socrates, essentially a philosopher,
believed that knowledge is virtue and virtue knowledge –
it is knowing the good and knowing how to seek it in any
circumstance. For Plato that journey would lead him ever
further away from the practical issues of living and working
that interested Socrates, far into the realm of abstract ideas,
the domain of philosophy which would for ever bear his
stamp. But his fellow student, Xenophon, would take a
very different course.

THE CASE OF THE YOUNG
CAVALRY COMMANDER

One day, Xenophon tells us, Socrates engaged in discussion
with a newly elected cavalry commander. As Xenophon
himself was elected to that office it is tempting to believe

that this is a piece of autobiography and he is describing here his first encounter with 'The Thinker'.

Under questioning from Socrates, the young man agreed that his seeking of the rank of commander could not have been because he wanted to be first in the cavalry charge, for, as Socrates pointed out, the mounted archers usually rode ahead of the commander into battle. Nor could it have been simply in order to get himself known by everyone – even madmen, he conceded, could achieve that. He accepted Socrates' suggestion that it must have been because he wanted to leave the Athenian cavalry in better condition than when he found it. Xenophon, both a renowned authority on horsemanship and the author of a textbook on commanding cavalry, had no difficulty in explaining what needs to be done to achieve that end. The young commander, for example, must improve the quality of the cavalry mounts; he must school new recruits – both horses and men – in equestrian skills and then teach the troopers their cavalry tactics. All these points emerged step by step out of the dialogue.

'And have you considered how to make the men obey you?' continued Socrates, 'Because without that, horses and men, however good and gallant, are of no use.'

'True, but what is the best way of encouraging them to obey, Socrates?' asked the young man.

'Well, I suppose you know that under all conditions human beings are most willing to obey those whom they believe to be the best. Thus in sickness they most readily obey the doctor, on board ship the pilot, on a farm the farmer, whom they think to be the most skilled in his business.'

'Yes, certainly,' said his student.

'Then it is likely that in horsemanship too, one who clearly knows best what ought to be done will most easily gain the obedience of the others.'

Xenophon captures here that very distinct theme in Socrates' teaching on leadership already identified above. In harmony with the rest of his doctrine (for, despite his pose of ignorance, Socrates had ideas of his own), it emphasizes the importance of *knowledge* in leadership. People will obey willingly only those whom they perceive to be better qualified or more knowledgeable than themselves in a particular situation.

THE CASE OF THE ASPIRING GENERAL

One of the young Athenians around Socrates announced that he wished to stand in the annual election of ten generals in the city's army. Socrates encouraged him to attend the classes of an itinerant teacher called Dionysodurus, who had recently arrived in Athens and advertised a course in generalship. When the young man returned he had to endure some good-humoured banter from Socrates and his friends.

'Don't you think, gentlemen,' said Socrates, 'that our friend looks more "majestic", as Homer called Agamemnon, now that he has learned generalship? For just as he who has learned to play the harp is a harper even when he does not play, and he who has studied medicine is a doctor even though he does not practise, so our friend will be a general for ever, even if no one votes for him. But an ignoramus is neither general nor doctor, even if he gets every vote. Now,' he continued, turning to the young Athenian, 'in order that any one of us who may happen to command a regiment or company under you may have a better knowledge of warfare, tell us the first lesson in generalship Dionysodurus gave you.'

'The first was like the last,' the young man replied. 'He taught me tactics – nothing else.'

'But that is only a small part of generalship,' replied Socrates. By question-and-answer he then led the young man into a much fuller understanding of the knowledge and abilities required for a successful military leader. A general must be good at administration, so that the army is properly supplied with military equipment and provisions. Moreover, as Xenophon knew from his own experience, a general should ideally possess a number of personal qualities and skills:

> He must be resourceful, active, careful, hardy and quick-witted; he must be both gentle and brutal, at once straightforward and designing, capable of both caution and surprise, lavish and rapacious, generous and mean, skilful in defence and attack, and there are many other qualifications, some natural, some acquired, that are necessary to one as a general.

Even on the all-important subject of tactics, Socrates found the instruction given to his young friend by Dionysodurus to be deficient. Did Dionysodurus give *no* advice on where and how to use each formation? Was *no* guidance given on when to modify deployments and tactics according to the needs of the many different kinds of situations one encounters in war? The young man insisted that this was the case. 'Then you must go back and ask for your money back,' said Socrates. 'For if Dionysodurus knows the answer to these questions and has a conscience, he will be ashamed to send you home ill-taught.'

In this Socratic dialogue, as in the previous one, Xenophon is offering instruction in the art of being a strategic
leader. What he is doing is helping his young listeners to
form a complete *concept* of strategic leadership, in contrast
to the limited or imperfect notion of it offered by Dionysodurus and his kind. The Socratic view is roughly that
what prevents you from being a good leader is – in the first
place – that you do not have a *true* concept of strategic
leadership. If you could but *see* the truth, then you could
hardly prevent yourself from moving towards it.

Although neither Athens nor any of the other Greek
cities had any business schools, the figure of the itinerant
guru speaking to large audiences for fat fees on such
subjects as the art of public speaking, generalship, or how
to be happy and successful was a familiar one. These
sophists, as they were called, were clever men, some more
than others, known for their adroit, subtle, plausible reason-
ing but lacking in substance. Socrates and other philoso-
phers regarded them as glib, superficial and out for money
(Socrates himself did not charge fees).

Often, as in the case of Dionysodurus, the sophists did
not really know what they were talking about. When
Hannibal – arguably one of the ten greatest generals of all
time – was in exile at the end of his long career, his host
Antiochus, the Greek king of Syria, took him to hear a
lecture by an elderly sophist who specialized in military
leadership. 'Well, what did you think of it?' Antiochus
inquired at the end. Hannibal looked at the king with his
one remaining eye and replied in his characteristically dry,
laconic, humorous way: 'In my time I have had to listen to
some old fools, but this one beats them all!'

THE CASE OF NICOMACHIDES

Once, on seeing Nicomachides returning from the elections, Socrates asked him, 'Who have been chosen generals, Nicomachides?'

'Isn't it just like the Athenians?' Nicomachides replied. 'They have not chosen me after all the hard work I have done since I was called up, in the command of company or regiment, though I have been so often wounded in action.' (Here he uncovered and showed his scars.) 'They have chosen Antisthenes, who has never served in a marching regiment nor distinguished himself in the cavalry and understands nothing but money-making.'

'Isn't that a recommendation,' said Socrates, 'supposing he proves capable of supplying the men's needs?'

'Why,' retorted Nicomachides, 'merchants also are capable of making money, but that doesn't make them fit to command an army!'

'But,' replied Socrates, 'Antisthenes also is eager for victory, and that is a good point in a general. Whenever he has been choir-master, you know, his choir has always won.'

'No doubt,' conceded Nicomachides, 'but there is no analogy between the handling of a choir and of an army.'

'But you see,' said Socrates, 'though Antisthenes knows nothing about music or choir training, he showed himself capable of finding the best experts in these activities. And therefore if he finds out and prefers the best men in warfare as in choir training, it is likely that he will be victorious in that too; and probably he will be more ready to spend money on winning a battle with the whole state than on winning a choral competition with his tribe.'

'Do you mean to say, Socrates, that the man who succeeds with a chorus will also succeed with an army?'

'I mean that, whatever a man controls, if he knows what he wants and can get it he will be a good controller, whether he controls a chorus, an estate, a city or an army.'

'Really, Socrates,' cried Nicomachides, 'I should never have thought to hear you say that a good businessman would make a good general!'

By his familiar method of patient cross-examination, Socrates won agreement from Nicomachides that successful businessmen and generals perform much the same functions. Then Socrates proceeded to identify six of these functions or skills:

- Selecting the right man for the right job;
- Punishing the bad and rewarding the good;
- Winning the goodwill of those under them;
- Attracting allies and helpers;
- Keeping what they have gained;
- Being strenuous and industrious in their own work.

'All these are common to both,' Nicomachides accepted, 'but fighting is not.'

'But surely both are bound to find enemies?'

'Oh yes, they are.'

'Then is it not important for both to get the better of them?'

'Undoubtedly; but you don't say how business capacity will help when it comes to fighting.'

'That is just where it will be most helpful,' Socrates concluded. 'For the good businessman, through his knowledge that nothing profits or pays like a victory in the field, and nothing is so utterly unprofitable and entails such heavy loss as a defeat, will be eager to seek and avoid what leads to defeat, will be prompt to engage the enemy if he sees he is strong enough to win, and, above all, will avoid an engagement when he is not ready.'

The amazement expressed by Nicomachides at Socrates' line of argument in this dialogue rings true. For the teaching of Socrates, that people will only follow leaders who have the authority of knowledge relevant to a given situation, must have been well known in Athens. Moreover, in that city, as in Britain during much of this century, businessmen were held in low social regard. Young gentlemen from good Athenian families would seek military and political careers, but they did not become merchants. Of course the scale of commerce and industry before the Industrial Revolution was relatively small and the scope for leadership was correspondingly limited. Armies and navies, by contrast, remained the largest and most important forms of common human enterprise until relatively recent times. In the mid-eighteenth century, for example, the Royal Navy was the largest industry in Western Europe.

Socrates did challenge this Athenian snobbery that has cast such a long shadow in history. 'Don't look down on businessmen, Nicomachides,' he said towards the end of their discussion. 'For the management of private concerns differs only in point of number from that of public affairs. In other respects they are much alike, and particularly in this, that neither can be carried on without men, and the men employed in private and public transactions are the same. For those who take charge of public affairs employ just the same men when they attend to their own; and those who do understand how to employ them are successful directors of public and private concerns, and those who do not, fail in both.'

AUTHORITY FLOWS TO THE
ONE WHO KNOWS

Socrates, then, clearly taught that professional or technical competence should be a prerequisite for holding a position of leadership responsibility. Here Xenophon and Plato are doing more than handing on that torch to us. 'You must have noticed', said Socrates, 'that a man who is incompetent does not attempt to exercise authority over our harpists, choristers, and dancers, nor over wrestlers. All who have authority over them can tell you where they learned their business.'

The tendency of people to follow a leader who knows what to do, observed Socrates, is strengthened in a time of crisis. In a discussion with Pericles, named after his father, the famous statesman, which took place when an army from the Greek state of Boeotia was threatening Athens, Socrates made the additional point that such a crisis should be more to an effective leader's liking than a period of ease and prosperity, for it is easier to make things happen. He illustrated this point with an analogy, the behaviour of sailors at sea:

> For confidence breeds carelessness, slackness, disobedience: fear makes men more attentive, more obedient, more amenable to discipline. The behaviour of sailors is a case in point. So long as they have nothing to fear, they are, I believe, an unruly lot, but when they expect a storm or an attack, they not only carry out all orders, but watch in silence for the word of command like choristers.

In spite of his own military experience which must have given many a glimpse from the serried ranks of the phalanx of the competencies or incompetencies of the various generals he had served under, Socrates conducted these discussions on a general level, as befits a philosopher and teacher. But Xenophon was shortly to find himself in military command and faced with a real crisis. The teaching of Socrates would now be tested and shaped in the hot forge of experience.

Apparently against the advice of Socrates, Xenophon enlisted in a Greek army which the Persian prince Cyrus the Younger hired in a bid to replace his brother Artaxerxes II on the throne of Persia. In 401 BC a decisive battle was fought at Cunaxa, not far from ancient Babylon. The 10,400 Greek hoplites acquitted themselves well on the day, but Cyrus lost both the battle and his life.

After the battle of Cunaxa, the Persians offered the Ten Thousand (as the Greeks were later known) surrender terms if they stayed where they were, but threatened to kill them all if they moved from their camp. In this crisis the man of authority was the most experienced of the six Greek generals – Clearchus the Spartan. He took the burden of decision upon himself.

Clearchus indicated that he would act as spokesman for his fellow generals to the Persian emissaries, but gave no indication to anyone what he was going to say. After sunset he summoned a meeting of the officers, briefly reviewed the options and then told them what they must do. They must head northwards that very night on the first stage of a long march to safety on the shores of the Black Sea, which lay some 800 miles away. As Xenophon records in *The Persian Expedition*, everyone sensed that only Clearchus could lead them out of mortal danger:

On receiving their instructions the generals and captains went away and carried them out; and from then on Clearchus was in command, and they were his subordinates. This was not the result of an election, but because they realized that he was the one man who had the right sort of mind for a commander, while the rest of them were inexperienced.

ARE KNOWLEDGE AND EXPERIENCE ENOUGH?

But is having knowledge and experience relevant to the situation – the general working field or the particular situation of crisis – the *whole* of leadership? Xenophon knew that it was not so. From his close observation of men in action, he made a distinction between those leaders who won *willing* obedience from their subordinates and colleagues, as compared to those who merely extracted compliance from them either out of fear or a grudging acceptance of the authority of knowledge.

Clearchus, the Spartan general who saved the day after Cunaxa, is a good example of such a limited leader. We can recognize men of his stamp again and again in military history. The Roman army depended upon men such as him. Their type would resurface in later armed forces: the Prussians of Frederick the Great, the British Royal Navy in Georgian times, the German *Wehrmacht* in the Second World War, and the American Army in Vietnam.

Clearchus was about fifty at the time of his death. He had spent much of his life at war, acquiring by hard experience a sound knowledge of his profession. But, as Xenophon noted, Clearchus never won the hearts of men.

He had no followers who were there because of friendship
or good feeling towards him. Xenophon continued:

As for his great qualities as a soldier, they appear in the facts
that he was fond of adventure, ready to lead an attack on the
enemy by day or night, and that, when he was in an
awkward position, he kept his head, as everyone agrees
who was with him anywhere. It was said that he had all the
qualities of leadership which a man of his sort could have.

He had an outstanding ability for planning means by
which an army could get supplies, and seeing that they
appeared; and he was also well able to impress on those
who were with him that Clearchus was a man to be obeyed.
He achieved this result by his toughness. He had a forbidding
appearance and a harsh voice. His punishments were severe
ones and were sometimes inflicted in anger, so that there
were times when he was sorry himself for what he had done.
With him punishment was a matter of principle, for he thought
that any army without discipline was good for nothing;
indeed, it is reported that he said that a soldier ought to be
more frightened of his own commander than of the enemy if
he was going to turn out one who could keep a good guard,
or abstain from doing harm to his own side, or going into
battle without second thoughts.

So it happened that in difficult positions the soldiers would
give him complete confidence and wished for no one better.
On these occasions, they said that his forbidding look seemed
positively cheerful, and his toughness appeared as confidence in the face of the enemy, so that it was no longer
toughness to them but something to make them feel safe. On
the other hand, when the danger was over and there was a
chance of going away to take service under someone else,
many of them deserted him, since he was invariably tough

and savage, so that the relations between his soldiers and
him were like those of boys to a schoolmaster.

It is tempting to conclude that while Clearchus had great
abilities as a soldier, and also as what we would now call a
manager, he fell far short as a leader. One reason why
people today often react so negatively to the idea of military
leadership is because they assume that all military leaders
are cast in the same mould as Clearchus. This is certainly
not the case.

Xenophon's last point, that Clearchus treated his soldiers
like a *pedagogue* (literally in Greek a 'leader of children') is
illuminating. The Greeks prided themselves on the belief
that they were the most intelligent people on the face of
the earth; they were deeply conscious, too, of their tradition
of equality and democracy. They did not like being bullied
or treated as children.

Xenophon, aged twenty-six, was elected as one of the
successors to Clearchus and the other five Greek generals
whom the Persians butchered in an act of treachery not
long after Cunaxa. Having been taught leadership by
Socrates, what style of leadership would Xenophon display?
Doubtless he thought hard about that question. Obviously
he did not want to be another Clearchus, nor did he want
to err too far in the opposite direction of courting popularity and appearing weak. Xenophon tells us that Proxenus
the Boeotian, one of the other murdered generals, had made
that mistake. It was he, incidentally, who had first invited
Xenophon to go on the Persian expedition, and so they
were probably friends. Proxenus was a very ambitious
young man and had spent much money on being educated
by a celebrated teacher called Gorgias of Leontini. 'After he
had been with him for a time,' wrote Xenophon, 'he came

to the conclusion that he was now capable of commanding an army and, if he became friends with the great, of doing them no less good than they did him; so he joined in this adventure planned by Cyrus, imagining that he would gain from it a great name, and great power, and plenty of money.' Yet, with all these ambitions, Proxenus made it clear to all that he wanted to acquire these things in a fair and honourable way or not at all. He liked to be liked, however, which led him into the mistake of appearing soft and of courting popularity for its own sake:

> He was a good commander for people of a gentlemanly type, but he was not capable of impressing his soldiers with a feeling of respect or fear for him. Indeed, he showed more diffidence in front of his soldiers than his subordinates showed in front of him, and it was obvious that he was more afraid of being unpopular with his troops than his troops were afraid of disobeying his orders. He imagined that to be a good general, and to gain the name for being one, it was enough to give praise to those who did well and to withhold it from those who did badly. The result was that decent people in his entourage liked him, but unprincipled people undermined his position, since they thought he was easily managed. At the time of his death he was about thirty years old.

It could be said that Proxenus was not right for the military situation and could not establish the right relationship with his soldiers. But he would probably have been just as ineffective in non-military spheres of leadership as well. For Proxenus' very virtues created a certain lack of firmness or toughness which can lead to a loss of respect. Without respect, leadership is fatally impaired. A weak leader exposes himself to exploitation by his more unscrupulous subordinates. Bad leadership of this kind looks remarkably the same whatever the field or area of human enterprise.

Xenophon, who sat at the feet of Socrates, the Western world's first great teacher of leadership, now shows us what *he* meant by leadership.

A LEADER IN ACTION

Imagine yourself on a sun-baked, stony hillside on the southern edge of Kurdistan (on the borders of what is now Iraq and Turkey) watching this scene unfold before you. It is about noon; the sky is clear blue except for a line of white clouds almost motionless above a distant mountain range. Marching through these foothills come the advance guards of the Ten Thousand. The hot sun glints and sparkles on their spears, helmets and breastplates. They are hurrying forward, eager to reach the safety of the mountains in order to be rid of the Persian cavalry snapping like hunting dogs at their heels. But first they have to cut their way through the Carduci, the warlike natives of the region. Across the pass you can see a strong contingent of these tribesmen already occupying the lower heights of a steep hill which commands the road. Now the Greek advance guard has spotted them too, and it halts. After some hurried deliberations you can see a messenger running back. A few minutes later a horseman – it is Xenophon – gallops up to the commander of the advance guard, a seasoned Spartan captain named Chirisophus. Xenophon tells him that he has not brought up a reinforcement of the light-armed troops that had been urgently requested because the rearguard – still under constant attack – could not be weakened. Then he carefully studies the lie of the land. Noticing that the Carduci have neglected to occupy the actual summit of the hill, he puts his plan to his Spartan colleague:

'The best thing to do, Chirisophus, is for us to advance on the summit as fast as we can. If we can occupy it, those who are commanding our road will not be able to maintain their position. If you like, you stay here with the main body. I will volunteer to go ahead. Or, if you prefer it, you march on the mountain and I will stay here.'

'I will give you the choice', replies Chirisophus, 'of doing whichever you like.'

It would be an arduous physical task, Xenophon points out, and he tactfully says that being the younger man he would be the best one to undertake it. Having chosen some 400 skirmishers, armed with targets and light javelins, together with 100 handpicked pikemen of the advance guard, he marches them off as fast as he can towards the summit. But when the enemy see what the Greeks are doing, they too begin to head for the highest ground as fast as they can go.

Then there was a lot of shouting, from the Greek army cheering on its men on the one side and from Tissaphernes' people cheering on their men on the other side. Xenophon rode along the ranks on horseback, urging them on. 'Soldiers,' he said, 'consider that it is for Greece you are fighting now, that you are fighting your way to your children and your wives, and that with a little hard work now, we shall go on the rest of our way unopposed.

Soteridas, a man from Sicyon, said: 'We are not on a

level, Xenophon. You are riding on horseback, while I am
wearing myself out with a shield to carry.'

Although he could conceivably have had him arrested and
punished later, Xenophon did not take this course. Writing
of himself in the third person, he tells us what happened
next:

> When Xenophon heard this, he jumped down from his horse,
> pushed Soteridas out of the ranks, took his shield away from
> him and went forward on foot as fast as he could, carrying
> the shield. He happened to be wearing a cavalry breastplate
> as well, so that it was heavy going for him. He kept on
> encouraging those in front to keep going and those behind
> to join up with them, though struggling along behind them
> himself. The other soldiers, however, struck Soteridas and
> threw stones at him and cursed him until they forced him to
> take back his shield and continue marching. Xenophon then
> remounted and, so long as the going was good, led the way
> on horseback. When it became impossible to ride, he left his
> horse behind and hurried ahead on foot. And so they got to
> the summit before the enemy.

Note that it was the other soldiers who shamed Soteridas
into taking back his shield. Although Xenophon, burdened
with a heavy cavalry breastplate, eventually fell back behind
the ranks as the men rushed up the hill, yet he encouraged
the men forward and urged them to keep their battle order.
Eventually he remounted and led his soldiers from the
front, at first on horse and then again on foot.

Once the Greeks had gained the summit the Carduci
turned and fled in all directions. The Persian cavalry under

Tissaphernes, who had been distant onlookers of the contest, also turned their bridles and withdrew.

Then Chirisophus' men in the vanguard of the army were able to descend through the mountain pass into a fertile plain beside the Tigris. There they refreshed themselves before facing the fearsome rigours of a winter march amid the snow-covered Armenian highlands. Eventually, in the summer of the following year, the army reached the safety of the Hellespont, the narrow straits dividing Europe from Asia. They owed much to Xenophon who, not long afterwards, became the sole commander of the Ten Thousand.

Anyone reading this story will recognize that in it Xenophon acted as a leader. He led by example. That is a universal principle or theme in the story of leadership. It is especially important where people face hardship or danger: they expect their leaders to run the same risks and shoulder the same burdens as themselves, or at least to show a willingness to do so.

The story of Xenophon's assault on the Carduci illustrates another cardinal principle of leadership. Leaders *encourage* people. They renew spirits, giving others fresh courage to pursue the common course of action. Xenophon's words and deeds infused the Greeks with new confidence and resolution. His brave example inspired them.

A LEADER IN ESTATE MANAGEMENT

After the expedition Xenophon continued to serve as a military commander. He seems to have fallen in love with the profession of arms, though he was also a man of wide-ranging interests. As Athens was in turmoil, Socrates was judicially put to death by enforced suicide about this time – Xenophon chose to live in exile with the Spartans whom he much admired. Not until towards the end of his life did he return home to Athens, and by then he had written some sixteen books and was renowned as one of the most prolific authors in antiquity. Contemporary history, tracts on hunting and horse riding, constitutional studies, texts for educating the young: all flowed from his ready pen. Alexander the Great and Hannibal read and profited from Xenophon's thoughts on leadership. The Romans especially admired him, Julius Caesar and Cicero foremost among them.

For his services to Sparta over many years Xenophon received as a reward a large estate at Scillus, near Mount Olympus, where he lived with his wife and family. It was run as a profit-making business as well as a private estate. Xenophon's book called *Oeconomicus* in Greek (from *oikono-mus*, household manager) is the world's first inquiry into the body of laws or branch of knowledge that relates to the management of estates. From the same word we derive our concept of *economy* and the study known today as *economics*. Incidentally, our English word *manage* also derives in part from the management or control of horses. (The first school of management that opened in London in the reign of Queen Elizabeth I was attended by horses and their riders.) Xenophon's book *On Horsemanship* is the oldest extant complete work on the subject, written with all the authority of an expert.

Xenophon did not have much to say about the management of accounts, the origin of our economics. But he was naturally interested in the way that an estate manager – if he was a good leader – could affect the spirits of men at work in the estate fields. He saw a clear parallel here between leadership in the harvest field and leadership on the battlefield: both, he observed with a scientist's eye, had the same positive effect on men.

'Nobody can be a good farmer,' Xenophon wrote,

> unless he makes his labourers both eager and obedient; and the captain who leads men against an enemy must contrive to secure the same results by rewarding those who act as brave men should act as punishing the disobedient. And it is no less necessary for the farmer to encourage his labourers often, than for a general to encourage his men. And slaves need the stimulus of good hopes no less, nay, even more than free men, to make them steadfast.

This general leadership ability, as relevant to agriculture as to politics or war, was often absent, he noted, in those who held positions of authority. Xenophon instanced the Greek warships of his day, which were rowed by free men and not by slaves.

> On a man-of-war, when the ship is on the high seas and the rowers must toil all day to reach port, some rowing-masters can say and do the right thing to sharpen the men's spirits and make them work with a will. Other boatswains are so unintelligent that it takes them more than twice the time to finish the same voyage. Here they land bathed in sweat, with mutual congratulations, rowing-master and seamen. There they arrive with dry skin; they hate their master and he hates them.

Xenophon's mind ranged back to the generals he had known, who also differed widely from one another in this respect.

> For some make their men unwilling to work and to take risks, disinclined and unwilling to obey, except under compulsion, and actually proud of defying their commander: yes, and they cause them to have no sense of dishonour when something disgraceful occurs. Contrast the genius, the brave and skilful leader: let him take over the command of these same troops, or of others if you like. What effect has he on them? They are ashamed to do a disgraceful act, think it better to obey, and take a pride in obedience, working cheerfully, every man and all together, when it is necessary to work. Just as a love of work may spring up in the mind of a private soldier here and there, so a whole army under the influence of a good leader is inspired by love of work and ambition to distinguish itself under the commander's eye. Let this be the feeling of the rank and file for their commander, then he is the best leader – it is not a matter of being the best with bow and javelin, nor riding the best horse and being foremost in danger, nor being the perfect mounted warrior, but of being able to make his soldiers feel that they must follow him through fire and in any adventure. So, too, in private industries, the man in authority – bailiff or manager – who can make the workers keen, industrious and persevering – he is the man who gives a lift to the business and swells the profits.

ARE LEADERS BORN OR MADE?

For Xenophon, this kind of leadership is quite simply 'the greatest thing in every operation that makes any demand on the labour of men'. If leaders are made in the sense that they can acquire the authority of knowledge, are they born as far as the capacity to inspire is concerned? It is tempting to conclude that this is the case. The ability to give people the intellectual and moral strength to venture or persevere in the presence of danger, fear or difficulty is not the common endowment of all men and women. Xenophon, however, did believe that at least the basic principles of it could be acquired through education, as he had experienced himself with Socrates.

'Mind you, I do not go as far as to say that this can be learnt at sight or at a single hearing,' he wrote in the conclusion of *Oeconomicus*. 'On the contrary, to acquire these powers a man needs education.' Natural potential is most important, he continues. But in some men leadership amounts to a gift, something akin to genius which suggests something more of divine origin than human. This 'power to win willing obedience' may seem ultimately as if it is a gift of the gods, writes Xenophon, but it is not capriciously bestowed. The true beneficiaries of it are 'those who devote themselves to seeking wisdom'. There speaks the voice of Socrates!

SUMMARY OF KEY POINTS

This chapter has been devoted to the world's first thoughts – in the person of Xenophon – on strategic leadership. He saw it as a transferable art or skill, and identified its essential principles for the first time. Although nature equipped men and women for leadership – some even having a gift for it – even the best could only develop their natural ability by experience and education. Here is Xenophon's legacy to us:

- Leadership is done from in front. Never ask others to do what you, if challenged, would not be willing to do yourself.

- A leader must be technically and professionally competent in his or her field. You must know your business. This is the main necessary condition for winning respect and trust. It applies to women as well as to men – Xenophon instanced the weaving industry in Athens as one where women were accepted as leaders. *Authority flows to the one who knows.*

- A leader shares fully in the risks, hardships and dangers of the army or workforce. 'Many have often seen him lying on the ground wrapped only in a military cloak amid the sentries and outposts of his soldiers,' wrote the Roman historian Livy of Rome's great enemy, Hannibal. Lead by example.

- A leader inspires others by encouraging them in times of difficulty or challenge, expressing confidence in them and in their ability to surmount the hurdles before them. You can lift people's spirits with a word of encouragement and support.

- A leader reminds people of why they are working and striving – for self, family and comrades certainly, but for that which transcends self.

- A leader has to be firm and just in maintaining necessary order. Without a certain toughness in this regard you will not win the respect of the group as a whole.

- A leader should show humanity, a basic empathy with people. Rejoice with others when any good befalls them, and sympathize when ills overtake them, as they can us all. Give practical help to individual team members in any kind of need where you can do so.

- Above all, a leader is *there* – at the right time and place.

Never underestimate the positive influence that your very presence can exert in a situation.

There is a small risk a leader will be regarded with contempt by those he leads if, whatever he may have to preach, he shows himself best able to perform.
Xenophon

2

THE MILITARY ROOTS OF STRATEGIC LEADERSHIP

Dux erat ille ducum.
(He was leader of leaders.)
Ovid, *Heroides*

'Do you know when managers began to talk about strategy?' Peter Drucker asked during the course of a seminar we were leading together.

'I imagine it was sometime . . . no, I really don't know,' I replied. 'When was it?'

'In 1964 I submitted a book to my American publisher,' he said, 'which I had called *Management Strategy*. They insisted that I should change the title as "strategy" was a military term and business executive readers would either not understand it or perceive it as irrelevant. So it appeared as *Management for Results*.'

'Where did the idea come from to bring in the concept in the first place?' I asked.

'I believe it stemmed from Robert McNamara in the Kennedy era,' Drucker replied. 'McNamara moved between heading up the Pentagon as Secretary of Defense to being President of the Ford Motor Company.'

In fact one or two books did appear about that time which used the word *strategy* in the business context, notably Alfred Chandler's *Strategy and Structure: Chapters in the History of American Enterprise* (1962) and Igor Ansoff's *Corporate Strategy* (1965). But, as far as I know, I was the first to introduce the concept of strategic leadership in the 1980s and it is now in wide use.

Originally, as we have seen, strategy (*strategia* in Greek) meant strategic leadership – the art of being a commander-in-chief. But the ancient Greek authors were reflecting military use where strategy is distinguished from tactics and studied as a thing in itself. In fact, strategy in this later and narrower sense is the *thinking* appropriate to a commander-in-chief, as opposed to the thinking required in commanders at lower levels. That is a subject I shall return to in Chapter 7.

Therefore, inadvertently and through no fault of their own, these early business gurus were making the same errors as Dionysodurus. They were mistaking a part for the whole and also teaching it in an academic and wooden manner.

'*Ad Fontes*' – 'Back to the Fountains' – was the personal motto of the Renaissance scholar Thomas Linacre, an eminent doctor and a founder member of the Royal College of Physicians. In order to understand the concept of strategic leadership we must explore its roots in the tangled undergrowth of military history which stretches back 2,500 years to the Age of Xenophon. Only by this process can we root out some of the misconceptions that, like gigantic weeds, tend to dominate the modern idea of a strategic leader.

THE OVER-EMPHASIS OF STRATEGY

Just as in the days of Xenophon battlefield tactics was only one aspect of *strategia*, not the whole, so in later times campaign strategy was only one aspect of being a commander-in-chief, not the whole. The misconception that campaign strategy is the *dominant* work of a general is comparatively recent in origin. It has led to an over-emphasis on the importance of strategic thinking.

Veni, vidi, vici. As the proverbial schoolboy knows, 'I came, I saw, I conquered' is Julius Caesar's laconic summary of his campaign in Gaul. Although not the first general to write a memoir of his campaigns – Xenophon has that to his credit – Caesar certainly was not the last. Like his successors, however, he tells us virtually nothing about strategy or about himself as a strategic thinker.

The tendency to equate strategy with strategic leadership or generalship in the military field really dates from the twentieth century, paradoxically at a time when the evolution of telecommunications was eroding more and more of a general's freedom of action.

Given the realities of the situation, strategy in the military field is usually simple. It is also commonly the product of many minds. When generals in modern times – Montgomery is a good example – write their memoirs, especially if they tend to be egotistical, they exaggerate their own role in devising strategy and correspondingly denigrate the contribution from others, be it their superiors, colleagues or predecessors.

CASE STUDY: LAWRENCE OF ARABIA

T. E. Lawrence was in his late twenties when he found himself in Cairo during the First World War, working in military intelligence. The Arab Revolt broke out when the Arabs in the Hejas (now part of Saudi Arabia) rose up against the Turks, who were allies of Germany. The British saw the opportunity of exploiting the rising to cause a diversion on the Turkish flank while their main forces under General Allenby advanced against the Turkish field army in the Sinai and Palestine. Lawrence was employed as a junior envoy to the members of Hashemite family who led the revolt, and then gradually became their resident political adviser.

Lawrence's main role was political liaison with Cairo. As such he was the principal conduit for British rifles, reinforcements and gold – especially important for keeping the irregular Bedouin tribal forces in the field. So he had some power and influence. Soon he began to stand out amongst the small community of British officers, soldiers and advisers who had been sent out to get the Sharif of Mecca's army into a state where it could afflict some damage on the Turks – no easy task.

Authority flows to the one who knows. Although totally lacking in military experience, Lawrence did have knowledge that few of the other British present possessed. Having been an archaeologist in the region, he had a good command of colloquial Arabic. He also had a detailed knowledge of the Turkish army and its neighbouring formations. Added to this situationally relevant knowledge, Lawrence had a natural gift for leadership which responded to and met the need of the moment. For Lawrence had a passion for the Arab cause – freedom and independence – which outstripped the rather more mixed motives of some of the Arab leaders themselves. To this zeal he added boundless energy, integrity, toughness of mind and body and the ability to communicate brilliantly by word or on paper.

To the amusement of the senior British officers, Lawrence cast himself in the role of commander-in-chief and principal strategist. He took part in military operations and as the Bedouin looked to British officers, however young, for leadership, he found himself expected to lead from the front, with the tribesmen eager to follow. Raids on the Hejaz railway, the capture of Aqaba and a major skirmish won him a decoration for gallantry – based solely on his own despatches it must be added, though there is no reason to doubt Lawrence's bravery. He was even recommended for the Victoria Cross, but, as he put it, they do not give that for 'brainy leadership' – his real contribution.

By 'brainy leadership' Lawrence implied that he thought up the tactics on hit-and-run raids on the Hejaz railway and the strategic direction of the Arab Revolt as a whole. Later British commentators tended to take him at his word and ascribe to Lawrence the concept of what we call now guerrilla warfare. Yet guerrilla war (from the Spanish *guerra*, war) – small bands operating independently against a stronger and more organized force with surprise attacks – dates back to the Peninsular War (1808–14).

Lawrence was above average in intelligence. He had gained a First in Modern History at Oxford and he was able to read the Greek classics in Greek. He studied Xenophon's account of the march of the Ten Thousand, an epic that served as a template for his own *Seven Pillars of Wisdom*. He was widely read, too, in the modern theorists of war, such as Clausewitz. Like Proxenus, Lawrence thought himself thereby qualified to be a commander-in-chief, the role he believed that *faute de mieux* he now occupied.

In his book Lawrence describes an episode early in 1917 when parts of the nascent Arab Army were half-heartedly attacking the Turkish garrison of Medina to their rear prior to moving northwards. Falling ill with dysentery and fever, he lay in his tent for eight days. It was here, he claimed, that he realized the unimportance of taking Medina. Why bother when out of every 1,000 miles of the Hejaz 999 were already free? The Hejaz War was already as good as won.

> When it grew too hot for dreamless dozing, I picked up my tangle again, and went on ravelling it out, considering now the whole house of war in its structural aspect, which was strategy, in its arrangements, which were tactics, and in the sentiment of its inhabitants, which was psychology; for my personal duty was command, and the commander, like the master architect, was responsible for all.

The commander-in-chief was in fact the Emir Feisal, whom Lawrence claimed to have more or less selected on behalf of the British in preference to his two brothers. As his chief political adviser, Lawrence was in a good position to influence Feisal to stir the Arab Army into moving northwards with more speed, so that it could thereby fulfil its (British) role as a diversionary side-show. According to Lawrence, in the course of the endless work chivvying the Arabs northwards, he was the first to identify Damascus as the strategic goal of the campaign.

Again we must take this claim with a pinch of salt. The ambitious Hashemite brothers already had their eye on the northern Arab states. Moreover, as a strategic goal for the campaign there was no other option but Damascus.

Jerusalem would fall to Allenby's army, Istanbul was an impossibility and Baghdad lay in the wrong direction. But an epic needs a destination! In fact the Bedouin irregulars of the Arab Army, accompanied by Lawrence, were not the first into Damascus – the Australians beat them to it – but at least they made it.

THE ART OF GENERALSHIP

If we look at it historically, strategy – strategic thinking and planning – is never more than half of what a commander-in-chief, the prototypical strategic leader, should be doing. War is like wrestling, playing chess or making love in that there are only a finite number of possibilities. These strategic options are easily available to a general of average or above-average intelligence who knows his business and has served his apprenticeship under other commanders good or bad.

WELLINGTON LEARNS HIS LESSONS

The British Army in the later eighteenth century was unprofessional, inadequately trained and under-resourced. Any coherent system of command and control and of administration, and any tradition of commitment and loyalty were lacking. Wellington had acquired first-hand experience of the situation during the Duke of York's disastrous campaign in the Netherlands in 1794–5, 'I learned more by seeing our own faults, and the defects of our system in the campaign in Holland than anywhere else,' he claimed and later observed that 'I learned what one ought not to do, and that is always something.' During the next twenty years, first in India, then in the Peninsula, he set about creating an army with a sense of confidence and achievement that could and would defeat Napoleon.

Even the strategic ideas are simple. Since the study of Napoleon's campaigns one of the chief ones has been 'concentration of force'. The underlying principle here is the concentration of superior force at the decisive time and place, the main point of effort, while economizing elsewhere. For it is impossible to be strong everywhere and, if decisive strength is to be concentrated at the critical time and place, there must be no wasteful expenditure of effort and resources which cannot significantly affect the issue.

'Surprise' is another example of a basic strategic idea. The Greeks called on artifice, or tricks, in war for surprising, deceiving and outwitting an enemy and a *stratagema*, (derived from *strategia*), to be a general. From it we derive our word stratagem. Surprise always acts as a bonus in war, and it can have a devastating effect on an enemy not least for psychological reasons: its elements are secrecy, timely intelligence, deception, concealment, audacity and speed. Timing is the key factor. It may be difficult to achieve at strategic level, but even so, it may still be achieved at operational and team levels. Surprise of itself doesn't deliver success, but it is often a principal factor in achieving it.

Strategy will always be a simple matter, with some surprises thrown in for good measure. But, as Clausewitz said, 'In war what counts is doing simple things, but in war it is very difficult to do simple things.' It is overcoming these areas of difficulty – quite apart from strategy – that constitutes the other core elements in the art of the commander-in-chief. 'Strategy' is only one exam paper that a general has to answer in the field; here are three others of equal importance.

MORALE

How do you build and sustain the spirit of the army as a whole? How can you restore confidence if it has suffered reverses? How can you generate the will to win?

General Eisenhower had to take a crash course in strategic leadership in order to pass this exam paper. He had no direct experience of war when he was appointed as commander-in-chief of the American Army which landed in North Africa in 1943. Rommel's experienced panzer troops inflicted a severe defeat on the Americans at Casserine Pass. In his headquarters in Gibraltar, Eisenhower was despondent. But he learned there the most important lesson of all. Optimism spreads down from the Supreme Commander, but pessimism spreads down even faster. He saw that it was critical in a leadership role to exude optimism and to radiate a sense of self-confidence. 'I firmly determined', he said later, 'that my mannerisms and speech would always reflect cheerful certainty. Without optimism in command, victory is scarcely attainable.'

Morale is the mental and emotional attitude of a person or a group to the function or task expected of them. It comes from the French *moral*, respelt to indicate stress of pronunciation (like the word *locale*). Cicero invented the word *moral* in Latin as a translation of the Greek *ethikos*, pertaining to a person's character.

Confidence, hope, zeal, willingness: all these are

expressions of morale. Rather like shares on the stock exchange, they fluctuate up and down. Sometimes these movements are so slight that you may hardly notice them. At other times, however, the fall is much more noticeable. It is an essential function of a strategic leader – in partnership with operational and team leaders – to build and maintain a high level of morale.

The reason for such a high strategic priority is that morale is a fuel gauge indicating the sense of common purpose with respect to a group – close to what the French call *esprit de corps*, the common spirit existing in members of a group and inspiring enthusiasm, devotion and a strong regard for its honour. That sense of common purpose is the aligned and focused energy of the group or organization. If that energy is diminished in any way, an organization's effectiveness is thereby depleted as well.

The military have long understood that fact, and also the dynamic relationship between leadership and morale. Since about 1830 the word *morale* has been used in English to cover the moral condition, conduct or behaviour of a body of soldiers when it comes to such matters as confidence, willingness to go forward and discipline in adversity. It has long been recognized as a battle-winning (or -losing) factor, and 'Maintenance of Morale' comes second in the list of Principles of War only to 'Selection and Maintenance of the Aim'.

Because success in military operations depends as much on the morale factor as upon the scale of personnel involved or the quantity and quality of material deployed, high morale is probably the single most important factor across the spectrum of conflict, ranging from full-scale war to peace-keeping activities. But the principle applies to all organizations.

The common issue of morale is the basic mental and emotional attitude to the common task. The confidence in question is the confidence of victory, success or achievement. That is why failures or reverses tend to lower morale. It follows that morale can only be boosted by successes or the prospect of ultimate success. To provide better food, better offices or better pay cannot have more than a momentary effect on morale. For money or material factors cannot buy what is essentially a matter of the spirit.

SUSTAINABILITY

Administration is the activity of sustaining an army during every stage of a campaign. Following French military usage, there is a distinction between *personnel* – the people involved – and *materiel* – the sum of equipment, weapons and expendable commodities. Administration encompasses all these aspects.

Logistics, (from the Greek *logistike*, the art of calculating), is the science of the procurement, maintenance and transportation of military *materiel*, facilities and personnel. In wider use it now refers to the detailed organization and implementation of a plan or operation. No plan can succeed without logistic support commensurate to the aim of the campaign or operation. It follows, therefore, that a strategic leader must have a degree of control over the logistical side of the plan which matches his level of accountability. Scarce resources should be controlled at the strategic level, and the logistic organization must be flexible enough to respond to changes of plan in the most economic way.

Great captains of war have always been strong on administration, not least because it directly effects battle effectiveness – even the bravest need ammunition – and because poor administration adversely effects morale. As armies grew in size and complexity, operating over great distances from home base, so administration called for a higher order of the art of calculating. 'You need to know mathematics,' Napoleon commented to one of his entourage, General Gourgaud, who accompanied him into exile on St Helena and subsequently wrote Napoleon's memoirs. 'That is useful in a thousand circumstances to correct ideas. Perhaps I owe my success to my mathematical ideas; a general must never make a picture for himself. That is the worst thing of all.'

Napoleon's tendency to calculate – to determine things by mathematical processes – applied to his military operations as well. 'I am used to thinking three or four months in advance about what I must do, and I calculate on the worst,' he explained to his brother Joseph. 'In war nothing is achieved except by calculations. Everything that is not soundly planned in its details yields no results.' Napoleon was not a man to leave things to chance.

Apart from inducing an almost scientific sense of objectivity and a natural ability to calculate the odds, the mathematics which Napoleon had acquired as a young artillery officer served him well as an administrator. His brain could work like a computer, which helped. 'A very curious thing about me is my memory,' he told Gaspard Gourgaud. 'As a young man I knew the logarithms of more than thirty to forty numbers. I knew, in France, not only the names of the officers of all regiments, but the places where the regiments were recruited and gained distinction.'

This prodigious memory and his infinite capacity for mastering detail – much of it administrative – set Napoleon apart from most men. He constantly fretted in letters to his generals about the need for them to pay strict attention to their muster rolls.

> The good condition of my armies comes from the fact that I devote an hour or two every day to them, and when I am sent the returns of my troops and my ships each month, which fills twenty large volumes, I set every other occupation aside to read them in detail in order to discern the difference that exists from one month to another. I take greater pleasure in this reading than a young lady would get from reading a novel.

Napoleon kept his critical eye on every detail of logistics. 'The direction of military affairs [i.e. strategy] is only half the work of a general,' he insisted. One large segment of the half centred upon morale, the maintenance of the *esprit de corps* of the army and its famous *élan* – the energy, ardour and dash arising from enthusiasm. But Napoleon may well have regarded the shielding of the 'sacred flame' as he called it, as part of the direction of military affairs, and needless to say he was a master of this aspect of personal leadership. His very presence could transform the mood of the army. Wellington once remarked: 'I used to say of him [Napoleon] that his presence on the field made the difference of forty thousand men.'

No, the other half was a detailed knowledge of the workings of the military machine. It is true that Napoleon delegated the day-to-day running of the machine to his various chiefs-of-staff. The greatest of them was Marshal Berthier, whose absence in the Waterloo campaign undoubtedly contributed to Napoleon's ultimate defeat. The Emperor's workload was made tolerable by his absorbing interest in the details of military activity, including everything to do with logistics. When asked one day how, after so many years, he could recall the statistics of his units and the names of their commanders, Napoleon replied: 'Madam, this is a lover's recollection of his former mistresses.'

Organization and administration go hand-in-hand. The prime purpose of the former is to establish a framework of responsibilities through and by means of which the concern may do its job. The prime purpose of the latter is to make the organization work; this includes, as one of its principal purposes, the removal of every avoidable obstacle from the way of the people who are actually doing the job. These obstacles may be material, human or organizational: but they all are fundamentally the concern of administration.

CASE STUDY: FIELD MARSHAL MONTGOMERY

On 13 August 1942 Montgomery arrived to take command of the Eighth Army, two months before the Battle of Alamein. 'The atmosphere was dismal and dreary,' he wrote in his diary. That evening he addressed the entire staff of Eighth Army Headquarters, between fifty and sixty officers. As he was their fourth Army Commander within a year, he faced a sceptical audience. The seasoned commanders and staff officers plainly doubted that this new general from Britain was the man to reverse their recent defeats and failures. Montgomery knew that he had to win their minds and hearts that evening if the morale of that broken army was to be restored to full pitch.

He stood on the steps of his predecessor's caravan and bade the gathering sit on the sand. He spoke without notes, looking straight at his audience. Here is what he said:

I want first of all to introduce myself to you. You do not know me. I do not know you. But we have got to work together; therefore we must understand each other and we must have confidence in one another. I have only been here a few hours. But from what I have seen and heard since I arrived I am prepared to say, here and now, that I have confidence in you. We will then work together as a team; and together we will gain the confidence of this great army and go forward to final victory in South Africa.

I believe that one of the first duties of a commander is to create what I call 'atmosphere'; and in that atmosphere, his staff, subordinate commanders and troops will live and work and fight.

I do not like the general atmosphere I find here. It is an atmosphere of doubt, of looking back to select the next place to which to withdraw, of loss of confidence in our ability to defeat Rommel, of desperate defence measures by reserves in preparing positions in Cairo and the Delta. All that must cease. Let us have a new atmosphere . . . We will stand and fight here. If we can't stay here alive, then let us stay here dead.

I want to impress on everyone that the bad times are over. Fresh divisions from the UK are now arriving in Egypt, together with ample reinforcements for our present divisions. We have 300 to 400 new Sherman tanks coming and these are actually being unloaded at Suez now. Our mandate from the Prime Minister is to destroy the Axis forces in North Africa; I have seen it written on half a sheet of notepaper. And it will be done. If anyone here thinks it can't be done, let him go at once; I don't want any doubters in this party. It can be done, and it will be done; beyond any possibility of doubt . . .

What I have done is to get over to you the atmosphere in which we will now work and fight; you must see that that atmosphere permeates right down through the Eighth Army to the most junior private soldier. All the soldiers must know what is wanted; when they see it coming to pass there will be a surge of confidence throughout the army.

I ask you to give me your confidence and to have faith that what I have said will come to pass.

There is much work to be done. The orders I have given about no further withdrawal will mean a complete change in the layout of our dispositions; also that we must begin to prepare for our great offensive . . .

'The great point to remember', Montgomery concluded at that famous initial briefing, 'is that we are going to finish with this chap Rommel once and for all. It will be quite easy. There is no doubt about it. He is definitely a nuisance. Therefore we will hit him a crack and finish with him.'

As Montgomery stepped down the officers rose and stood to attention. 'One could have heard a pin drop if such a thing were possible in the sand of the desert,' recollected Montgomery. 'But it certainly had a profound effect, and a spirit of hope, anyway of clarity, was born that evening.' His Chief-of-Staff, General de Guingand, agreed: 'It was one of his greatest efforts,' he wrote. 'The effect of the address was electric – it was terrific! And we all went to bed that night with new hope in our hearts, and a great confidence in the future of our Army. I wish someone had taken it down in shorthand, for it would have become a classic of its kind.' Fortunately, it *was* taken down in shorthand and filed away for many years before appearing in print for the first time in 1981.

COOPERATION

Napoleon was beaten at Waterloo not by Wellington alone but by the combination of the British and Prussian armies. Most successful military operations are joint enterprises, involving in these days cooperation between the three services, the civil authorities, and between allies. Goodwill, a common aim and a clear division of responsibilities, based upon an understanding of the capabilities and limitations of the others involved, are necessary conditions for such cooperation. A strategic leader's role includes forging alliances and making them work well.

Within alliances and conditions, where nations may not have identical interests but share a specific common aim, that key strategic responsibility may call for considerable political skills if the alliance is to be kept healthy. The Duke of Marlborough's dealings with Britain's Dutch ally in the early eighteenth-century wars against France is a copy-book example of how it should be done. But some generals fail this particular exam paper in strategic leadership in a spectacular way. Montgomery, for example, was unable to work harmoniously with his American counterparts nor under Eisenhower as Allied Supreme Commander. In his own phrase, he had reached his ceiling. By contrast, Generals Alexander and Slim were both exceptionally good at building strong relations with their allies.

Not that it was always easy. After his lecture to managers on leadership in 1948, Slim was asked if there were any parallels with negotiations with trade unions in the forces, a pressing topic for a British industry divided between the 'us' and 'them' of unionized labour and management. Slim drew an analogy with dealing with allies:

I speak from very little experience of trade unions but with a great deal of experience of allies. Russians, Chinese, French, Americans, Iraqis, Syrians, the Lord knows what! They were all at times absolutely exasperating. Try conducting negotiations with a Chinese general or a Russian, and see how you get on! But what I always found was that I could get the thing in perspective by remembering that I was an 'ally' myself.

'Get the trade union leaders to see that you are both on the same side, like allies in a common cause, he concluded.'

POLITICS

As a general principle the consequence of moving to the strategic level of leadership responsibility is that you move either suddenly or imperceptibly into the domain of politics. This principle in turn is part of an even wider one, namely that it is increasing complexity which distinguishes one level of leadership from another.

It follows that a mind honed to deal with military complexity by reducing it to simple essentials may not be equally equipped to handle political complexity. As we have just seen, the ability to cooperate effectively with allies implies an understanding of their different political agendas and some tact if not diplomatic skill. Similar political awareness, understanding and skill is called for in relation to what generals in democratic countries tend to refer to as their 'political masters'. Politicians are not always universally esteemed, but in a democracy they are on top and – subject to certain safeguards – military forces owe their loyalty to their elected governments. Moreover, the principle articulated by Clausewitz (but certainly not invented by him), that war is never an end in itself but always a means to a political end, ordains that a commander-in-chief must work in harmony with the political leader-in-chief. For the latter, in our Clausewitzian world, is the ultimate arbiter of strategy.

Like all human relations, the basis for a successful partnership between a military commander-in-chief and a political strategic leader-in-chief is mutual trust and respect. That in turn implies good communication. For the better the communicator, the more the trust; the more trust, the more that can be communicated. As the proverb says, *'The wing carries the bird, but the bird carries the wings.'*

In the Second World War some British generals like Wavell and Auchinleck, who were 'stiff upper-lipped' in the mould of Wellington, lost their jobs because Churchill found them too inarticulate. They were not men who would stoop to trying to sell themselves. Both had strong professional reputations. Wavell could certainly communicate well in other situations – he lectured on leadership at St Andrew's University and wrote an essay 'On Generalship'. But he failed one of the examination papers of modern military strategic leadership: he seemed tongue-tied in Churchill's presence and could not throw that first line across the river which would eventually lead to the building of a bridge of trust.

Other generals could do it. Eisenhower was gifted in this respect. As Allied Supreme Commander he forged an excellent working relationship with Churchill based on mutual confidence in each other's qualities as leaders in their respective fields.

When Sir Winston Churchill died, the spontaneous outpouring of admiration and affection from all over the world was a tribute to a great and noble man. But it was more than that; it was also a shining testimonial to the qualities of leadership. This world has always set a high value on leadership, and in the person of Sir Winston people everywhere found a superb combination of those characteristics which lift and inspire the human spirit.

I have long suspected that men who possess the capacity for leadership are always among us – waiting in the wings – but it sometimes takes a great crisis to bring them to prominence. The turbulent period in which I have lived has produced its share of outstanding leaders, and it has been my good fortune to know a number of them.

These were the opening words of Eisenhower's article on 'What is Leadership?' (*The Reader's Digest*, July 1965). It gives us some glimpses of Eisenhower's extraordinary ability to establish partnerships with supervisors of very different personalities, such as the American chief-of-staff, General Marshall, and Churchill.

It would be hard to imagine two men more unlike, in external traits, than General Marshall and Winston Churchill. Marshall was remote in manner, often abrupt. I knew no man who could call him an intimate friend. Churchill was convivial, outgoing, full of humour. The give-and-take of conferences delighted him; he liked people, and people instantly liked him. Yet both men had the same inner qualities of heart and mind that made them great leaders.

Mutual liking is not enough, it has to be backed by mutual respect. Here a political leader-in-chief has to demonstrate a grasp of the broad strategic issues, not least because the one or two big strategic decisions in a war have to be taken by the politician acting on professional advice, not by the commander-in-chief alone. General MacArthur, commander-in-chief in the Korean War, lost his job for appearing to challenge President Truman's prerogative to decide on such a major strategic issue as the employment of tactical nuclear weapons against the Chinese.

President Truman had served as a front-line artillery officer in the First World War, but his predecessor Franklin D. Roosevelt had no military experience; indeed, crippled by polio as a young man, he was bound to a wheelchair. Yet Eisenhower was impressed by his strategic grasp and sheer application:

> I never knew President Roosevelt as well as I did some of the other world leaders, but in the few conferences I had with him I was impressed, not only by his inspirational qualities, but by his amazing grasp of the whole complex war effort. He could discuss strategy on equal terms with his generals and admirals. His knowledge of the geography of the war theatres was so encyclopaedic that the most obscure places in far-away countries were always accurately sited on his mental map. President Roosevelt possessed personality, but as his nation's leader, in a global conflict, he also did his homework – thoroughly.

All strategic leaders have to find their way through complex political situations. Some – the strategic leaders in charge of large government departments, for example, or chief executives in local government – will have direct deals with elected political leaders. They will need Eisenhower's ability to establish common ground and build a professional but warm partnership. Equally, however, political leaders must learn to be *leaders* – strategic leaders of the calibre of Churchill and Roosevelt who command respect by their strategic grasp of the business in question. Who is to train senior politicians throughout the world to be such effective strategic leaders? Solve that problem and the world takes a quantum step forwards.

ON GENERALSHIP

It is interesting to see the role of a *strategos* – the leader of a whole army – through the eyes of a chief-of-staff. By definition a chief-of-staff works closely with a commander-in-chief and their roles are complementary, and so it is a professional equivalent to marriage. Indeed, a chief-of-staff can fulfil some of the functions of a wife in restoring a degree of harmony when her difficult spouse is apparently intent on disrupting them. Montgomery was fortunate to have as his Chief-of-Staff a man with a talent for diplomacy.

In 1946 Sir Francis de Guingand, a knight and a major-general at the age of forty-four, retired from the army. He had been Field Marshal Montgomery's Chief-of-Staff from the Battle of El Alamein until the end of the war in Europe, and Montgomery, on becoming Chief of the General Staff, failed to appoint him as his Vice, contrary to his previously stated intentions.

In his autobiography *From Brass Hat to Bowler Hat* de Guingand tells of the events leading to his resignation and of the way in which he employed the talents that had made him an outstanding chief-of-staff to carve out a second career as an industrialist in South Africa. Interesting as these reminiscences are, the book is more important for the light that the author, who was closely involved with all three, throws on the characters and relationships of Auchinleck, Montgomery and Eisenhower.

Perhaps the greatest contribution de Guingand made to the Allied victory was in preventing an outright breach between Montgomery and Eisenhower while remaining loyal to the one and retaining the friendship of the other. Of Auchinleck he writes:

> Montgomery detested him . . . This was a shame, for Auchinleck's contribution to ultimate British victory in the Western Desert is indisputable . . . When Rommel subsequently counter-attacked . . . it was Auchinleck's personal assumption of command that restored the situation and paved the way for the successful defence of Alam Halfa.

De Guingand remained on close terms with Eisenhower and Montgomery until the end of their lives and indeed helped to smooth ruffled feathers in what might be termed the 'Battle of the Memoirs'. As he writes: 'Once more, as in the war, I found myself trying to keep the peace between Eisenhower and Montgomery, not always an easy task. They were in almost every respect opposites; yet each in his own way a genius.'

Montgomery, he adds, 'never possessed Eisenhower's breadth of vision, transparent humility or nobility: but at the deadly business of war, the task of making a largely amateur army first equal, then superior to, a highly disciplined, indoctrinated enemy he had no rival.'

In his earlier book *Operation Victory* (1947) de Guingand offered 'six points for successful generalship' that apply to any strategic leader, not merely military ones. A general must:

- know his 'stuff' thoroughly;
- be known and recognized by the troops;
- ensure that the troops are given tasks that are within their powers. Success means mutual confidence – failure the reverse;
- see that his subordinate commanders are disturbed as little as possible in carrying out their tasks;
- command by personal contact;
- be human and study the human factor.

De Guingand continues: 'Many times during the war I have tried to analyse the ingredients of the "big man". The following are the points that I consider important:'

- he should be able to sit back and avoid getting immersed in detail;
- he must be a good 'picker' of men;
- he should trust those under him, and let them get on with their job without interference;
- he must have the power of clear decision;
- he should inspire confidence;
- he should not be pompous.

A business leader who read this list commented to me: 'Any good chairman or chief executive should be able to identify with those qualities. More importantly, perhaps, his or her board colleagues should be able to recognize them when appointments are being made.'

De Guingand's profile tells us much about what a chief-of-staff *expects* from a commander-in-chief. It is the work of a general. In order to make it possible the staff, under direction of its chief, have to take as much as possible of the load of detailed planning, logistics and administration off the general's shoulders, leaving him free to think, to lead and to oversee the whole operation – including key relations with allies and political leaders. Behind every great commander-in-chief lies a great chief-of-staff. What would Napoleon have been without Marshal Berthier? Have a look at the Battle of Waterloo and there is your answer!

THE ROLE OF A STRATEGIC LEADER

'The Leaders of Industry', wrote Thomas Carlyle in 1843, 'are virtually Captains of the World.' Although Xenophon had first explored the parallels between war and business it was not until the rise of industrial giants – notably the railways – in the nineteenth century that business leaders could be mentioned in the same breath as the great captains – Wellington and Napoleon, Grant and Lee. It was perhaps symbolic that General Robert E. Lee became president of the first business school in America. Were not men like Andrew Carnegie or John D. Rockefeller, heads of organizations that dwarfed armies in size and resources, the new commanders-in-chief of the post Industrial Revolution?

To those industrial organizations of all shapes and sizes we must add others in many fields – such as health, education, science, sport, the arts, politics and religion. Given that the roots of strategic leadership go down so deeply into the military tradition, is it really possible to disentangle them, as it were, from their bloodstained soil and come up with a generic set of functions?

That is a question I shall leave hanging tantalizingly in the air. For the way to answer it is, in my opinion, not to try to work directly from military to civilian practice, modifying or adapting one to the other. It is better to be radical and explore the deeper common root which feeds all particular manifestations or field-specific forms – leadership.

SUMMARY OF KEY POINTS

- Strategy as a word is a fairly recent borrowing from the military vocabulary. It reflects its more modern military usage – strategy as opposed to tactics.
- In fact this modern idea of strategy is far too narrow. Strategy or *strategia*, properly understood, is the leadership of a large body of people, such as a *stratos* – an army spread out. As armies were the largest work-related organizations for some 3,000 years before the rise of big business in the nineteenth century, it is not surprising that the concept of strategic leadership developed into its first full-blown form in the role of a commander-in-chief.
- The contemporary tendency to equate strategic leadership with formulating strategy reflects a basic misunderstanding of the concept. If you look closely at effective military leaders, strategy in the narrow sense occupies only a small amount of their time.
- Some writers of military memoirs, such as T. E. Lawrence, have described how they alone solved what appears to be a complex strategic problem. In fact strategy is usually simple and obvious to someone of above-average common sense. It does not require what Lawrence called 'brainy leadership'. Moreover, strategy evolves – it is almost invariably the product of more than one mind.
- Lawrence himself, in his self-appointed and partly imagined role as commander-in-chief, showed real flair in some of the other aspects that make up effective strategic leader-

ship. He was an inspirational leader, with a clear grasp of the importance of morale. He secured the trust both of Allenby and Feisal, so he became the chief hinge of the British–Arab alliance. He understood the politics of the situation. As a skilled adviser he worked through Feisal who was commander-in-chief.

- A large amount of any general's daily work is administration – ensuring the sustainability of an army. Much of it, given the military staff system that has evolved over centuries, can be delegated. But delegation is not the same as abdication. Sustainability is so important that a commander-in-chief must always have oversight of it.

- The parallels between leadership in different fields soon become apparent to those who study them. The higher the level of leadership responsibility, the closer they seem to become.

- This suggests that leadership – be it teams or organizations – is like a substance that can be moulded into different forms without losing its intrinsic nature. An exploration of that 'substance', with examples from different fields to make it concrete, should lead us to a more generic role of strategic leadership than this review of generalship can afford us. It's worth a try!

> *'He has a look upon his face that I would*
> *fain call master.'*
> *'What is that?'*
> *'Authority.'*
> Shakespeare, *King Lear*

3

WHAT IS LEADERSHIP?

*Not the cry but the flight of the wild duck leads the flock
to fly and to follow.*

Chinese proverb

What is leadership? I first asked myself this question when
I was just eighteen and coming to the end of my schooldays
at St Paul's School in London. I had chosen to give a lecture
on the subject 'Leadership in History' to the school historical society which I had founded. Someone present wrote
this brief summary of my talk for the school magazine:

> Leadership, he said, could be defined as the activity of
> influencing people to pursue a certain course; there must also
> be some power of mind behind the leader. Leadership is not
> merely the authority of the commander, but contains by
> necessity some strange strength of personality which attracts
> the ordinary man. It is only when the times are favourable that
> a man of destiny can come into his own. Although leadership
> may change in this aspect from age to age, the qualities of a
> leader are the same.

Many years later, having devoted much of my professional
life to leadership and leadership development, I find that
this summary is not far off the mark in reflecting what I
think today. Sometimes first thoughts are best.

The year was 1952, seven years after the end of the Second World War. A week later Field Marshal Montgomery came to lecture to the sixth form. He had been a pupil at St Paul's School and he had also used our red-brick school building in Hammersmith to house his planning staff before Operation Overlord in 1944. We gathered to hear him in the lecture room where he and Eisenhower had once briefed King George VI and Winston Churchill on the plans for D-Day.

At precisely 11.00 a.m. Monty, as we all called him, strode on to the platform, wearing battle-dress with ten rows of coloured medal ribbons. He had a narrow, foxy face, sharp, intelligent and tenacious, with very bright and clear blue eyes and a small, light, spare body. He had a look on his face of extreme attention and sagacity, like a very alert terrier. This was the completely self-confident man who had taken over command of a somewhat demoralized Eighth Army, restored its fighting spirit and led it to the first British victory of the Second World War.

Alone on the platform with a large map as a visual aid, Monty spoke to us about the Alamein campaign for an hour without notes, as if he had been briefing his divisional commanders. Clarity and confidence hallmarked every sentence. As Brigadier Essame wrote about him in Ronald Levin's *Montgomery as a Military Commander* (1971):

> He could describe a complex situation with amazing lucidity and sum up a long exercise without the use of a single note. He looked straight into the eyes of the audience when he spoke. He had a remarkable flair for picking out the essence of a problem, and for indicating its solution with startling clarity, It was almost impossible to misunderstand his meaning, however unpalatable it might be.

Such was the impression he made on me. Over lunch in the High Master's room I asked Monty his secret of leadership. How did he lead such a large army to victory? Of his reply I can remember now only one sentence: 'I made my soldiers partners with me in the battle.' When my first book *Training for Leadership* appeared in 1968, Monty took the trouble to write to me in his own clear hand:

> Leadership is an immense subject. In 1961 I published a book entitled *The Path to Leadership* (Collins), in which I tried to show the way towards it. And in 1945 I gave a lecture at St Andrew's University in Scotland on 'Military Leadership'.
>
> Nowhere is it more important to teach it than at Sandhurst and in our universities; in fact to youth, since it falls on dead ground with the older generation.

By 1952 there were political moves afoot to abolish military conscription, which Churchill had insisted should be called National Service. In the context of the Cold War, Montgomery insisted upon its retention, and so I owe it in part to him that I served as a soldier for a compulsory two years after leaving school. Not that I minded – I was looking forward to the adventure.

In the army I encountered two theories of leadership, as they might be called. One – the Qualities or Traits Approach – I had largely been working with already. The other – the Functional Approach, as I named it – was implicit in the selection system for officers but not overt. Long after my military service I came to see that there were in fact *three* distinct approaches to understanding leadership – Qualities, Situational and Functional – and it is that fuller conceptual sketch map that I follow below.

THE QUALITIES APPROACH

'The qualities of a leader are the same,' I had said at St Paul's School. When I eventually got to Eaton Hall Officer Training Unit in 1953 we were given a student précis that defined leadership as 'the art of influencing a body of people to follow a certain course of action; the art of controlling them, directing them and getting the best out of them'. Seventeen qualities were then listed, each with a brief note of explanation:

Ability to make decisions	Initiative
Energy	Pride in command
Assurance (confidence)	Loyalty
Determination	Sense of duty
Example	Humour
Resolute courage	Ability to accept responsibility
Calmness in crisis	Physical fitness
Sense of justice	Enthusiasm
Human element	

'These qualities make a good leader but never imagine you have learnt all about leadership,' concluded the précis. 'You will always have something more to learn, so be prepared to profit by experience. Experience helps a great deal. Take every opportunity of gaining experience in leadership. Being an officer and a leader is a big job, a fine job and a thoroughly worthwhile job. See that you become a leader in the early and best sense of the word.' That was all that we were taught directly about leadership.

Meanwhile the Qualities Approach – the above was an instance of it – was falling out of favour in the United

States. Some psychologists had already pointed out the discrepancies between the various lists of leadership qualities derived from what purported to be objective or empirical studies of actual leaders. The assumption that there is a set of leadership qualities which characterized all leaders in all fields at all times was questioned and then abandoned. In its place came the view that leadership was situationally determined. There were no universal qualities: it all depended upon what attributes were required in a specific situation. In the box below you will find some examples of these early research findings, but feel free to skip them if your interests are not academic.

RESEARCH INTO LEADERSHIP QUALITIES

1. Professor Bird of the University of Minnesota looked at approximately twenty studies 'bearing some resemblance to controlled investigations' which contained seventy-nine traits. 'Surprisingly little overlapping is found from study to study. Actually, 51 or 65 per cent are mentioned once, 16 or 20 per cent are common to two lists, 4 or 5 per cent are found in three, and another 5 per cent in four lists. Two traits are common to five lists, and one trait, namely, initiative, to six, and another one, high intelligence, to ten lists.
(C. Bird, *Social Psychology* (D. Appleton-Century, New York and London, 1940) pp. 378–9).

2. The writers of one article have 17,000 words used to describe qualities of personality.
(G. W. Allport and H. A. Odbert, 'Trait-names: A Psycholexical Study', *Psychological Monographs*, no. 211 (1936)).

3. R. M. Stogdill, who studied the evidence for twenty-nine qualities appearing in 124 studies, concluded that although

---

intelligence, scholarliness, dependability, social participation and socio-economic status were found to bear some relation to leadership, the evidence suggests that leadership is a relationship that exists between persons in a social situation, and that persons who are leaders in one situation may not necessarily be leaders in other situations.

(R. M. Stogdill, 'Personal Factors Associated with Leadership: A Survey of the Literature', *Journal of Psychology*, vol. 25 (1948), pp. 35–71.)

4. Another study by W. O. Jenkins, published a year earlier in 1947, supports this conclusion. After reviewing seventy-four studies on military leadership the author wrote:

> Leadership is specific to the particular situation under investigation. Who becomes the leader of a particular group engaging in a particular activity and what the leadership characteristics are in the given case are a function of the specific situation . . . [there are] wide variations in the characteristics of individuals who become leaders in similar situations and even great divergence in leadership behaviour in difference situations . . . The only common factor appeared to be that leaders in a particular field need and tend to possess superior general or technical competence or knowledge in that area. General intelligence does not seem to be the answer . . .

(W. O. Jenkins, 'A Review of Leadership Studies with Particular Reference to Military Problems', *Psychological Bulletin*, vol. 44 (1947), pp. 54–79.)

The intellectual and emotional rejection of the Qualities Approach reflected some of the cultural values in American society in the post-Second World War period. Many of those in the burgeoning field of the social or behavioural sciences had emigrated from a Europe where the German and Italian words for leader were *Führer* and *Duce*. It was an anti-leadership culture, in so far as leadership was seen to be vested in an individual by virtue of possessing the 'qualities of leadership'. The group replaced the leader as the centre of attention.

William H. Whyte caught this mood perfectly in *The Organization Man* (1955). 'Anti-authoritarianism is becoming anti-leadership,' he wrote. 'In group doctrine the strong personality is viewed with overwhelming suspicion. The cooperative are those who take a stance directly over the keel; the man with ideas – in translation, prejudices – leans to one side or, worse yet, heads for the rudder.'

The trouble with 'group leadership' was that, while it may have been effective in the artificial situations for research and training known in America as 'group laboratories', it could not be and was not effective in the real world of work. One of the first to see this truth was Douglas McGregor, a former professor of psychology at the Massachusetts Institute of Technology and author of the widely influential book *The Human Side of Enterprise* (1960). In 1948 McGregor was appointed head of Antioch University and there he learnt that being a college president meant exercising personal leadership. Here are his conclusions:

The first is a conviction that has been derived from my personal struggle with the rôle of college president. Before coming to Antioch I had observed and worked with top executives as an adviser in a number of organizations. I thought I knew how they felt about their responsibilities and what led them to behave as they did. I even thought that I could create a rôle for myself that would enable me to avoid some of the difficulties they encountered. I was wrong! It took the direct experience of becoming a line executive, and meeting personally the problems involved, to teach me what no amount of observation of other people could have taught.

I believed, for example, that a leader could operate successfully as a kind of adviser to his organization. I thought I could avoid being a 'boss'. Unconsciously, I suspect, I hoped to duck the unpleasant necessity of making difficult decisions, of taking the responsibility for one course of action among many uncertain alternatives, of making mistakes and taking the consequences. I thought that maybe I could operate so that everyone would like me – that 'good human relations' would eliminate all discord and disagreement.

I could not have been more wrong. It took a couple of years, but I finally began to realize that a leader cannot avoid the exercise of authority any more than he can avoid responsibility for what happens to his organization. In fact, it is a major function of the top executive to take on his own shoulders the responsibility for resolving the uncertainties that are always involved in important decisions. Moreover, since no important decision ever pleases everyone in the organization, he must also absorb the displeasure, and sometimes severe hostility, of those who would have taken a different course.

A colleague recently summed up what my experience has taught me in these words: 'A good leader must be tough enough to win a fight, but not tough enough to kick a man when he is down.' This notion is not in the least consistent with humane, democratic leadership. Good human relations develop out of strength, not of weakness.

One of Douglas McGregor's students who acted as a joint editor of the collection of essays entitled *Leadership and Motivation* (1966) in which this passage appears was Warren Bennis. The youngest American company commander in Europe at the end of the Second World War, Bennis also became a university president. It was he more than any other with his book *Leaders* (1985) who launched the revival of interest in organizational leaders. The major contribution of the new school lay in emphasizing the nexus between leadership and vision.

Those in the military field at such institutions as West Point and Sandhurst, with their own traditions of leadership, never abandoned the Qualities Approach. It reaches back to Xenophon, for he listed the qualities of an ideal leader as *temperance, justice, sagacity, amiability, presence of mind, tactfulness, humanity, sympathy, helpfulness, courage, magnanimity, generosity* and *considerateness*.

At Sandhurst the basic list was derived from a lecture on leadership given there by General Slim. His qualities are *courage, willpower, judgement, knowledge, flexibility of mind* and *integrity*. These also formed the substance of his lectures on leadership to management audiences. For his part, Montgomery mentioned with approval Aristotle's four leadership virtues : *justice, temperance, prudence* and *fortitude*.

My own view is that a leader should possess and exemplify the qualities expected or required in his or her field. So a military leader, for example, will need physical courage as well as the other characteristics of any good soldier. But there are some more generic leadership qualities, such as *enthusiasm, integrity* – the quality that makes people trust you – the combination of *toughness* or demandingness and *fairness*, *warmth* or humanity and *energy* and *resilience*.

This list is not exhaustive, for with leadership there are always facets of the diamond that catch the light in some individuals in certain circumstances and not in others. So you can always study the qualities of leaders and see – or see afresh – new facets. *Humour*, for example, not mentioned above, can be a powerful leadership quality. No one has the sum of all these contributory qualities, for the ideal leader is a concept not a person. But you should aim to develop the natural qualities that you have which fall within the general flight-path indicated above. If you try and fail, the good news is that you will tend to become more humble – and humility is the most useful leadership quality as well!

THE SITUATIONAL APPROACH

Enough has been said about the Situational Approach not to warrant more here. Suffice to say that in its classical form it lays more emphasis upon the technical or professional competence – in a word, *knowledge* – of the leader, than upon his or her qualities of personality or character (not that these are unimportant in the true classic tradition).

You may have noticed that General Slim put *knowledge* on his list. Speaking within the military context, then an all-male environment, this is what he had to say in his lecture on 'Leadership in Management', given in 1957 in Australia when he was Governor-General.

> I said he must have knowledge. A man has no right to set himself up as a leader – or to be set up as a leader – unless

he knows more than those he is to lead. In a small unit, a platoon say – or maybe a workshop gang – the leader should be able to do the job of any man in the outfit better than he can. That is a standard that should be required from all junior leaders. As the leader rises higher in the scale, he can no longer, of course, be expected to show such mastery of the detail of all the activities under him. A Divisional Commander need not know how to coax a wireless set, drive a tank, preach a sermon or take out an appendix as well as the people in his division who are trained to do those things. But he has got to know how long these jobs should take, what their difficulties are, what they need in training and equipment and the strain they entail. As the leader moves towards the top of the ladder, he must be able to judge between experts and technicians and to use their advice although he will not need their knowledge. One kind of knowledge that he must always keep in his own hands – is that of men.

Although one may question all of that last sentence, it certainly points to a more generic knowledge – a knowledge about human nature and how best people might work together in organizations – which is characteristically present in effective leaders. Whether or not that wider knowledge of human nature, of 'the human side of enterprise', knowing how to lead, is present in any given individuals can be principally judged by their actions.

Knowing what to do in situations is partly a factor of technical/professional knowledge and partly a factor of knowledge about people (if those situations involve people, as in the case of leadership they invariably will). But two other factors – *intelligence* and *experience* – also come into the equation. In the Socratic concept of *knowledge*, you could say, *intelligence* and *experience* are in-built. That may be so, but it is worth artificially separating them out here for the sake of understanding.

As a general common-sense principle, a leader should be at least as intelligent as the average if not above average. As Ordway Tead wrote in *The Art of Leadership* (1935): 'What little scientific evidence there is above the consensus of observable facts seems to point to the truth that, *other qualities being equal*, the person of greater intelligence will probably make the better leader.'

Intelligence is the faculty of understanding. Mental alertness, problem-solving ability and keen perception of relationships are all implicit in *intelligence*. Mental ability in this wider and more informal sense is obviously more transferable than any specific technical know-how. 'The few studies available', continues Tead,

> indicate also that this higher intelligence factor in leaders correlates with *versatility*. The tentative conclusion seems to be that those capable of leading in one field are likely to be found potentially high in capacity to lead in several fields. The kind of eager, alert, outreaching mental quality which marks the leader predisposes him to use his powers in several directions.

Intelligence in this context includes the ability:

- to see the point;
- to sense relationships and analogies quickly;
- to identify the essentials in a complex picture;
- to 'put two and two together';
- to find the salient factors in past experience which are helpful in shedding light on present difficulties;

- to be able to distinguish clearly between ends and means;
- to appraise situations readily;
- to see their significance in the total setting of present and past experience;
- to get the cue as to the likely line of wise action.

These overlap considerably, but taken together they offer an idea of the kind of intelligence we are talking about.

In the list above the interdependence of *intelligence* with *experience* is evident. Experience can be either experience of life in general, which of course only comes with age, or relevant experience to a given situation. Familiarity is based upon considerable actual practice. You have personally encountered, undergone or lived through situations not unlike the one now faced. By implication, this past immersion in a subject or field has resulted in superior understanding. Sometimes, however, gain in wisdom need not be suggested by the word so much as a piling-up of involvement. Marshal Saxe's donkey, it is said, went on twenty campaigns carrying his master's baggage, but learned nothing about the art of war.

The Greeks had a word for this combination of intelligence and experience in practical affairs – *phronesis*. It was translated into Latin as *prudentia* and thence into English as *prudence*. Essentially, *prudent* suggests action that is the outcome of wisdom gained by experience. The ability to govern and discipline oneself by the use of reason, sagacity or shrewdness in the management of affairs, prudence in the use of resources, caution or circumspection as to danger or risk – you can see why Aristotle placed *phronesis* among the 'Intellectual Virtues'. As prudence carries a slight overtone of restraint, a better translation of *phronesis* today is practical wisdom.

THE FUNCTIONAL APPROACH

My first encounter with the Functional Approach to leadership was on the receiving end. In 1953, a month or two into National Service, I was sent to the War Office Selection Board for it to determine whether or not I should be offered a commission as an officer. It was a fair, interesting and impressive experience, and I do not say that simply because I passed! Not that I understood all the theory behind it – nor, I suspect, did those officers who staffed it.

WOSBs, as they were known – the grandparent of all assessment centres today – had been introduced in 1942 while the British Army was expanding rapidly from a few hundred thousand to some six million men and women. The traditional interview method of officer selection from the public schools was clearly not working effectively. The Adjutant-General of the day, Sir Ronald Adam, convened a working party of soldiers and psychologists in uniform who jointly designed the three-day selection process.

Dr Henry Harris, one of the psychologists involved from 1943 onwards, wrote a book on this remarkable innovation, entitled *The Group Approach to Leadership Testing* (1949). The essential problem, he wrote, was how to select the right man for the right group, given that small military groups which would have to operate in the stress conditions of the battlefields needed a leader who could function efficiently under stress.

WOSB's answer was to test and evaluate him in the context of a small experimental group submitted to considerable time and problem stress, i.e. required to execute a difficult task against time. That which one sought to observe and evaluate one might call his group effectiveness, the sum total of his contribution to the group and its task.

Group effectiveness was broken down into *task functioning*, such as planning and organizing the available abilities, materials and time, and *group-cohesiveness functioning*, notably the ability to bind the group in the direction of the common task and to relate its members emotionally to each other and to the task. Also observed and noted was the ability of the candidate to withstand the effects of stress, which today we would call resilience. 'One selects and *tests* him *in* a group and *for* a group': that was the essential principle.

It is clear that in these early days the elements of the Functional Approach were available and put to use for leadership selection. In his thoughtful summary Henry Harris writes:

> One may suggest provisionally that leadership is the measure and degree of an individual's ability to influence — and be influenced by — a group in the implementation of a common task. This circumscribes three important aspects of leadership function: the *individual*, the *group* and the *task*; and indicates leadership as a functional relationship between these three basic variables.

Personally I hate war, necessary evil though it may sometimes be, and I am eternally grateful to those whose labours and sacrifices have removed the threat of it for most of us. Yet war is often the matrix of accelerated technological development, witness the computers and jet engines that emerged from the Second World War. The Functional

Approach and its massive testing in the WOSB application is another such example.

My own work in the 1960s at Sandhurst could be interpreted as the application of the Functional Approach to the issue of *training* leaders as opposed to *selecting* them. The approach focused in a two-day practical course of exercises, group discussions, film and case study proved to be successful, and became widely adopted in the British Armed Services and overseas. Renamed 'Action-Centred Leadership' (ACL), it was introduced to industry by me, and more than one million managers and supervisors participated in the programme.

One key break-through that made this success possible was relating the three elements of 'need' – *task*, *group* (renamed *team*) and *individual* – in a simple diagram. As the Chinese proverb says, *a picture is worth a thousand words.*

Figure 3.1 *The Interaction of Areas of Need*

If you place a disc over the 'Task' circle in the figure above, it will immediately cover segments of the other two circles as well. In other words, lack of task or failure to achieve it will affect both team maintenance, e.g. increasing disruptive tendencies, and also the area of individual needs, lowering member satisfaction within the group. Move the disc on to the 'Team' circle, and again the impact of a near-complete lack of relationships in the group on both task and individual needs may be seen at a glance.

Conversely, when a group achieves its task the degree of group cohesiveness and enjoyment of membership should go up. Morale, both corporate and individual, will be higher. And if the members of a group happen to get on extremely well together and find that they can work closely as a team, this will increase their work performance and also meet some important needs which individuals bring with them into common life.

These three interlocking circles therefore illustrate the general point that each area of need exerts an influence upon the other two; they do not form watertight compartments.

Clearly, in order that the group should fulfil its task and be held together as a working team, certain functions will have to be performed. By 'function' in this context we mean any behaviour, words or actions which meet one or more spheres of 'need', or *areas of leadership responsibility* as they may also be called. Defining the aim, planning, and encouraging the group, are examples of what is meant by the word 'function'. (See the box below for other examples.)

SOME KEY LEADERSHIP FUNCTIONS

PLANNING
    Seeking all available information
    Defining group task, purpose or goal

Making a workable plan (in the right decision-making framework)

INITIATING
Briefing team on the aims and the plan
Explaining *why* aim or plan is necessary
Allocating tasks to group members
Setting team standards

CONTROLLING
Maintaining group standards
Influencing tempo
Ensuring all actions are taken towards objectives
Keeping discussion relevant
Prodding group to action/decision

SUPPORTING
Expressing acceptance of persons and their contribution
Encouraging team/individuals
Disciplining team/individuals
Creating team spirit
Relieving tension with humour
Reconciling disagreements or getting others to explore them

INFORMING
Clarifying task and play
Giving new information to the group, keeping them 'in the picture'
Receiving information from the group
Summarizing suggestions and ideas coherently

EVALUATING
Checking feasibility of an idea

> Testing the consequences of proposed solution
> Evaluating team performance
> Helping team or individual to evaluate their own performance
>   against standards.

This three-circle model also served as a framework for other satellite theories or models, such as Abraham Maslow's theory of a hierarchy of individual needs and the model which represented the different ways a leader could share a decision with a group or individual – starting with *telling* and becoming progressively more participative – seen as points on a decision-making continuum (for details of both see my other books in this series). The general principle that emerges is that the more you share decisions the better, for the people involved will feel more committed to carrying them out. But there are natural factors – shortage of time, extent of knowledge and experience of the group or individual – which may limit how far you can go.

In summary, a leader is the sort of person with the appropriate *qualities* and *knowledge* – which is more than technical or professional – who is able to provide the necessary *functions* to enable a team to achieve its task and to hold it together as a working unity. And this is done not by the leader alone but by eliciting the contributions and willing cooperation of all involved. As Sir John Smyth, VC wrote:

> A good leader is someone whom people will follow through thick and thin, in good times and in bad, because they have confidence in him as a person, his ability and his knowledge of the job and *because they know they matter to him.*

THE THREE-CIRCLE MODEL IN PERSPECTIVE

The three-circle Functional Leadership concept is now the best-known and most widely used leadership–development model in the world. Many models and theories have come and gone, but none other has been consistently employed in selection and development for fifty years and has, in that time, grown in reputation. *Time tries truth*, as the English proverb says. In this field time does help to sift out the merely ephemeral or fashionable so-called theories of leadership.

There are, however, two respects that have come to my notice in that long period in which the three-circle model is not fool-proof. First, the equal size of the three circles has led a few tyro-leaders to assume that they always spend *equal* time and energy on the task, team and individual. In fact, as most people realize, one circle may be much 'larger' than another in the sense that in some situations you may have to focus mainly upon one area at the temporary expense of the other two. A good leader may well redress the balance when circumstances allow. But the three-circle model is dynamic rather than static; the shape or pattern is constantly changing.

Second, it has been argued that the model encourages mediocrity in that it assumes a team that merely accomplishes a task given to it: it does not *improve* on the task or come up with a *better* one. But this is a misconception, a reading of something into the model which is not there. In fact it encompasses the creative group or team which invents its own task or chooses to transcend the already defined task it has been given. Indeed, the degree of creativity in any one of the three circles will – following the interactive principle – affect both the other circles. If, for example, you give a team a creative task to do, it will evoke the latent creativity in both group and individuals. If you introduce a highly creative person into the team, the task will be seen and approached in a more creative way and the group as a whole may well become more effective.

By the light of experience it now seems as if the three-circle model is – in the sphere of leadership – the modest equivalent to Einstein's General Theory of Relativity. For it obeys Einstein's principle that 'Everything should be made as simple as possible, but not more simple.' The model is simple and true, which means that it can never be simplistic or superficial.

LEVELS OF LEADERSHIP

Leadership exists on different levels. Thinking of organizations, there are three broad levels or domains of leadership:

Team	The leader of a team of some ten to twenty people with clearly specified tasks to achieve.
Operational	The leader of one of the main parts of the organization and more than one team leader are under one's control. It is already a case of being a leader of leaders.
Strategic	The leader of a whole organization, with a number of operational leaders under one's personal direction.

A simple recipe for organizational success is to have effective leaders occupying these roles and working together in harmony as a team. That is simple enough to say: I am implying that it is easy either to achieve or to maintain that state of affairs under the pressures of life today. But what is your alternative?

Within each broad level there may be subdivisions. The levels also overlap considerably. But the distinction is still worth making.

Sometimes, however, these three floor levels of the organizational house are disguised by the elaborate façade of hierarchy. A *hierarchy* (from Greek *hierus*, sacred) originally meant a ruling body of priests or clergy organized into orders or ranks each subordinate to the one above. The Greek *archos* was a generic term for a man who was in authority over others, their leader. It comes from a verb which means both to begin and to take the lead. Hence our English word-ending *-archy*, which means government or leadership of or by an *arch*. An *archbishop*, for example, is the first or leader among bishops, whereas *monarchy* is rule by one person – a king or emperor.

In Greek phalanxes and Roman formations there were *archoi* of various names among the rank-and-file. But once battle was joined, formations tended to disintegrate and the natural 'leaders of ten' emerged to rally and lead their comrades forward.

The foundation is the team leader, a truth that continues to evade many large organizations today. 'Ten soldiers wisely led will beat one hundred without a head,' wrote the Greek poet Euripides. A *decanus* in Greek and Latin was the leader of ten soldiers. From its use in monastic orders for a monk in charge of ten others, the word comes down to us in the form of dean – the dean of a cathedral or the dean of a university faculty. Our military equivalent is corporal, which derives, like captain, from Latin *caput*, head. *Chief*, coming from *chef*, the French for a head, has the same meaning. Because as humans we stand erect, we tend to assume that a head is a hierarchical model: the head is on top so it is important. But look at any other animal: the head always goes *first* – it is the body's leader.

In war tactical formation is no substitute for team leaders. General Slim once recounted a conversation on that very point:

I remember a long time ago, when I was a very earnest young staff officer, a lot of us – even in those days we did a certain amount of work in the army – were studying how a battalion should be formed up to attack. We had all sorts of ideas and argued them with tremendous enthusiasm. Watching and listening was an elderly man, a very fine fighting soldier, and we turned to him and said: 'What do you think, sir?'

'Well,' he answered, 'I can tell you one thing. It does not matter what formation your battalion starts in – square, diamond, arrow, line, column, or squashing matchbox – it will always end up in the same formation – small groups rallying around the bravest men.' I have since seen a lot of battalions go into action, in all sorts of formations, but in the end they have always been like that – small groups round the natural leaders.

A TEAM LEADER IN ACTION

A special correspondent representing the combined British Press writes from one of the beach-heads, dated Wednesday:

Down here on the beaches today I have been listening to stories of heroism at the first assault. The first men to hit the beaches were Commando units, and their boats were raked with mortar and machine-gun fire as they rode the surf into the assault area.

A young Commando corporal from one boat was seen by many of his comrades to sink to his knees half-way up a section of the beach towards a pill-box. He was quickly on his feet again and shouting: 'Come on mates,' rushed right into the mouth of the pill box from which half a dozen machine guns were firing. He fell again in the doorway and this time did not get up. He had led his men right to the death and his body had more than fifty wounds in it. The ten Germans inside the pill-box surrendered to the survivors of that gallant assault.

The Times, 9 June 1944

Even a very large and globally wide spread organization can exhibit in classic form the three levels of leadership. If you are a Roman Catholic, for example, in a Church which has millions of members throughout the world, there are only three leaders that come within your mental and spiritual compass: the *parish priest*, the diocesan *bishop* and the *pope* as head of the Church. Of course there are other ranks and grades of clergy in the hierarchy, but they do not obscure that essential three-level pattern. One of the strengths of the Catholic Church lies in the basic simplicity of its organization, world-wide though it is.

SUMMARY OF KEY POINTS

- There are three main approaches to understanding leader-ship, like paths converging towards the mist-shrouded summit of a mountain: Qualities, Situational and Func-tional. Each makes a vital contribution.

- A leader should personify the qualities expected in any worker in their field, as well as some of the more generic attributes of a leader – for instance, enthusiasm, integrity, toughness and fairness, humanity, energy and resilience.
- As Socrates first pointed out, a leader should know his or her business. To that technical/professional knowledge must be added knowledge of human nature. Knowing what to do in situations calls for what the Greeks called *phronesis*, practical wisdom – a blend of intelligence and experience serviced by character.
- The Functional Approach integrates the other two in the 'breakthrough' model of the three circles – task, team and individual. The role of any leader can be defined by the model, and then further broken down for selection or training purposes into *functions*.

    There are a set of common *functions* – things you have to do – if these three overlapping areas of responsibility are to be met:

Defining the task	What are the purpose, aims and objectives? Why is this work worthwhile?
Planning	A plan answers the question of *how* you are going to get from where you are now to where you want to be. There is nothing like a bad plan to break up a group or frustrate individuals.
Briefing	The ability to communicate, to get across to people the task and the plan.
Controlling	Making sure that all resources and energies are properly harnessed.
Supporting	Setting and maintaining organizational and team values and standards.

Informing	Bringing information to the group and from the group – the *linking* function of leadership.
Reviewing	Establishing and applying the success criteria appropriate to the field.

These are best called *leadership functions*. Together they constitute the *role* of a leader, but leadership is more than the sum of those parts.

- Which circle is dominant in the mind of a leader at any one time depends upon the circumstances. For the model is dynamic and not static. It does suggest, however, the need for a balance over the longer term.
- Leadership is discernible on three broad levels: team, operational and strategic. These constitute the natural hierarchy in all working organizations, although the levels overlap and may be subdivided in a variety of ways.

Keep your fears to yourself but share your courage with others.

Robert Louis Stevenson

4

THE ROLE OF STRATEGIC LEADER

*No one would have doubted his ability to reign if he
had never become emperor.*
Tacitus, Roman historian, of Emperor Galba

We are now approaching the summit of the mountain. The distinguishing characteristic of the strategic leadership level, as we have seen, is that it implies responsibility for the *whole* as contrasted to the *part*, be it large (operational) or small (team). The three-circle model, however, applies to organizations as well as teams. It is worth dwelling on this point for a moment because it is not widely recognized (functional leadership is often – and wrongly – assumed to relate to *teams* only).

UNDERSTANDING ORGANIZATION

To *organize* means arranging so that the whole aggregate works as a unit, with each element having a proper function. The Greek *organon* meant literally 'that with which one works' and is related to *ergon*, work. It meant a tool or instrument, especially a musical instrument or a surgical instrument. But it was also used figuratively of the parts of the human body that were regarded as instruments of sense of faculty.

That sense of something made deliberately for man's use carries over into our concept of an organization. The *-ation* at the end of these long Latin-derived words means the action or process itself or the resulting condition. So an organization is what you get as a result of organizing, which in turn means systematic arranging for a definite purpose.

There is a useful distinction to be made between an *organization* and a *community*, though both are the products of humans imposing order on chaos. A community derives from the family, kindred group or tribe and has order through acceptance of common law and a form of government. Our nation states stand in this line of descent. Organizations, by contrast, are hunting parties at large. They are formed and developed with a particular form of work or – in the most general sense – task in mind.

You can eat apples, pears, grapes or bananas, but you cannot eat *fruit*. For fruit is a generic and therefore abstract concept. In a similar vein, you can see and experience life in organizations like an army, church, government department, bank or computer company, but you will never encounter *organization* as such, apart from its forms. You cannot see or touch it. It is an abstract concept too, like fruit.

Why bother with such an abstract concept? Because the world of organizations is extremely complex. They differ in size and shape, in purpose or function. Some are young and thrusting, others are old and venerable institutions. Not only does national culture colour them, but they develop their own organizational cultures. Faced with this bewildering variety, it is natural for the human mind to search for what is generic and common. It is a seeking of simplicity in the face of apparent complexity, but not for a purely academic end. For the concept of strategic leadership as at least theoretically a transferable art depends upon organizations having — beneath the surface — a generic unity. So organization is worth exploring further.

The only way we can think about something as abstract as organizations is by analogy or metaphor. One of the oldest metaphors used to help us understand is the human body. An organization — any organization — is a form of a whole made up of interdependent parts. Those two aspects — whole and parts — is generic; it is the essence of organization. The human body metaphor gives us some of our generic language about organization, such as *head* or *chief*, *corporate* and *member*.

THE THREE-CIRCLE MODEL

If we widen the metaphor and think of the human *person* and not just the body, that suggests two ideas. First, just as we are all unique and have our own distinctive personality, so groups — if they stay together — develop a *group personality*. And organizations, which are teams writ large, also form an *organizational personality*, or corporate culture as it is commonly called. It finds expression in the behaviour typical in that group or organization. Remember, therefore, that every organization you encounter is unique, and one of your first requirements as its strategic leader will be to be aware of that uniqueness.

Different though we all are as individual persons, however, we share some things in common, such as the attribute of personality itself. Most obviously, we all have needs — for food, drink and shelter, for example. Following that analogy, all organizations have three areas of need present in them:

- The need to accomplish the common task. Why is an organization formed? To achieve a task which an individual or small group cannot do on its own.
- The need to be held together and maintained as a working unity – a whole and not just a collection of discordant parts.
- The need which individuals bring with them into any organization.

Clearly we are back now to the three-circle model – the great discovery that the three areas of 'need' in *any* organization will act upon each other in an inter-influential way for good or ill. Therefore the role of a strategic leader is to do for the *whole* what other leaders should accomplish for the parts.

THE RELATION OF THE WHOLE TO THE PARTS

Under the microscope, the abstract invisible *organization* that informs all the organizations you or I have ever known turns out to have an atomic structure – the three interacting areas of forces I have called needs. As if in response to these needs a simple *hierarchy* of three levels of *leader* can be observed. By some subatomic work the six or seven main *functions* which compose their *roles* can also be mapped. So enormous strides have been made in the understanding of *organization*, though the many and various applications of that knowledge in the world of actual organizations lag far behind.

From this analysis it is clear that one major issue in all organization is *getting the right balance between the whole and the parts.*

Alfred P. Sloan who, along with Pierre DuPont, had an immense influence on corporate organization in the United States, saw that key issue in managerial teams. Writing in *My Years with General Motors* (1964), he expressed it thus: 'Good management rests on a reconciliation of centralization and decentralization, or "decentralization with coordinated control."' For 'centralization' read *whole*, and for 'decentralization' read *part*. Sloan's solution, as he hinted in his last phrase, is a *both-and-one*: decentralization but maintaining some control from the centre.

That sounds simple, but in practice it is not easy to achieve. No formula exists, whatever the popular pundits or gurus with their quick-fix solutions may say. As a strategic leader you have to be able to think it out for yourself. As Sloan continued:

> There is no hard and fast rule for sorting out the various responsibilities and the best way to assign them. The balance which is struck ... varies according to *what is being decided*, the *circumstances of the time, past experience*, and the *temperaments and skills of the executive involved*.

The relation of the whole to the parts as a perennial issue applies in both *unitary* and *federal* organizations. For there are *unitary* organizations, the ones that resemble your body; and there are *federal* ones, which are more like your family. In the political field, federal (from the Latin *foedus*, compact or league) set-ups are composed of political units that surrender their individual sovereignty to a central authority, but retain limited residuary powers of self-government. Power is distributed between that central authority and its constituent territorial units. The degree to which they are integrated varies from a *union*, where there is virtually one

political identity, to a loose *federation* which functions more
like an alliance whose members can choose to leave if they
wish. You will be familiar with the debates raging in
Europe about the nature of the European Union. Does
having its own currency and military force constitute steps
towards a strong federalist super-state on the model of the
United States?

Unitary organizations tend to resemble armies in that
you can theoretically tell people what to do and they will
do it. In modern jargon they are 'command and control
organizations'. As the Roman centurion put it simply to
Jesus: 'I am a man under authority, with soldiers under
me; and I say to one, "Go", and he goes, and to another,
"Come", and he comes, and to my slave, "Do this", and he
does it' (Matthew 8:9).

In federal organizations it is all very different. As the
federal leader you can lead but you cannot command. For
example, in the Church of England — a federation of forty-
three dioceses each headed by a bishop with its own
diocesan synod and administration — the Archbishop of
Canterbury supported by his brother Archbishop of York
who presides over the northern of the two provinces and
their new Archbishop's Council, can only make things
happen by carrying the dioceses with him.

Beneath the surface here you can identify the perennial
and ever-present issue of the relations of the *whole* to the
parts. That in turn is a reflection of the still deeper tensions
between the values of *order* and *freedom*. They appear to be
opposites, but the true function of *order* is to create *freedom*.

Where *all* leaders — not just those at strategic levels —
are committed to the whole as well as to their particular
part, and where each fulfils his role with all the qualities of
a good leader, the organization is dancing. The teamwork

of the leaders produces an effect that is best described as
harmony – the Greek work *harmos*, joint, also gives us words
like *arm*. All the arms or parts move and work together in
a pleasing and even graceful cooperation like the chords of
a musical composition or dancers in a chorus-line.

In this respect a great orchestra is a strong metaphor
illuminating that underlying concept of organization which
all organizations must express. The parts are the individual
players, grouped together in four teams – strings, wood-
wind, brass and percussion, each with its own 'first' player
or leader. In rehearsal and performance a conductor is the
operational leader, whose conducting holds the teams
together in an artistically expressive interpretation of
the composer's score. The conductor – from the Latin word
for one who leads people together or jointly – provides
both direction in the performance and cohesion in the
orchestra.

Yet an orchestra is a relatively small organization, and a
good conductor can establish rapport with all the players
literally over the heads of the section leaders as well as with
those playing solo parts. In very large organizations, say an
army of hundreds of thousands, it is obviously much more
difficult for the strategic leader to relate directly to people
in that way, but great leaders achieve just that.

In summary, three important things are common to
organization is a generic sense – that which applies to *all*
organizations as if they were manifestations of a platonic
idea:

- The three interacting circles of 'need' apply in every
  instance, just as needs for food, security and recognition
  are common to us all.
- Every organization, like every individual person, is unique;

it has a distinct group personality or corporate culture that is its generic fingerprints.

• The issue of the relation of the whole to the parts, the balance of order and freedom, is common to all.

It could be added, too, that all organizations are like fish: whether they are whale-sized or sprat-sized, they swim in the sea of society.

THE FUNCTIONS OF STRATEGIC LEADERSHIP

Although it has been a recent fashion to produce long lists of leadership 'competencies' – some as thick as telephone books – the essential requirements of a leader are simple. The core role at any level refracts into broad functions derived from the three-circle model. The three general functions are:

Figure 4.1 *The Broad Functions of Strategic Leadership*

This role, of course, has to be fulfilled against a background of a society which has many continuities, but is subject to a manner of changes which constantly impact on each of the three areas and the organization as a whole. Working from some first principles of organization, I think at present the generic role of strategic leadership (or *strategia*) refracts into seven colours or functions – in no order of importance:

Providing Direction for the Organization as a Whole	*Purpose/Vision*
Getting Strategy and Policy Right	*Strategic Thinking and Planning*
Making it Happen (Overall Executive Responsibility	*Operational/Administration*
Organizing or Reorganizing (Balance of Whole and Parts)	*Organization Fitness to Situational Requirement*
Releasing the Corporate Spirit	*Energy, Morale, Confidence, Espirit de corps*
Relating the Organization to other Organizations and Society as a whole	*Allies and Partners, Stakeholders, Political*
Choosing Today's Leaders and Developing Tomorrow's Leaders	*Teaching and leading the learning by example*

What fits a person to fulfil this role? It is clearly a demanding and challenging one, even though there are professional staff at hand – sometimes in cohorts to help the strategic leader where the responsibilities are great.

Let us assume that the strategic leader has awareness, understanding and skill in the three-circle model. Assume, too, that he or she knows their business. Take for granted as well personal leadership qualities such as enthusiasm, integrity, fairness, toughness, calmness, humanity and resilience. What is important next is the *mind* of the strategic leader as opposed to his or her heart and spirit.

INTELLIGENCE

The primary responsibility of the strategic leader is for the *whole* of the organization, as opposed to its *parts*, however large or significant they may be. And, by definition, a whole is more complex than a part. Add to this factor of complexity another: the positioning and relationship of the whole organization within a rapidly changing and highly complex social, political, economic and technological environment – and a global one at that. In order to fulfil effectively the strategic leadership role at that level, a person needs an above-average level of *intelligence*. Or, putting it another way, above-average intelligence is a necessary condition for a strategic leader but not a sufficient one. You may well fail without it, but it is not a single guarantee of success. It is right that at a strategic level it is less easy for leaders today than it was – due to an increase in complexity – to make up for the absence of intelligence by persistence or dogged determination, or by integrity and friendliness, to offset their limitations in mental ability.

Of course the complexity was always there, for strategic leaders have always had to deal with a more complex task, a more complex group and more complex individuals in their top teams than leaders at lower levels in the hierarchy. But the nature and extent of change have certainly made things considerably more complex than the days when the river of life moved forward in a slower and more placid way.

The principle is clear: 'The general truth still stands out', as Ordway Tead wrote over sixty years ago, 'that one should not assume a leadership role with which one's intelligence is not able to cope. No leader can [or should?]

rise higher than his mentality will allow.' Here mentality (or intelligence) means a person's all-round effectiveness in activities that depend upon thought.

THEMISTOCLES

The intellectual powers required in a leader are exemplified by this Athenian statesman and general who lived in the fourth century BC. Born of a father of no particular distinction and an alien mother, as a boy Themistocles showed unusual ability and application. Indeed, his career proved a point made by Pericles, that in Athens 'what counts is not membership of a particular class, but the actual ability which the man possesses'. As Thucydides wrote in his history of the war between Athens and Sparta, few surpassed Themistocles in practical wisdom:

> Themistocles was a man who showed an unmistakable natural genius; in this respect he was quite exceptional, and beyond all others deserves our admiration. Without studying a subject in advance or deliberating over it later, but using simply the intelligence that was his by nature, he had the power to reach the right conclusion in matters that have to be settled on the spur of the moment and do not admit of long discussions, and in estimating what was likely to happen, his forecasts of the future were always more reliable than those of others. He could perfectly well explain any subject with which he was familiar, and even outside his own department he was still capable of giving an excellent opinion. He was particularly remarkable at looking into the future and seeing there the hidden possibilities for good or evil. To sum him up in a few words, it may be said that through force of genius and by rapidity

of action this man was supreme at doing precisely the right thing at precisely the right moment.

As a young man Themistocles fought at Marathon, the battle in which the Persian invasion of Greece by Darius was defeated. But he foresaw that the Persians would be back. He persuaded his fellow Athenians to build a fleet. There was not a day to spare, for the Persians returned under Xerxes thirsting for revenge. Themistocles showed his greatness as a leader by abandoning Athens to the invaders, concentrating the Greek fleet at Salamis and, by a clever stratagem, tricking the Persian fleet into attacking his triremes in narrow straits where it was utterly defeated.

I have listed some of the aspects of intelligence above (pages 72–3). Especially important in strategic leadership, is the ability to step back from the complexity of detail and to see the 'wood for the trees' or 'the whole picture', so that its simple essentials or salient features stand out. Today this faculty is sometimes called 'taking the helicopter view', though it is no good going up in the metaphorical helicopter unless you have a trained analytical eye and some competence as a map-maker in your field.

Although Field Marshal Montgomery lacked some elements of *phronesis*, he excelled in this aspect of practical intelligence. Sticking to the strategic level of thought meant ruthlessly standing back from the complexity of the detail, except where detail was important enough to warrant the strategic leader's attention. In a lecture on 'Military Leadership' to the University of St Andrews in 1945, he made that point with characteristic clarity and vigour:

No man can be a great military leader unless he has the ability to cut through overlying difficulties, and to see clearly the few essentials in any problem with which he is faced. In any problem there are never more than a few essentials which are vital *to that problem*. These must be grasped out of the mass of details and must never be lost sight of. If in battle a commander loses sight of the few essentials that matter, he will suffer defeat.

But to see the essentials clearly he must not himself get too immersed in detail. Every great commander has had a chief of staff whose main task was the mastery of detail, thus leaving his master free to tackle the essentials of the problem together with those details, and only those details, which were vital to that problem. For though there is much detail with which a commander cannot and must not bother himself, it is interesting to note that every great commander has always concerned himself with certain of the details of his problems. Napoleon and Wellington are two good cases in point.

Strategy entails seeing the big picture and working on a large canvas. But pictures are made up of details. When Monet steps back from a giant picture of water-lilies and then steps forward to touch in a spot of colour with the tip of his brush, that detail matters. The art is to know what details should concern you, and what are best left to your staff. Do not, like Admiral Beatty, check every officer's mess bill in the Fleet!

'Too much intellect is not necessary in war,' Napoleon once wrote to his brother Joseph. 'Probably the most desirable attribute of all', or so he told Emmanuel Las Cases the French historian who accompanied him into exile on St Helena, 'is that a man's judgement should be above the common level. Success in war is based upon prudence, good conduct, and experience.'

That generic strand in practical wisdom – Napoleon called it prudence – of seeing things as they really are, not distorted by wishful thinking or unhinged by false assumptions, or restricted by a tunnel vision, 'he believed he had to an extraordinary degree'. He once remarked to General Gourgaud that 'the one that distinguishes me the most, *is to see the entire picture distinctly*'.

At Waterloo, Napoleon lost the day – just – to a general who also shared that attribute. 'Wellington's real gift was transcendent common sense,' wrote J. W. Fortescue, 'the rare power (shared also by Marlborough) of seeing things as they are, which signifies genius.' It is a comment that reminds me of the Spanish saying, *El sentido commun es el menos commun de los sentidos* – 'common sense is the least common of the senses'. To possess it to an above-average level is essential in a leader.

The ability to see the realities of a situation as a whole in this way sounds more like common sense than anything requiring intelligence. But remember that I said you do not have to be brilliant!

This clarity or freshness of vision – seeing the situation steadily as a whole with all its complex elements but also discerning its essentials – calls for what the Japanese call the *sunao* mind. Konosuke Matsushita, one of the most celebrated Japanese business leaders of the last century, strove for it all his life, as his close associate Toru Yamaguchi informed me:

> The *sunao* mind or the untrapped mind is calm and highly adaptable. It enables its owner to free himself of preconceived notions so that he can see things as they are. Managers who

don't have the *sunao* mind are often swayed by their own interests in decision-making, inevitably leading to corporate failure. Since managers, just like everyone else, are creatures of habit and prejudice, they have to cultivate the *sunao* mind to judge the situation accurately and lead the way to corporate success. Konosuke always said that cultivating the *sunao* mind is important, and that it wasn't easy, but he continued to his final days the constant work of developing it.

This freedom from preconceived notions, from subconscious assumptions and wishful thinking, is one of the marks of a person with the degree of *phronesis* required at all strategic leadership levels. There are countless examples of bad strategic decisions resulting from a failure to look at the world with a steady, unself-centred and dispassionate *sunao* mind, seeing it as it is and not as one would wish it to be. 'Without it,' Konosuke Matsushita wrote, 'one can enjoy neither genuine success in management nor genuine happiness in life.'

IMAGINATION

Themistocles exemplified *phronesis* – 'doing precisely the right thing at the right time' – but he also possessed another mental power valuable in a strategic leader – imagination. This is more highly desirable than essential, for others may well have creative ideas or imaginative suggestions. You do not have to be a creative thinker in the sense of being a person who reaches valuable new combinations of ideas. But strategic leaders need imagination to see new possibilities in the present or the future. They should also be leaders in innovation – the process of bringing those valuable new ideas to the market place or community in the shape of new products or services because for most organizations today innovation is strategically important. Nor must one expect from a strategic leader who lacks imagination that priceless gift in any organization – vision.

Imagination refers to the mind's power to call up images, to picture or conceive things that are not actually before the eye or within the experience. And so it may apply to the representation of what is remembered, or of what has never been experienced in its entirety, or indeed of what is actually non-existent. For as humans we have this extraordinary and unique faculty to consider actions or events not yet in existence.

Imagination is linked to *phronesis* in so far as the latter includes the power to *foresee* – to see some development beforehand, as Themistocles foresaw that the Persians would return to invade Greece again. 'Forewarned, forearmed', says the proverb. Such a strategic leader will then *anticipate* the foreseen development – responding mentally to it and taking action before it happens. Foresight of this nature, however, may simply be knowledge derived from ordinary reason and experience, either at the conscious level or subconsciously through the process of information-gathering, analysing and synthesizing we call *intuition*. In other words, it is not creative.

Creativity is about bringing something into existence that did not exist before. Whatever the merits of this book, it did not exist a year ago. We are *synthesizing* all the time – a word that means in Greek 'putting together' as opposed to *analysing*, separating. But we do not usually describe that as being creative unless the raw material and the finished product are very different. We then recognize that imaginative skill of a rare order – which belongs to an artist – has been at work.

Creative, imaginative, ingenious, inventive, original, resourceful – all these words apply to the active, exploratory mind and to its products, describing creators or creations that employ ordinary materials in extraordinary ways. *Creative* suggests the entire process whereby things that did not exist are conceived, given form, and brought into being.

On this spectrum, it is worth noting, an effective military strategic leader – a *strategos* or general – will certainly need to be *resourceful* – solving his problems despite limitation, finding whatever means are available and adapting them to his ends. He should also be *ingenious* in devising those stratagems which surprise, mislead or trick the enemy. But it is not a form of strategic leadership that calls for an *imaginative* mind – at least it did not in the past – still less for a *creative* one. A great general may create a fine army out of a rabble or create a high morale out of despair, but no one pretends that war itself is anything but destructive – an evil if somewhat necessary one. In the majority of strategic leadership roles, however, there is a clear and ever stronger call for imagination and creativity as well as practical wisdom.

HUMILITY

In his book on ethics Aristotle placed *phronesis* among the 'Intellectual Virtues', as it played a vital part in guiding a person to what is good or right conduct. Humility does not accompany it, which is surprising when you consider that

its opposite, *hubris* – pride or arrogance – and its consequences are the stuff of Greek tragedies. What claim does
humility have to be numbered among the intellectual
virtues of an excellent strategic leader?

Humility is by origin a religious concept. The excessive
self-confidence of *hubris* was interpreted as a form of inso-
lence against the gods, who in Greek tragedy redress the
balance by humiliating the offender. In the biblical tradition humility is the result of seeing God. In our more
secular age it takes the form of having a sense of one's
relative insignificance before something infinitely greater
and better. You may know that you are very good, even
the best in your field – humility does not imply lack of
self-confidence or belief in yourself – but measured against
the source and sum of all reality, what are you?

Because humility is a reflection, like the light of the
moon, it is pointless to try to gauge your own degree of
humility. If you feel that you are humble already compared
to others you will be tempted to congratulate yourself, and
pride comes on stage again! But you can see humility in
the actions or words of others, providing they are sincere
and not put on for the sake of show. Sir Isaac Newton, one
of the great scientists of all time, once said;

> I do not know what I may appear to the world, but to myself I
> seem to have been only like a boy playing on the seashore,
> and diverting myself in now and then finding a smoother
> pebble or a prettier shell than ordinary, whilst the great ocean
> of truth lay all undiscovered before me.

Nor would Newton accept the fame thrust upon him. 'If I
have seen further,' he wrote to Robert Hooke in 1975, 'it
is by standing on the shoulders of giants.'

HUMILITY – A TEST OF GREATNESS

'I believe the first test of a truly great man is his humility. I do not mean by humility, doubt of his own power, or hesitation in speaking his opinions; but a right understanding of the relation between what *he* can do and say, and the rest of the world's sayings and doings. All great men not only know their business, but usually know that they know it, and are not only right in their main opinions, but they usually know that they are right in them; only, they do not think much of themselves on that account. Arnolfo knows he can build a good dome at Florence; Albrecht Dürer writes clearly to one who had found fault in his work, "It could not have been done better"; Sir Isaac Newton knows that he has worked out a problem or two that would have puzzled anybody else; – only they do not expect their fellow-men therefore to fall down and worship them; they have a curious under-sense of powerlessness, feeling that the greatness is not *in* them, but *through* them; that they could not do or be anything else than God made them. And they see something Divine and God-made in every other man they meet, and are endlessly, foolishly, incredibly merciful.'

John Ruskin, *Modern Painters* (1843)

In the Western tradition leadership is associated with strong self-confidence and a powerful egotism – breeding-grounds for the kind of *hubris* that the world witnessed in Hitler, Mussolini and Stalin. Although Montgomery was a Christian by belief, he was not untouched by arrogance as a leader. T. E. Lawrence was not noted for humility either, though he was aware of the problem and welcomed humiliation – even created his own – like the hero of a Greek tragedy. As far as I know, the word humility was never applied to him.

Yet part of the effectiveness of three of the great Second World War generals – Slim, Alexander and Eisenhower – lay in the very fact that they possessed the personal grace and intellectual virtue of humility, as their biographers testify. My own conversations with Slim and Alexander left me with that impression as well. General Sir John Glubb, as Glubb Pasha and Commander-in-chief of the Arab Legion in which I served, was the only general I have come to know really well personally. A deeply religious man, Glubb had a transparent humility about him.

'Humility must always be the portion of any man who receives acclaim earned in the blood of his followers and the sacrifices of his friends,' said Eisenhower. It was a quality he regarded as essential in a leader:

> A sense of humility is a quality I have observed in every leader whom I have deeply admired. I have seen Winston Churchill with humble tears of gratitude on his cheeks as he thanked people for their help to Britain and the Allied cause.
>
> My own conviction is that every leader should have enough humility to accept, publicly, the responsibility for the mistakes of the subordinates he has himself selected and, likewise, to give them credit, publicly, for their triumphs. I am aware that some popular theories of leadership hold that the top man must always keep his 'image' bright and shining. I believe, however, that in the long run fairness and honesty, and a generous attitude towards subordinates and associates, pay off.

A good strategic leader will certainly accept complete personal responsibility if the decision he or she has made leads to failure. He will not 'pass the buck' to his colleagues or subordinates. After the failure of his first attack on Quebec, General Wolfe wrote: 'The blame I take entirely upon my shoulders and I expect to suffer for it. Accidents cannot be helped. As much of the plan as was defective falls justly on me.'

Eisenhower also shouldered the responsibility of failure. The weather conditions in the first few days of June 1944 caused his Air Commander to argue for further postponement of the invasion of Europe. After consultation with his generals and specialist advisers, Eisenhower himself took the momentous decision to take the risk and go ahead on 6 June 1944. Before the invasion fleet set out he wrote this press release, to be used if necessary:

> Our landings have failed and I have withdrawn the troops. My decision to attack at this time and place was based upon the best information available. The troops, the Air and the Navy did all that bravery and devotion to duty could do. If any blame or fault is attached to the attempt it is mine alone.

Hitler exemplified the opposite side of the coin – irresponsibility. He persistently blamed the failure of his military plans upon the incompetence of his subordinates or their lack of will-power, while taking for himself the credit of the early successes. When the roof fell in Hitler castigated the German people for letting him down. He could neither see nor face his ultimate responsibility as leader.

Yet why is humility an *intellectual* virtue, as I have

suggested it is? To accept that one may have been wrong after a decision and to accept the consequences is only one aspect of humility. To be open to others and their ideas before a decision means that you do not believe you are a genius who alone knows what to do – this is an equally important facet of humility. As the Scottish proverb says, *The clan is greater than the chief.* A chief who believes that is more likely to consult the clan and listen to their ideas. As G. K. Chesterton said, 'It is always the secure who are humble.'

The principal contribution of humility to the mind of a strategic leader is that it signifies a marked lack of self in mental perception and calculations. Self is like an ever-present shadow, it can obscure the clarity of the *sunao* or untrapped mind. In the original metaphor, to see God is to see reality as it is and all else including self in the blinding light of that Sun. Putting it another way, if you and I could but see reality as it is – not just that which presents itself to our senses – we should reflect it as humility. And the more humble we are, the more likely it is that we shall see life and its changing situations and other people as they really are. Humble people are standing in front of their own shadows. They see clearly relations and proportions with the scheme of things.

'If you lack humility,' said James Blyth, a former chairman and chief executive of Boots, in a lecture on leadership, 'you are not a leader, not perhaps even a true person.' Blyth suggested that humility as a leader means:

- you acknowledge the common bond of humanity;
- you accept that you are less than perfect;
- you are willing to listen;
- you have the resilience to try again.

He quoted Peter Drucker: 'The leader of the past knows how to tell; the leader of the future will know how to ask.' A belief in oneself is not arrogance, he continued, but more confidence in that part of one's self that 'looks on tempests and is never shaken'. It is the ability to be closely in touch with the passing show, but not embroiled in it.

THE ANATOMY OF WISDOM

Wisdom outranks all other words – discernment, discrimination, judgement, sagacity, sense – when it comes to denoting mental qualities that have to do with the ability to understand situations, anticipate consequences and make sound decisions. For it suggests a rare combination of discretion, maturity, keenness of intellect, broad experience, extensive learning, profound thought, and compassionate understanding. In its wider application wisdom implies the highest and noblest exercise of the faculties of moral nature as well as of the intellect. In the slightly narrower compass of *phronesis*, wisdom can be analysed into three elements: intelligence, experience and goodness.

> Experience is by industry achiev'd
> And perfected by the swift course of time.

Apart from this vocational experience of which Shakespeare wrote in *The Two Gentlemen of Verona*, a broader experience of life is needed. Matched with intelligence, which I have sketched in above, the two work together like two eyes joined in sight. But why *goodness*?

The Greeks sensibly had two different words for *good* – *kalos* (skilled in, proficient at) and *agathos* (good in the moral sense). Originally, in Homeric times, *agathos* described how a man discharged his functions as king or warrior, judge or shepherd. To inquire if a Homeric nobleman was *agathos* meant was he courageous, wise and kingly? In other words, did he, fight, manage and rule with success? Virtue or normal excellence referred to his art or skill in performing his socially allotted role. Later, *agathos* came to refer not to the qualities required to fulfil a role but to certain human qualities we call *goodness*.

Something of that original sense remains in the leadership context. For *integrity* and being *just* or fair are essential leadership qualities, but both are also moral virtues. Therefore it is not strictly true that you can be a *good* leader without being a *leader for good*. Integrity, from the Latin *integer*, whole, implies a moral soundness and unity created by adherence to values as if outside oneself, notably truth. So integrity is close to honesty. They always breed trust. And what is more strategically important in all human relations than trust? 'Trust being lost,' wrote the Roman historian Livy, 'all the social intercourse of men is brought to nought.'

The element of *goodness* in wisdom could almost be described as *character*. By saying that a person has character (as opposed to personality and temperament) we mean that he or she has:

- a conception of what they should be and what others may rightly expect of them;
- principles that they will not be likely to betray;
- loyalties and commitments of an enduring kind;
- firmness when subject to attractive temptations;
- responsibility for their own actions and an expectation that others will be responsible too;

- a sense of the reality of moral values, so that they are not a matter of personal preference.

Character, from the name of the Greek tool used for engraving on stone or metal, consists of the attributes or features which mark out an individual. In this context, it applies more specifically to the aggregate of moral qualities by which a person is judged, apart from his intelligence, competence or special talents.

Why *goodness*? Because many of the decisions which will face you as a strategic leader will have a moral dimension to them. If you lack wisdom – intelligence, experience and goodness – your judgement will be fatally impaired. Not to know right from wrong as a leader is worse than not knowing port from starboard. A ship with such a morally blind leader at the helm is bound to crash into the rocks.

SUMMARY OF KEY POINTS

- An organization is the product of the activity of *organizing*. It is an instrument designed or evolved for a purpose and it can be best understood in terms of that purpose, the reason for its existence.
- Although we only know organizations, it is possible to think of human organization in the abstract. It has three elements which are found genetically and generically in all working organizations:

  1. The three-circle model – the interaction of task, group and individual.
  2. Being human, organizations always manifest a group personality or culture that distinguishes one from

another, even in the same social setting and field of enterprise.

3. The relation of the whole to the parts – order and freedom – is a fundamental issue in organization.

- The leadership role has evolved in response to the three interlocking areas of need. At strategic level the broad functions of achieving the task, building the team and developing the individual which constitute it, can be broken down further into seven generic functions, like light refracted into seven colours of the rainbow:

  - Providing direction for the organization as a whole
  - Getting strategy and policy right
  - Making it happen
  - Organizing or reorganizing

  - Releasing the corporate spirit
  - Relating the organization to other organizations and society as a whole
  - Developing tomorrow's leaders

- Strategic leadership differs not in kind but in magnitude of issues and scale of complexity encountered. It calls for a commensurate level of what the Greeks called *phronesis*, practical wisdom. 'A leader is not so much clever', said Henry Kissinger, 'as lucid and clear-sighted.'
- As distinct from *phronesis*, the intellectual qualities of being imaginative and creative are desirable if not essential.
- Humility may seem an unlikely virtue in a leader, but who wants to work for an arrogant chief executive? It contributes to the mental clarity of a thinker by reducing subjectivity.
- Wisdom – the mind of a *wita*, leader – is composed of three elements: intelligence, experience and goodness.

Character matters in all true leadership, not least at strategic level where it can be most under siege.

These are hard times in which a genius would wish to live.
Great necessities call forth great leaders.
Abigail Adams, writing to Thomas Jefferson (1790)

PART TWO

LEADING THE WAY

5

THE FIRST HUNDRED DAYS

A good beginning makes a good ending.
English proverb

'I may be accused of rashness, but not of sluggishness,' Napoleon once told Marshal Berthier. Escaping from prison on Elba with a few aides, he landed in France and he won over the troops sent to arrest him, marched at their head into Paris, ejected the restored French king, resumed his imperial authority, reorganized the government, regrouped the *Grande Armée* and fought the decisive Battle of Waterloo. It almost came off – Wellington always described the battle as a close-run thing – but in fact those three months of dynamic activity only led Napoleon back into a second exile on the tiny island of St Helena in the middle of the Atlantic.

'A hundred days, sire, have elapsed since the fatal moment when Your Majesty was forced to quit your capital in the midst of tears,' begins the address of Count de Chambord, the prefect, after the signing of the abdication. This is the origin of our phrase 'The First Hundred Days' – in Napoleon's case the days between 20 March 1815 when he reached Paris and 28 June, the date of the second restoration of Louis XVIII.

'Let me assert my firm belief that the only thing we have to fear is fear itself,' declared President Franklin D.

Roosevelt in a ringing voice during his First Inaugural Address on a chilly day in March 1933. Like a general taking over a dispirited army, Roosevelt set about changing the 'atmosphere' of America so that it reflected his own confident, positive and forward-looking spirit. His first one hundred days, when he initiated the major recovery measures of what he called the New Deal for America, did much to bring about that change of mood. America awoke the morning after the address feeling that an optimistic and constructive leader was now at the helm of its fortunes.

How do strategic leaders in business face the challenge of making their first one hundred days equally decisive? A year or two ago I suggested to Caroline Kennedy, then editor of the *Director* magazine in the United Kingdom, that some research into the question might lead to an interesting article – and so it did. The following two case studies are taken from her article 'The First Hundred Days' (March 1995).

Why the opportunity? Most organizations have an established *status quo*, an existing state of affairs. People know the familiar geography: what is important, where influence lies, what ideas are likely to be accepted, who has prestige, how things are done, what enhances one's career. They know where the land mines are. The arrival of a new chief executive unbalances all this for an all-too-brief period. Everything is temporarily up in the air; nothing can be taken for granted, and expectations of change are high. There is a willingness to listen and learn, a tacit agreement to suspend judgement and to give the newcomer the chance to show some leadership. It is the honeymoon period. Now or never. As Shakespeare wrote in *Julius Caesar*:

We, at the height, are ready to decline.
There is a tide in the affairs of men,
Which, taken at the flood, leads on to fortune;
Omitted, all the voyage of their life
Is bound in shallows and in miseries.
On such a full sea are we now afloat,
And we must take the current when it serves,
Or lose our ventures.

Used well, this unique opportunity to challenge the *status quo* provides the new strategic leader with the chance to initiate a new order. Changes that you wish to make across the whole organization can be identified and signposted. What begins to be clear is what legacy you wish to leave behind you, the organization as it will be at the end of your last one hundred days – whenever that will be. If the new order is not established and does not start to settle in during or within reach of that short but critical first period, what happens? Yes, you are right, the old order reasserts itself. The organization is then moving quickly upon what Keats called 'the journey homewards to habitual self'.

To use this time well you, as the new strategic leader, need to have a clear picture of what you are trying to achieve and how you are going to go about it. Remember the military maxim, *Time spent on reconnaissance is seldom wasted.* Find out as much as you can about the organization. Talk to some of the key people. Make some visits. Formulate some working hypotheses – they are no more than that. Then you will be able to 'hit the deck running'.

CASE STUDY:

ALAN SHEPPARD AT GRAND METROPOLITAN

'If you don't do it in the first hundred days, you won't do it in a hundred years.' So says Lord Sheppard, the feisty, lead-from-the-front chairman of Grand Metropolitan. As chief executive and combined CEO/chairman from 1986 to 1993, Sheppard steered the strategy which has transformed GrandMet from a conglomerate of assorted businesses into a focused food-and-drink giant and the owner of key US businesses such as Pilsbury, Pet and Häagen-Dazs.

Sheppard was talking mainly in the context of acquisition and divestment, particularly in relation to making big changes in newly acquired businesses. When GrandMet bought Pilsbury, major organizational changes were completed in weeks. 'We are very fast, so we are termed frenetic,' says Sheppard. 'But we can be fast because we have very short lines of communication; there is a two-way dialogue with almost daily exchanges that hone the process.'

Among landmarks of Sheppard's own first hundred days in late 1986/early 1987 were the acquisition of Heublein, the wine and spirit arm of RJR Nabisco, for $1.2 billion, the sale of a Scottish brewing and pubs business to Allied Lyons, and a number of new appointments including the new post of group strategy development director.

The direction that had been identified for the company, whether by predecessors or by Alan Sheppard himself, was clear: to move from being a collection of assorted businesses to a food-and-drink major player with a strong base in the United States.

With that in mind he could move swiftly in terms of acquisitions and divestments. Presumably the Scottish brewing and pubs business did not fit in with his vision of what GrandMet should be in, say, three years' time and he was sufficiently sure of that fact to dispose of it.

Organizational changes were needed in new acquisitions such as Pilsbury as part of the digestion process. Notice that a flat structure at the top and good two-way communication on a daily basis enabled Alan Sheppard to move fast and carry his team with him. In today's business conditions, the capability for fast action when it is called for is absolutely essential. A business today needs to be able, in Mohammed Ali's famous words, *to float like a butterfly and sting like a bee.*

The appointments that you as a strategic leader make in the first hundred days are also key signals to the organization. I shall discuss this aspect more fully in the following chapter, but it is worth noting here that, by creating the new post of group strategy development director, Alan Sheppard was signalling the need for the *group* as a whole to have a common strategy, not merely its constituent parts or member businesses.

CASE STUDY:

JAN LESCHLY AT SMITHKLINE BEECHAM

Jan Leschly's first hundred days at SmithKline Beecham (SB) had barely progressed beyond a fortnight when the company announced a dramatic acquisition which fairly bowled the financial commentators over, though in fact negotiations had been under way since the previous summer. The sense of dynamic action was undoubtedly reinforced by Leschly's charismatic style, his youthful career as a competitor in championship tennis and his restless body language and emphatic, Danish-accented voice – all very different from the average executive 'suit'.

Recruited from the US Squibb Corporation in 1990, shortly after the Anglo-American merger of Beecham and SmithKline Beckman, Leschly ran SB's world-wide pharmaceuticals business for just over four years before moving up to the chief executive's chair. He had the great benefit, as he points out, of a transition year working with the outgoing chief executive, Robert Bauman, on strategy for the group and on forming a 'Vision 2000' management team to fine-tune the details of that strategy.

It was clearly a stimulating time for both men. 'Bob was involved but knew he was not going to be implementing the results. I had a wonderful period working with Bob but not being responsible. I can certainly recommend this to any CEO. The key is to have a proper transition. During this transition period, SB was adapting to 'a whole new environment' in the drugs industry, in which governmental pressures on health care costs were pointing to new integrated alliances between pharmaceutical and healthcare companies. Internally, SB was also undergoing major restructuring into individual business units and replacing management functions by processes, as Leschly puts it, 'turning the silos 180 degrees on their side'.

Leschly took over as CEO on 25 April 1994, the day of his first annual meeting. The decision to buy Diversified Pharmaceutical Services, a US healthcare management group, was taken by the management team the following day and an hour later the board was reconvened to approve the $2 billion purchase. It was announced on 3 May. A bunch of formidable new executive directors had recently joined the board, including Sir Christopher Hogg of Courtaulds and Reuters and Paul Allaire of the Xerox Corporation. Leschly had already spent a good deal of time in getting to know them on an individual basis – a tip he hands on to every new CEO of a major company.

Unknown to the outside world, work also started at this time on bidding for Stirling Winthrop, Inc, an acquisition sealed in August for $2.92 billion and another key step towards SB's goal of becoming the world's leading player in over-the-counter medicines.

The gradual transition meant that 'only natural changes' were required within the top management team: the two leaders, who were retiring, Chairman Henry Wendt and Chief Executive Bob Bauman, and two others who were retiring with them. Replacements for the latter were already decided, and Sir Peter Walters of Blue Circle and the Midland Bank was coming in as non-executive chairman.

Reflecting in the New Year on his first eventful months of acquisition and divestment to focus SB as an integrated healthcare player, Leschly was patently gratified that the company had just rated four mentions in the *Wall Street Journal*'s review of the year – more than any other corporation.

'What do I spend my time on?' he asks rhetorically. 'I believe the key change from being an operator to being CEO is that I do a lot more strategic thinking. Notice that I did not say planning – strategic planning is different from strategic thinking.'

'I spend a lot of time outside – talking to customers, suppliers, and also working with my management team and spending time talking around the table. The other key is the communication process, talking directly to employees. I have what I call "all-hands meetings" wherever I go – to a plant in Brazil, say. It is important to meet 'live' with employees, my internal customers. After Christmas I meet all headquarters employees at breakfast meetings: I go through the highlights of the year and set out goals for the year ahead.

'Ninety-six per cent of all our grade 8 and up managers – perhaps 15,000 – are fully aware of our strategic intent and are aligning their work accordingly.

'Strategy is an involving process. What do we want to focus the business on? For example, there is our huge investment in genetics, something that will not yield until years down the line.'

At the same time as the company was 'going more and more towards process management', identifying core competencies and adapting its resource allocations, what should be done internally and what should be brought in?

Then, Leschly adds, there is the whole question of incentives: 'What drives us? We are a very transnational company, moving more towards giving incentives for the economic value that every business adds to the whole.'

A long time ago, Leschly told himself he only wanted the CEO job 'if I can make a difference. In 1994 we came a long way towards how we want the business to be in five to ten years' time. When I leave the company *I want it to be among a handful of major successful global players in healthcare.*'

At this point he recommends new CEOs to cultivate in-depth knowledge of their non-executives. 'Don't underestimate the time spent with them. You can't achieve your goals unless the board is behind you. Appreciate that you can't do it all on your own.'

Jan Leschly is one of the new breed of business strategic leaders that emerged in the 1990s. These are men and women who clearly saw the difference between management and leadership, and are in no doubt that their role is to provide strategic leadership. They applied what General Slim called 'the principle of personal leadership' to their role as chief executives.

Significantly Leschly had a clear idea of how best to spend his time. For example, he saw that a key difference between being an operational leader and a strategic leader is 'that I do a lot more strategic thinking', which he distinguishes from the processes of corporate strategic planning. He needed time to think.

Paradoxically, the higher you rise in an organization, the more time you spend out of it (see Chapter 8). But there is a balance to be struck here between *outside* involvements – talking to customers, suppliers, financiers – and *inside* requirements, especially time with your top management team. This is where your practical wisdom comes into play, for there are no rules. Every situation is different.

Notice that a good time-manager like Leschly also has time to communicate to the whole organization. Both personal and direct, this communication extends beyond the upper crust of management, and touches as many people as possible. The aim is to align a critical mass of the operational and team leaders, and ultimately everyone, with the broad strategic direction. That in turn will inform goals and the setting of objectives in all parts of the organization.

You can sense, too, the vision behind Leschly's approach to being a chief executive – 'When I leave the company I want it to be among a handful of major successful global players in healthcare.' His own personal motivation was equally clear: it was 'to make a difference' in bringing about that desired result. Within those first hundred days he had identified clearly the leadership legacy he wished to leave behind him. Have you done that yet?

How far was Jan Leschly successful as a strategic leader? His final act before leaving the company was to engineer a major merger with Glaxo. As I have some shares in the company I received this report from my portfolio manager seven years after Leschly's first hundred days at SB:

> Glaxo Wellcome and SmithKline Beecham have now obtained all the regulatory approvals necessary to complete their merger, and the new company, Glaxo SmithKline has now been formed.
>
> The combined Glaxo SmithKline is an exceptionally strong company, with global market share of around 7 per cent. Given the benefits that should come from combining Glaxo's strength in pharmaceutical research and development with SmithKline's tremendous sales and marketing capabilities, the merged group will have the potential to achieve far greater growth than either Glaxo or SmithKline alone.

CASE STUDY:

JOHN JACKSON AT SKETCHLEY

One CEO who has followed the hundred-day rubric is John Jackson of Sketchley, the dry-cleaning group which has seen some radical management shake-ups in recent years. Taking charge in October 1994, Jackson reported his working principles to *Director* magazine as he reached day sixty-four.

First thirty days:

1. Take a very good look at what is really going on by meeting a large number of managers, shopfloor employees, bankers, investors, customers and suppliers. Keep asking questions, questions and questions – and double-check the answers.

2. Take a good look at the strengths and weaknesses of your directors and their first-line managers. For each key employee ask the question: 'Are they good enough to achieve the goals you are going to set the company'? If not, can you coach and redirect their talents? If the answer is no to these two questions, start the process of replacement.

3. Identify the culture, and working standards of the various facets of the organization.

Second thirty days:

1. 'Prepare the strategic plan for the short and long term. State where you want each division of the company to be at in terms of *financial performance*, *market share*, *quality standards*, *customer service* and *employee relations* by the end of the first twelve months.

2. Let each divisional managing director work out a plan to achieve these goals, and agree priorities and resources required to meet the plan.

3. At the group monthly board meeting, set out clearly your plans for the year ahead. Ensure they understand, have an input into, and support the plan.

Next forty days and onwards:

1. *Clearly communicate* to all levels of employees the tasks that lie ahead of them.

2. Set up a concise and clear communication process throughout the organization to keep them updated on

progress being made within their area, and by the
company overall.

3. *Bring about a culture change. Put the customer first. Attend* to
detail and speed up *the pace of the* organization. Get
employees to buy into the change process, and feel they
are making a contribution and that it is appreciated.

The main obstacles to change are: apathy and speed of
response.

Jackson's advice to new CEOs would be:

- Observe and identify (first thirty days).
- Preparation and selling of strategic plans and vision for
the company (next thirty days);
- Avoid setting standards and expectations too low.
- Set out your stall and make it happen (ongoing), and don't
accept second-best.

CASE STUDY:
JOHN HARVEY-JONES AT ICI

Sir John Harvey-Jones has written his own autobiographical
account of his first hundred days as Chairman/Chief Executive of ICI, as well as a best-selling book on his philosophy
of leadership and management, *Making It Happen*. Without
repeating the whole story I thought I would share with you
my personal glimpse of this outstanding business strategic
leader in action during that critical first 'window of opportunity' period of three months.

In September 1981 Bill Stead and Edgar Vincent – the
two senior managers responsible for group personnel in ICI

– came to see me at the University of Surrey. They gave me some background about the plight of ICI – 1980 had been a disastrous year in which profits fell by 48 per cent and the dividend was cut for the first time since the company's formation in 1926 – and told me that the executive directors had decided that the first priority in personnel strategy should be the development of what they called manager-leaders. They wished me to act as outside consultant.

Edgar Vincent asked me if I could suggest other organizations that had used my ideas to grow leaders, with the exception of the Army which he and his colleague had already visited. I remember being stuck for an answer. There were of course many organizations – some 2,000 of them in 1981 – which were sending managers and supervisors on ACL courses, or even putting the entire management through an ACL programme but that was not the question put to me. I could think of no organizations that were *growing* leaders in the ways I had been recommending. I suggested that ICI might like to be the first real guinea-pig, and Bill Stead and Edgar Vincent thought that would be an excellent idea. They also suggested that in exchange such a project should prove an extremely valuable opportunity within the context of my own research into leadership and leadership development.

After some further discussions with Edgar, now Group Personnel Manager, we agreed upon a plan to get the ball rolling. Instead of my writing a paper on strategy or the board issuing a set of edicts, it was decided that a major conference would be convened at Warren House, ICI's conference centre, at which a cross-section of able top managers in the company's nine divisions could meet and discuss the matter, hearing from various specialists like me in the course of three days. Then it would be left up to them to identify the right strategy for ICI, and for their own divisions within it, in order to achieve the first of the company's key personnel policies – the development of manager-leaders.

The Warren House conference took place in January 1982, based upon a programme that Edgar Vincent and I had worked out together. As consultant I was present throughout.

Since my initial meeting with Edgar and his colleagues, ICI had appointed in November a new chairman from among its three deputy chairmen – not the one that had been mentioned to me as the most likely candidate. Edgar evidently regarded his appointment as a considerable bonus to the enterprise of leadership development that was engaged upon. I met John Harvey-Jones for the first time in the bar at Warren House that evening (27 January) and he spoke to the conference informally after supper.

The chairman began by saying that ICI was wrongly positioned in terms of where its hardware was, its type of products, and its over-capacity in some areas. Above all, it was not well positioned in the real growth markets of the Far East and the United States. This picture had implications for management style/leadership pattern. 'We have first class management,' he said, 'but it has become excessively bureaucratic and political. We've adopted a value system that is ponderous, negative, unanxious to share risk and not willing to give headroom.'

'What's the pattern for the next ten years? Instability and change will characterize it. It will be a repositioning decade, with lots of new patterns and shifts of power. Growth, as we've known it, will be greatly reduced. No company can exist without growth, therefore we have to make it by pinching the markets of competitors, outdating his products and developing new ones,' John Harvey-Jones continued. He talked some more about how he saw the emergence of some giants in the chemicals industry in Europe, a pattern like the one in America. Technologically we were in for enormous change.

'What do we need to work in this environment?' he asked next. 'A new attitude to risk – we minimize risk, we don't maximize opportunities. But the biggest risk of all is to take no risk. We have to be flexible, because we won't read the future right. We need to have an ability to move fast, more market sensitivity, more openness and trust, greater tolerance of differences and more courage in dealings with others. Individuals have the answers, not ICI as a group.'

John Harvey-Jones then turned to his work plans after he formally became chairman in April. He would start at the top with the board. 'Let's meet in the middle. We haven't got time for a slow trickle-down.' 'Double-guessing would be cut out by having fewer people – the size of the board would be reduced for a start.' The discussion that followed was exceptionally frank on all sides. In response to one question the chairman pointed to 'the catalytic things we can do' to encourage entrepreneurial enterprise. 'The ICI system will kill any business! The dynamic has been increasingly centralized. One of my jobs at entry level has been to hold an umbrella over my chaps' heads. Senior management is about getting people to own the problem and to do something about it, not passing it up. Our system must be not to have a system.'

A sense of urgency coloured his closing remarks. It is a race against time – we are too late – the world is breaking up – bits to be grabbed now. His vision of an adaptable, open, flexible, fast-moving ICI – ready to move quickly in perceived thrusts or directions. 'We've got to grow this new ICI.' Asked about the attitude of his fellow directors, he said that he couldn't order them. 'I have to lead the board to lead. They voted for me. There is no such thing as one leader. What matters most is a common sense of values. Leadership is about getting extraordinary performance out of ordinary people. In ICI we have got extraordinary people to begin with.'

In answer to another question, John Harvey-Jones highlighted another strength. 'ICI exists through its ability to work informal systems. We have got the ability to work together informally. I'm keen on clarity of organizational responsibilities, but we've got to keep this informal ability to work together, because we'll never get the structure right. We start miles ahead of any other European chemical company; we have shown in the last two years that we can be unbelievably fast. We've got a lot going for us, such as a good technological basis. In other respects I could wish we were better placed. But we can knock the hell out of the opposition.'

Inspired by those words and determined to end the 'treacle', as they called it, which the ICI bureaucratic culture had created, the participants in the conference continued working all next day on their strategic action plans for liberating the leadership and enterprise within ICI.

Among the recommendations each of the nine divisional teams resolved to introduce leadership training based upon the three-circles approach – task, team and individual – which I had outlined. In keeping with the new emphasis on decentralization, it was left to the divisions to devise their own leadership training programmes, using me as a resource. My contribution varied accordingly. Looking through my diaries, I see that I spoke to all the senior managers in one division; spent three days at Warren House with all the finance directors and their teams; advised one division on its leadership course and did some on-the-spot 'training of the trainers' after the first one; did some counselling sessions with some divisional directors on an individual basis; advised four managers who had been asked to make recommendations on the key issue of leadership to the board of the Organics Division; reviewed ICI's method of selecting graduates; and carried out an evaluation survey of all the external leadership courses currently being used by ICI. But perhaps my most important contribution was to lead a one-day seminar each year for four years with Edgar Vincent for the nine divisional training managers responsible for the functional leadership courses in their various forms.

It is not within my compass here to say more about the radical changes that have taken place during the chairmanship of Sir John Harvey-Jones, which ended in 1987, especially as Sir John himself is writing a book on the subject. As I mentioned earlier, in 1984 ICI was the first British company to break the £1 billion profit barrier (the second, National Westminster Bank, has also made continual use of ACL since its introduction in 1969).

Of course, the success of ICI in the period under review cannot be ascribed entirely to leadership, although I don't suppose that anyone would deny the importance of leadership as shown by Sir John Harvey-Jones and by many other ICI manager-leaders at every level in the divisions. As for leadership development, it can be safely said that it has proved to be not incompatible with business success.

Leadership is about getting extraordinary performance out of ordinary people.

Sir John Harvey-Jones

THE FIRST CHALLENGE TO YOUR PRACTICAL WISDOM

'There are no precise or determined rules,' Napoleon declared. 'Everything depends on the character that nature has given to the general, on his qualities, his shortcomings, on the nature of the troops, on the range of firearms, on the season and on a thousand other circumstances which are never the same.' So the commander-in-chief has to think for himself, 'guided by their own experience or genius'. You may not be a genius, but you certainly have an above-average degree of what, as we have seen, Napoleon called prudence – our old friend *phronesis*. Probably the most desirable attribute of all in a strategic leader, or so he told Las Cases, 'is that a man's judgement should be above the common level'. By prudence, incidentally, Napoleon did not mean that a good general should be cautious in the conduct of affairs. *Au contraire*: a good general 'must be slow in deliberation and quick in execution'. Whenever Napoleon used the word prudence he meant the exercise of intelligence and experience before making decisions, careful management and presence of mind. 'But all that will be of little use to him,' he warned, 'if he does not have the sacred fire in the depths of his heart, this driving ambition which alone can enable one to perform great deeds.'

You can see that Napoleon was not a man to waste the opportunities of those first hundred days. Success may have eluded him, but he cannot be faulted for giving it less than his all. How about you?

Remember those words 'slow in deliberation and quick in execution'. Don't rush in where the proverbial angels fear to tread. Take your time. Listen and observe, give your mind time to weigh things up in its own way; and test out your provisional decisions on those whom you can trust before you go public. But leave people in no doubt that within a limited period of time – it may not be the hundredth day – you will either be placing your seal on the present *status quo* or introducing changes. 'What do you have in mind?' you will be asked. 'Wait and see,' you should reply. A little suspense does an organization no harm at all, providing you do not prolong it unnecessarily.

Setting a deadline, even if it is in your own diary, inoculates you against any tendency to procrastinate. The sheer unexpected complexity of things can propel you into an endless orbit of discussions, meetings – and more meetings – with the prospect of ever reaching conclusions and making decisions which lead to action receding over the horizon. Before you know it's happened, the jungle of the *status quo* has reclaimed the clearing that your arrival made. It's back to business as usual.

For those who enjoy intellectual debate and who can easily be seduced into endless discussion it is worth taking on board the advice of President Woodrow Wilson – himself temperamentally inclined that way – to anyone in an executive strategic leadership position:

> In an executive job we intellectuals are dangerous, unless we are aware of our limitations and take measure to stop our everlasting disposition to think, to listen, to – not act. I made up my mind long ago, when I got into my first executive job,

to open my mind for a while, hear everybody who came to
me with advice, information – what you will – then, some
day, the day when my mind felt like deciding, to shut it up
and act. My decision might be right; it might be wrong. No
matter, I would take a chance and do – something.

For in the conduct of affairs any decision is better than no
decision. You only have to be 80 per cent right. In real life
as much depends upon the way you execute decisions as
upon the decision itself. Generals such as Napoleon and
Wellington were well aware of this fact, and did not delay
decisions beyond the time when they needed to be made –
whatever the shortfalls in information. The same principle
applies in business, at least according to Percy Barnevik,
chairman of the ABB group of 1,200 companies that is
now the world's largest single supplier to the electricity
industry:

> I would say that in any business decision 90 per cent of
> success is execution, ten per cent strategy. And of that 10 per
> cent, only 2 per cent is really analysis and 8 per cent is guts
> to take uncomfortable decisions . . . *The question is, how do
> you mobilize people? How do you make 25,000 managers
> move like a big army?* It doesn't matter so much if you move
> in the right direction or not, as long as you move. I tell people
> that if we make 100 decisions and seventy turn out right,
> that's good enough.

I think the most difficult situation you will face is an
organization where you get the feeling as you go round
that everybody reckons they're doing all right. That is the
hardest organization in which to bring about change.
These organizations tend to be ones that have been

around quite a long time and are doing reasonably well and may have no obvious crisis looming, yet you know that if they just continue on that plateau the whole thing will erode. It's an interesting point whether or not as a strategic leader you need to introduce change for change's sake – like an unnecessary reorganization or selling the head office – just to wake up the organization.

Organizational complacency – or worse, corporate arrogance – is the deadliest enemy you will face as a strategic leader. If that is your fate, you must put on your prophet's mantle and, go out on the highways and byways to proclaim high and low within the organization that it is *not* the best. Produce evidence, if need be, to support your case at every point. In this way you will plough the frost-bound hardened earth into furrows with the iron-tipped ploughshare of truth, ready for the seeds of change. The true leaders in the organization will know what you are talking about, not to mention its staff who face the daily realities of the business.

> Everyone knows at any given moment which is the best company in its field. Not necessarily in terms of size or profits, though it could be. I mean the best in bringing new products, market sensitivity, presence, range, quality, how we deal with our people, ethical, environmental and safety standards – all of these things.
>
> Sir John Harvey-Jones

Only *phronesis*, practical wisdom – yours and other people's – will tell you what potential there is in an organization to change for the better. Perhaps you and it will not know before you try. By the end of the first hundred days you should have received your own marching orders. A test is to ask 'What would be my number one regret if I had to leave without achieving it?' and its corollary, 'What is the one thing that could derail that, now or in the future?'

SUMMARY OF KEY POINTS

- You will never have a second chance to make a good first impression in an organization. It is worth giving some time and thought to evolve your personal strategy during those critical first three months in office.
- The arrival of a new strategic leader always opens the door – or pushes it further open – for change. The *status quo* is on trial. A new order may emerge. Expectations may be high, which fuels the energy for overcoming inertia and making positive changes.
- First you've got to understand thoroughly how the existing system is working. Having come in as a new chairman or chief executive there is a window of opportunity and you have to make use of that, so it is a question of judgement and how quickly you can act.
- You may want to signal quite early that you think there are changes you will want to make, but make it absolutely clear that you're prepared to listen to what everyone else has to say. You're going to have to carry people with you, but you should also be absolutely firm. Find out, listen, act.
- Get a grasp of the organization by getting around, meeting people and getting a feel for the actual business. As it is a going concern, you certainly want to do any research you can to find out in which direction it is going.
- The other issue is relationships. You're going to have to work with people as individuals and collectively as a team.

The role of the strategic leader includes getting the best of that collective group. That is going to take time, but one of the first things to do is to try to establish some sort of personal link with people in the business.

- Think of that legacy, what you want to leave behind. As one chief executive of a company said, 'There is nothing more important than to leave behind an organization that feels confident of its future and feels like a winner.'

We must obey the greatest law of change. It is the most powerful law of nature.

Edmund Burke

6

BUILDING THE TOP TEAM

But of a good leader, who talks little,
When his work is done, his aim fulfilled,
They will all say 'We did this ourselves.'
Lao Tzu (third century BC)

Teamwork at the top – individuals working in harmony together towards a common end – gives an organization an enormous strength. It sounds so simple and so obvious, but it seems strangely difficult to achieve. Organizations lacking in it exhibit some well-known symptoms: intrigue, politicking and back-biting. Much of their energy is turned inwards upon itself in these internal feuds, clashes of ego and turf-wars. A knock-on effect in the organization can always be felt, like earth tremors spreading out from the epicentre. 'When the elephants fight, the grass gets trampled down', as the African proverb puts it.

How do you achieve teamwork at the top? In this chapter I shall identify some of the areas of team composition and team maintenance that you should consider carefully. This is the necessary prelude before making any changes. The first area to look at is your own role.

WHAT IS YOUR OWN ROLE?

Let's assume, at least as far as Part Two of this book is concerned, that you are in a strategic leadership role or, in other words, you're the leader of a discrete organization. Is your leadership of the whole vested in you alone, or do you share the overall responsibility with a colleague? In British business terminology, are you chairman of the board *and* chief executive (officer) or managing director? Or do you hold only one of these roles?

Splitting the strategic leadership role may seem odd, but there are two principal arguments for doing so. First, especially in a very large organization, there is too much work for one person to do on their own. Second, good corporate governance demands it. Since, in Lord Acton's well-known words, 'power tends to corrupt, and absolute power corrupts absolutely', the chief executive should be monitored by a yet more senior leader, who chairs the board of directors, governors, trustees or the like – the chairman, say, supported by some non-executive directors.

The counter-argument is the advantages of what the military call unity of command. Moreover, in some fields – whatever the workload – it is impractical to divide the top job. You cannot have two popes. If one person is in charge, and that person has the necessary authority and power to act, then in theory at least, decisions get made more promptly and change can be more easily implemented. Not that the history of dictators always bears out this claim. Certainly strategic leadership without the substance of the power to act, hedged in by only the minimum restrictions, becomes a most frustrating business. Unlike the proverbial gift-horse, you should always look a strategic leadership role very carefully in the mouth before you accept it. Sometimes titles do not signify the role content.

Writing in *Management Week* (16 October 1991) after his spell at ICI, Sir John Harvey-Jones reflected on the pros and cons in this way:

I am very uncertain about whether the top job should really be two jobs or not. I have seen successful examples both of a combination of chairman and chief executive in the one, and an admittedly small number but nevertheless very successful examples of where a non-executive chairman has worked well and happily with a chief executive. There is no doubt that if the top job of chairman and principal executive officer are combined in one, the job is a killer. The outside, representational role is immensely time-consuming. The better known and more successful you are at projecting the image of your company, the more you are requested to do so.

There are real advantages to having the top job split between two people. It is easier to replace either one of them if some disaster happens, or if one or the other begins to be 'off the boil'. It is extremely difficult to replace a combined chairman and chief executive. You take a double risk for a start, and the actual mechanisms of replacement are difficult to effect. It is relatively easy to draw up the fields of responsibility of two people who share the top job. The non-executive job should be primarily directed to the management of the actual board, and the external environment, as well as ensuring that mechanisms are in place to develop strategies and clear policies on the many issues for which a board has responsibility. The other, the executive role, is then responsible for that process. The chairman is responsible for seeing that the board checks that their policies have been carried out by the chief executive.

The difficulty in such organizations is one of split responsibilities. An organization of this type calls for a degree of integration and understanding between the two top people which is often difficult to achieve. Moreover, it can fall into the trap which the Americans dislike so much, of a lack of clarity as to who is ultimately in charge, and where the buck actually stops.

While it does have some highly desirable characteristics of flexibility, it lacks some of the crispness of having the whole thing tied into one person. Certainly such an approach is an unpopular one in America, where again organizational theory seems to be rather starker than in the United Kingdom.

One advocate for the American model – an executive chairman or chairman of the board with full executive powers which he or she may share by delegation with another officer (formerly called a managing director or chief operating officer) is Hugh Parker, a former regional head of McKinsey. Writing in the *Director* (April 1990) he delineated their respective roles in the process of what he called 'corporate renewal', taking over Sir John Harvey-Jones's definition of it as 'creating tomorrow's company out of today's'.

It is the chairman's role to:

- Create and work with a board that is capable of helping and supporting him in the overall direction and governance of the enterprise.
- Create a strategic vision for the business that derives realistically from the company's existing strengths, and that builds on its distinctive competitive advantages.
- Establish the basic properties, ethical values, policies and

attitudes within the company that will transform it from being a 'repeating' culture into a 'learning' culture.
- Set standards of performance in terms of such criteria as product quality, customer service, technological leadership, market share, and financial measures that will ensure an above-average p/e ratio.
- Appoint a managing director with a clear mandate to achieve established standards of operating and financial performance. Monitor the managing director's performance against these standards, help and support him. But if and when necessary, replace him.

It is the role of the managing director, together with his top management team, to:

- Ensure that operational planning and financial control systems are in place, appropriate to the new management organizational structures of each business unit.
- Ensure that operating objectives and standards of performance are not only understood but also 'owned' at all levels of the enterprise – i.e. are seen to be challenging, but realistic and attainable.
- Closely monitor operating and financial results of each business against agreed plans and budgets. Take remedial action where necessary.
- Develop business strategies and operating plans that reflect the longer-term corporate objectives and priorities established by the board. Maintain an ongoing conversation with the chairman and board to ensure that these objectives and priorities are constantly adjusted to reflect changes in the external environment.
- Restructure the business portfolio in line with the board's decisions that determine the future shape and strategy of

the business. Redraw the management organization
structure to reflect the restructured business.

- Undertake a programme for systematically strengthening
management at all levels – but especially at the higher
levels – by training, retraining, development, delegation,
motivation, recruitment and replacement.

If you compare these two lists of functions with the
seven generic functions which compose the role of a strategic leader (see page 95), you can see that what is happening
here is essentially the sharing of one role. There are not two
archetypal roles, as it were, in the generic script – only one.
Perhaps the most outstanding business leader over a period
of twenty years has been Jack Welch of General Electric in
the United States and he was in sole charge.

The point is that in an organizational situation where
there is a split role, everything depends upon the ability of
the two parties to work out a division of labour that makes
sense to them both. So numerous are the variables of
experience, temperament, tradition and personal chemistry
that there are no rules or principles, except that each should
be clear about what is expected and what they expect. The
resulting sub-roles are bound to overlap, and both parties
must be able to cope with some ambiguity and handle
issues where the shoe is pinching as they arise. If either the
chairman or the chief executive/managing director are lacking in sufficient practical wisdom, the relationship will end
up in divorce.

The essence of a successful 'job-sharing' relationship at
the top is that it should be a true partnership of minds and
spirits, but with complementary rather than identical
interests, abilities and temperaments. There should be
mutuality of trust and understanding between chairman

and chief executive, there should be a shared set of strategic objectives, and above all there should be so much sharing of perceptions and values that each can coordinate with the other, almost without having to discuss an issue at all.

CHOOSING THE TOP TEAM

Few strategic leaders apart from democratically elected strategic leaders such as the American President and the British Prime Minister have the luxury of choosing their team from scratch. Most inherit a top team and can only make changes if they move people out or replace those who leave or retire. The latter can be a lengthy process, and it takes some strategic leaders years to achieve the team they want. Yet there are few more important things you can do than to choose the right people for the top jobs.

As a general observation, the most common weakness of strategic leaders is lack of judgement about people. It is rather like driving a car: we all think we are good at it, but how many of us really are? Believing that you can 'spot a winner' is as hazardous in organizations as it is on the race-course. It is lack of judgement about people that leads to wrong choices in the first place or over-promotion. The deployment of carefully designed and led selection boards can compensate in part, but even so the strategic leader's influence tends to be decisive for or against. For the most senior appointments you should always be on the selection board – if not in the chair.

'Two minds are better than one' when it comes to judging the fitness of a person for a role – providing both minds are wise. For judgement about people is really just one aspect of *phronesis*. The best case studies I have come across of the process whereby a person with *phronesis* in this respect forms a judgement of another person in interactions over a course of time are the six novels of Jane Austen. There is a price to be paid in getting judgements of people wrong. If someone is not up to the mark and you have to find a replacement, think of the extra time and cost. Yes, you have learnt a lesson. It is a cheque paid into your experience bank. But think of the cost! 'Experience is the best of schoolmasters,' said Thomas Carlyle, 'only the school fees are heavy.' Get it right first time. Here are five tips for team-building, whether it be the board or the executive team that directly reports to you, gleaned from my own experience:

- Avoid selecting clones of yourself. You are looking for a balanced team, with complementary mental gifts of intelligence and imagination, technical and professional experience and interests relevant to your field.
- Always choose a person of real ability and stature, not those who can be guaranteed to accept the party line, agree with what you say and never challenge you in debate before decisions. If you appoint 'safe' people who will do your bidding without a word, you are only advertising your own weakness and insecurity.
- You are taking on a whole person, and great strengths are usually accompanied by great weaknesses. A wise and mature team can accommodate far more idiosyncrasies in the best people – providing they *are* the best – than a fragile one.
- Never write off a new team member too quickly. A person of ability may have been placed – by you or your predecessor – in the wrong role. Reassigned to another, that person may grow wings and fly.

- The opinion of the team on a prospective new member is always worth seeking. But remember that new appointments are ways of changing and improving the team, lifting it out of its comfort zone. Don't expect the team to see the pearl when you present them with someone who looks like grit.

The sign of a great strategic leader, one who is both excellent in leadership and credited with unassailable professional reputation, is his or her ability to lead highly complex and often over-confident individuals. Who, one might ask, would be able to hold together brilliant but wayward contributors such as Montgomery and Patton in the same top team? Yet Alexander and Eisenhower both achieved that difficult feat. It is significant, as I have said above, that both these Supreme Commanders were men of genuine humility.

CASE STUDY: LINCOLN AND STANTON

Edwin M. Stanton first met the future President Abraham Lincoln in 1855 when both men, as attorneys, were involved in the same court case. Stanton, renowned as a lawyer, evidently insulted the less well-known Lincoln, allegedly calling him a giraffe. He was equally critical of Lincoln during his rise to power, talking dismissively of him as a man with 'no token of any intelligent understanding'.

Yet despite this negative attitude towards him personally, Lincoln made Stanton the new Secretary of War in his Cabinet team, for he knew him to be the best man for the role. Stanton took on the challenge with enthusiasm and set about fully justifying his selection. Within a few months he reorganized the War Department and led it into becoming a much more effective body. Tireless in his efforts, he worked all hours of the day to merit the trust that Lincoln had placed in him.

Stanton soon revised his early opinion of Lincoln, while the President for his part appreciated more and more the reliable administrative abilities of the Secretary of War, and the solid worth of the man as opposed to his somewhat surly appearance and manner. As their mutual trust grew, Lincoln was able to delegate most completely to him. On 9 April 1865, on Lincoln's return to Washington, it was Stanton who greeted him with a warm embrace and the news that Lee had surrendered at Appomattox. And no man wept more when Lincoln was assassinated than Stanton.

CHALLENGES TO TEAMWORK

Whether you are leading a board of directors or its equivalent (such as a cabinet or council of governors) or a senior executive team of operational leaders and staff specialists, you should expect to deal with the complexity that arises from the tendency of senior and really able people to be complex. Sometimes they will be more complex than you are, just as T. E. Lawrence and Orde Wingate were, compared respectively to Allenby and Slim. Gifted but complex individuals are usually highly idiosyncratic: they evolve their own ways of doing things and need to be broken in gently, like wild mustangs, to the necessity of teamwork.

With all individual team members – and you as their leader are no exception – there is always a balance between their actual or potential contribution to the task and their eccentricity – some characteristic, action, practice or habit that differs in some way from what is usual or expected. An eccentric individual presents a strangeness or irregularity that may be harmless, but that is an ingrained part of the personality. Idiosyncrasy also suggests a strangeness of nature but less a divergence from the general (with a suggestion sometimes of at least mild mental aberration) evidence of a strongly independent personality – the following of one's own bent or temperament with strong individuality and independence of action.

A mature team will always live with idiosyncrasy and reasonable eccentricity (if there is such a thing!), providing the gift or talent is there. It would have been most unwise of a commander-in-chief to dismiss Nelson before Trafalgar because he flaunted social custom and propriety by living openly with his mistress. Not that his sailors would have cared tuppence.

In all teams, experience suggests, there are potential 'team maintenance' cracks, fissures as invisible as metal fatigue cracks on the wing of an aircraft which will give way under pressure. It may be a matter of interpersonal chemistry – X does not get on well with Y. Under normal circumstances all is well, but if things go badly X will tend to blame Y, and vice versa. They fall into the kind of conflict that Milton described so well in *Paradise Lost*:

> Thus they the fruitless hours
> In mutual accusation spent
> Neither self-condemning.

Or there could be a potential division – a hairline crack – along the lines of gender or ethnic background or profession. In some companies that are struggling, for example, you may find that sales and marketing blame production and vice versa, or there is a civil war between the accountants and the rest. Nor have all traces disappeared of that deeply ingrained divide between 'management' and 'work people', especially where the latter are strongly unionized.

Don't imagine that because you have reached the top of an organization you have passed beyond 'team maintenance' problems. If you lead the board in the context of the British business system or similar ones, for example, you will have a potential crack on your plate between executive and non-executive directors (in Japan the latter do not exist). As a business strategic leader with board responsibility in such a context you will need to think out carefully the qualities and abilities you are looking for in *both* kinds of director. Non-executive directors should have *phronesis* that commands respect from their executive colleagues, and if they have that they will acquire what knowledge they need of the actual business to perform their role as informed but independent and wise counsel.

Teamwork in the boardroom is essential, not least because it sends a positive message throughout the organization. 'Example is not the main thing in influencing others – it is the only thing,' said Albert Schweitzer. It has immense practical value, too, in that it affects the speed and quality of decisions.

Sir John Harvey-Jones, a former Royal Navy officer, believes that a board should be like Nelson's band of brothers:

> 'The speed at which a company can move depends, to a large extent, on the speed at which the board itself can move, for, while boards can seldom create the opportunities

which exist for businesses further down the line, they have demonstrated over and over again their ability to stop such opportunities being seized or developed. My ideal board is an enabling board, which adds value to the effort of people below and enables everyone, from the top to the bottom of the company, to give of his best. *To achieve this it is really essential that the board itself should be a team.* It is impossible to act as an enabling mechanism if there are unresolved fundamental differences between parts of the group which shares the responsibility for the direction of the company.

PROBLEMS WITH TOP LEADERSHIP TEAMS

Strategic leadership of an enterprise is a shared activity. To be successful you need a capable and effective top leadership team – your senior operational or executive leaders, including heads of staff functions such as finance. These teams characteristically range in size from five to fourteen, and that sort of span does not have any correlation with the size of organization. There are five main types of problem that arise in top teams.

Problem 1: Inadequate capabilities of an individual operational leader

Sometimes an operational leader will fail to grasp the strategic implications, such as when they deliver short-term profits by using short-sighted means which are detrimental to the values and longer-term interests that you are working for. Or you may have concerns about their style, such as lack of personal time management or failing to do what they said they would do, or lack of a sense of urgency. Arrogance or overt ambition may constitute other causes for concern.

Often the problematic person is more of a manager – competent in running the day-to-day business and an adequate staff administrator – than a leader. He or she lacks a strategic perspective and personal leadership and team-working skills. Such a person can manage a business but cannot *grow* the business. Counselling and coaching seldom do much good. Either you or your predecessor made an error in selection, and you should consider replacing the inadequate operational leader. It is never a mistake to turn back if you are on the wrong road. As a strategic leader you are paid to face unpleasant situations and make tough decisions such as sacking colleagues. Too often chief executives press ahead despite problems with individuals instead of confronting embarrassing or awkward issues and dealing with them at board level. In Japan this evasion reaches an art form!

Problem 2: Common team-wide shortcomings

As a new strategic leader you may come to the conclusion sooner or later that your top team as a whole – usually with one or two exceptions – is not up to either the challenges of its new competitive environment or the complexity and magnitude of the organization they are supposed to be leading. Swift growth, geographical expansion and diversification tend to breed this mismatch between today's opportunities and a top team that belongs to yesterday. Bringing the capabilities of the top team into balance with present realities and future aspirations is a complex challenge for any strategic leader, however experienced.

Problem 3: Harmful rivalries

These usually manifest as a particular rivalry between two individuals. They tend to start out as disagreements, often legitimate, over some aspect of the common business, before they blossom into full-blown feuds complete with personal abuse. Before you as the leader realize how serious it is, personal acrimony has flared out of control like a fire and threatens ever more serious consequences. Even after you or someone else – perhaps a wise non-executive director – have attempted to mediate, the issue may not so much go away as go to ground. At least if the rivalry is submerged it can do less damage.

Harmful rivalries of this politico-personal nature are symptoms of lack of team spirit and they should never happen. A friendly rivalry between parts of the whole is natural and, within reason, to be encouraged; there is a tension between certain individuals that can be positive rather than negative. But a good leader today is 100 per cent in the role of a leader (the three circles), 100 per cent in the role of colleague and 100 per cent in the role of subordinate. Nelson achieved full marks in all three roles, and so you must expect something more than pass marks for your top team.

Problem 4: Groupthink

Unexamined and unconscious assumptions, too easy agreement, a low tolerance for any conflicting debate about ideas, an unwillingness to confront, an implicit belief that what is unanimous must be right – these are some of the symptoms of groupthink. Superficially a team affected with this disease may appear healthy to an observer, in that its discussions are amicable, smooth-running and harmonious, often punctuated by much laughter. But look at the quality of its decisions, for 'by their fruits you shall know them'.

Cohesiveness in your top team, and a degree of like-mindedness in terms of purpose and values, is essential. But you should make it clear that you expect people to voice the truth as they see it. You and others may not agree, but that is a secondary matter. To put group cohesion – in mind – over and above the task, which in the case of the board or senior executive group is to make the best decision, is to invert the three-circle model and to court disaster.

THE NECESSITY FOR DISAGREEMENT

Unless one has considered alternatives, one has a closed mind.

This, above all, explains why effective decision-makers deliberately disregard the second major command of the textbooks on decision-making and create dissension and disagreement, rather than consensus.

Decisions of the kind the executive has to make are not made well by acclamation. They are made well only if based on the clash of conflicting views, with dialogue between different points of view, the choice between different judgements. The first rule in decision-making is that one does not make a decision unless there is disagreement.

Alfred P. Sloan is reported to have said at a meeting of one of his top committees: 'Gentlemen, I take it we are all in complete agreement on the decision here.' Everyone around the table nodded assent. 'Then,' continued Mr Sloan, 'I propose we postpone further discussion of this matter until our next meeting to give ourselves time to develop disagreement and perhaps gain some understanding of what the decision is all about.'

Sloan was anything but an 'intuitive' decision-maker. He always emphasized the need to test opinions against facts and the need to make absolutely sure that one did not start out with the conclusion and then look for the facts that would support it. But he knew that the right decision demands adequate disagreement.

Peter Drucker, *The Effective Executive* (1967)

Problem 5: Fragmentation

Some top teams are in name only – part of the rhetoric which second-rate chairmen and chief executives pick up and use but don't have written on their hearts. A group of individuals is not a team. Even if they meet together from time to time, operational leaders in charge of relatively independent spheres will not feel part of a team unless they view and share the common purpose of the whole enterprise, perceive themselves as stakeholders in that vision, and can see that their part – however important and relatively autonomous – is complementary to other parts in the organization.

Symptoms of fragmentation include lack of cooperation between the parts, failure to share information, decision-making regardless of the broad strategic direction, meetings of the top 'team' that are perfunctory and marred by absenteeism, the growth of separate agendas, and a particularism – exclusive or special devotion to a particular interest – that informs the thinking and action of each of the individuals in the team. The only person concerned or caring about the whole as opposed to the parts is *you*. If you are interested in having heart attacks, remember this simple equation: Fragmentalization = Hospitalization.

Of course, strategic leadership works in the opposite

direction. The chief issue in all organizations is getting the balance of the parts and the whole right. The operational leader should be *both* head of a part *and* a member of the strategic leadership team which, under your direction, is responsible for the whole. All that fragmentation at the top reveals is that you have failed to fulfil one essential function in your role as a strategic leader.

CASE STUDY:

HOW TO WIN TOP TEAM COMMITMENT

Horatio Nelson was born on 29 September 1758 at Burnham Thorpe in Norfolk. Forty years later he destroyed Napoleon's fleet at the Battle of the Nile and turned the great war with France in Britain's favour. Then, in 1805, he led a fleet which he had kept in fighting trim at sea for two years, mainly from its own resources, 3,000 miles across the Atlantic and back again. Finally, his victory at Trafalgar raised the reputation of the Royal Navy to such a height that it was not challenged again for over a hundred years, and laid the foundations of the British Empire.

Nelson's lifelong friend Collingwood wrote of him: 'He possessed the zeal of an enthusiast, directed by talents which nature had very boastfully bestowed on him, and everything seemed, as if by enchantment, to prosper under his direction. But it was the effect of system, and nice calculation, not of chance.'

It was in the art of leading men in war that Nelson's genius shone most brightly. In command of the inshore squadron at Cadiz and in the gallant failure of Tenerife he had shown courage, energy and readiness to risk not only his life but his reputation for the sake of getting at the enemy – a good example and a source of confidence to his followers. But there was more than this. Hitherto Nelson had commanded detachments; in the campaign which ended in the victory of the Nile he was in sole command.

'It was his practice during the whole of his cruise,' wrote Berry, his fleet captain, 'whenever the weather and circumstances would permit, to have his captains on board the *Vanguard*, where he would fully develop to them his own ideas of the different and best modes of attack, in all possible positions.' In eight weeks he had made of them a band of brothers. Admiral Lord Hone said of the victory to Berry: 'It stood unparalleled and singular in this instance, that every captain distinguished himself.'

In other words, Nelson gave only the simplest directions to his captains, relying on the intelligent responses of his 'band of brothers' as they faced particular opportunities, And it worked. For example, at the Nile it was Captain Foley of the *Goliath* who saw that the shoal water between the anchored line of French ships and the shore was just deep enough to allow a British attack on the unprepared landward quarter. As the US Admiral Mahan put it, 'It is in entire keeping with Nelson's well-known character, that, after discussing all likely positions and ascertaining that his captains understood his views, he should with perfect and generous confidence have left all the details of immediate action with them.' His book, *The Influence of Sea Power upon the French Revolution and Empire* carried Nelson's leadership style to generations of later natural strategic leaders.

Although you could say that Nelson's discussions with his captains centred more on tactics than strategy, the principle holds good. You need to share your strategic overview and strategic ideas with your operational leaders, leaving them free to plan and act in an opportunity-centred, entrepreneurial way. By entrepreneurial here I mean someone who bears the risk of success or failure, profit or loss.

As a strategic leader you can reduce the risks by holding the kind of discussions with your top team that Nelson conducted informally around the dinner table in his cabin. By revealing your thinking in that way you will convey to operational leaders what decisions you expect them to make themselves and what decisions they should naturally discuss first with you. The latter will obviously include, for example, any course of action where the downside of the risk – the consequences of failure – could hole your enterprise below the waterline.

I shall discuss corporate culture in Chapter 10, but it is relevant to say here that a blame culture is extremely counter-productive in the world of the new organization. You should expect plenty of errors. It's a healthy sign. Each error is a valuable attempt to seize an opportunity or solve a problem. Neither you nor the operational leader will learn much from your successes. But your failures come with potential gifts: of knowledge, of understanding, of future achievement, of growth.

First your team must learn self-trust from your example. The journey ahead will then be an adventure. Moreover, when you have freed your top team from the fear of failure you will have opened their eyes to all possibilities. And when they see possibilities in abundance, then they can make better decisions. The following model highlights the part played in creative possibilities, visible only to those who are unafraid to consider them in the decision-making process.

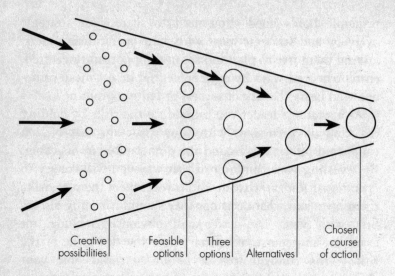

Figure 6.1 *The Lobster Pot Model of Decision-making*

THE HALLMARKS OF TEAM EXCELLENCE

How can you improve your powers as team-builder, given the complexities, potential problems and challenges outlined above? The answer is simple: form a clear concept in your mind of what an excellent team looks like. Then, like an automatic pilot, that concept will serve to guide you in all that you do and say to achieve it.

Hallmarks (from Goldsmiths' Hall in London, where gold and silver articles were assayed and stamped) are official marks stamped on gold and silver articles in England to attest their purity. Here are the characteristics or features that distinguish an excellent team from its copper or brass fellows:

- *Clear, realistic and challenging objectives*
  The team is focused on what has to be done – broken
  down into stretching but feasible goals, both team and
  individual. Everyone knows what is expected of him or
  her.
- *Shared sense of purpose*
  This doesn't mean that the team can recite the mission
  statement in unison! Purpose here is energy plus direction
  – what engineers call a vector. It should animate and
  invigorate the whole team. All share a sense of ownership
  and responsibility for team success.
- *Best use of resources*
  A high-performance team means that resources are
  allocated for strategic reasons for the good of the whole.
  They are not seen as the private property of any part of the
  organization. Resources include people and their time, not
  just money and material.
- *Progress review*
  The willingness to monitor its own progress and to
  generate improvements characterizes excellent teams.
  These improvements encompass process – *how* we work
  together – as well as tasks – *what* we do together.
- *Building on experience*
  A blame culture mars any team. Errors will be made, but
  the greatest error of all is to do nothing so as to avoid
  making any! A wise team learns from failure, realizing
  that success teaches us nothing and continual success may
  breed arrogance.
- *Mutual trust and support*
  A good team trusts its members to pursue their part in
  the common task. Appreciation is expressed and
  recognition given. People play to each other's strengths
  and cover each other's weaknesses. The level of mutual

support is high. The atmosphere is one of openness and
trust.

- *Communication*
  People listen to one another and build on one another's
  contributions. They communicate openly, freely and with
  skill (clear, concise, simple and with tact), Issues,
  problems and weaknesses are not sidestepped. Differences
  of opinion are respected. Team members know when to be
  very supportive and sensitive, and when to challenge and
  be intellectually tough.
- *Riding out the storms*
  In times of turbulent change it is never going to be all
  plain sailing. When unavoidable storms and crises arise,
  an excellent team rises to the challenge and demonstrates
  its sterling worth. It has resilience.

Where these eight hallmarks – in no order of importance
– are present, people enjoy working together as a team
more deeply. They have fun, like other teams, but so rare
is the experience of working in an excellent team that the
enjoyment and fun are transformed by hindsight into the
true gold and silver of enduring satisfaction and a sense of
gratitude.

SUMMARY OF KEY POINTS

- Who is your top team? That depends upon your own
  allotted role. You may be a leader of the board or council
  (the strategy- and policy-making body) and leader of the
  executive team. Or the role of strategic leader may be split
  into two.
- That is nothing new – Sparta always had two kings and

republican Rome two consuls. It helps with the workload and provides a check against abuse of power. On the other hand, a single strategic leader enjoys the advantages of 'unity of command', especially useful in times of crisis.

- In split-role situations it is vitally important to establish a truly complementary and harmonious working partnership, so that the expectations of both persons and their respective sub-roles are as clear as possible. There will be overlaps, so constant communication is necessary.

- Organizations take their drumbeat from the top. If the board of directors (or its equivalent) works as a team, then you have more than half solved the problem of getting the whole organization to see itself as one great team and to act like one.

- One of your major challenges as a strategic leader is to ensure that the calibre and capability of your top executive team match the complexity of its environment, the turbulent seas through which it must navigate the ship.

- Whatever its shape or composition, *your* team at the top should have the following hallmarks:

• Clear, realistic and challenging objectives	• Building on experience
• Shared sense of purpose	• Mutual trust and support
• Best use of resources	• Communication
• Progress review	• Riding out the storms

How do you know you have won? When the energy is coming the other way and when your people are visibly growing individually and as a group.
Sir John Harvey-Jones

7

GETTING THE STRATEGY RIGHT

*All men can see the tactics whereby I conquer,
but what none can see is the strategy out of which
great victory evolved.*
Sun Tzu (fourth century, BC)

As a strategic leader your prime responsibility is to ensure that your organization is going in the right direction. That sounds simple enough, but it is not always easy to achieve. What *is* the right strategic direction? How or where do you establish it? Why is implementation so difficult?

We can break the problem into two parts: identifying the best strategy and pursuing it to the desired result. Although these two parts in reality are interwoven, it makes sense to separate out the *thinking* side of it. That is what I call *strategic thinking*.

It is useful, I think, to distinguish between such *strategic thinking* on the one hand and *strategic planning* on the other. Strategic thinking is thinking about the longer term and the more important ends in any situation – including your own life – and the pathways that may or may not lead to them. If and when you can identify such an end or set of ends, and choose among the possible pathways the ones that make most sense, the process of corporate planning can get under way. It is daft to launch into a strategic planning exercise before your strategic thought has come to some working conclusions, although, believe me, that does happen.

It is not possible to teach anyone to think strategically if they cannot do it, for strategic thinking is a function of *phronesis*, practical wisdom, which is neither an art nor a science nor a skill. Therefore this chapter will be short! All that I can do is to remove some common misconceptions about strategic thinking. I must be honest and admit that these are misconceptions I have harboured myself, and only my customary struggle to be clear has revealed to me my own hidden assumptions. Not that I am entirely clear even now, but let me share with you what I have learned so far. These are all things that have helped me to become a better strategic thinker.

'But you said just now that strategic thinking is something that you either can do or you can't.'

You shouldn't believe everything I say. Perhaps I meant that it cannot be *taught*, but you can certainly *learn* to do it better. Remember that *phronesis* includes the capacity to learn, not least through experience.

THE INVENTION OF STRATEGY

It helps me to remember that strategy really doesn't exist! To remind you, *strategy* in ancient Greek meant the whole art of a commander-in-chief, including leadership, administration and working with allies, as well as knowing how to bring an enemy to battle and what tactics to employ. Strategy, if you like, was the thinking of a *strategos*, a general, and he had a lot to think about apart from the conduct of military operations. As armies became larger and warfare more complex, strategy was introduced as a new concept in contrast to tactics. But strategy was still about what a general thought it best to do in order to achieve victory. It was not something which existed, so to speak, separately, that you could read in a book or learn on a course.

That began to change when General Henri Jomini wrote a book on the principles that guided Napoleon in his strategic thinking and his art of generalship, an art for which he claimed, not entirely immodestly, that he had genius. Napoleon read the book with some alarm – 'It teaches my whole system of war to my enemies,' he muttered to a friend. Then he quickly regained his composure, saying with a smile: 'The old generals who command against me will never read it, and the young men who read it do not command!'

The study by Henri Jomini and Carl von Clausewitz of how Napoleon's mind worked gave rise to the Principles of War (which cover the whole art of generalship), including some strategic ideas such as that of concentrating decisive force at the critical point – though Alexander the Great, Hannibal or Caesar could also have thought up that one. But there was no strategy. Captain Sir Basil Liddell-Hart, who called himself a military strategist, claimed that he had discovered the strategy of the indirect approach. Wavell pointed out to him that he could have written an equally weighted book on the strategy of the direct approach! Direct or indirect, it all depends on the situation. We don't think any the worse of Montgomery as a general because he made a direct frontal assault at Alamein, for he had no alternative.

If you cannot find a thing called strategy in the military field, the source of the term, what were the first business writers actually borrowing? If you look at their books you will find a muddled understanding.

The first of these was William Newman's *Administrative Action: The Techniques of Organization and Management* (1951). Remarking that 'the matter of strategy' is little discussed, he defined its usage in his book as 'the adjustment of a plan to the anticipated reaction of those who will be affected by the plan'. You don't get more muddled than that.

The first serious writer on business strategy was Alfred Chandler. His *Chapters in the History of American Enterprise* (1962) began as a study of how large corporations had responded to the new environment of post-war expansion in the United States. He focused on nine companies who had innovated with new organizational designs, some dating back to the 1920s, and then on four of them – General Motors, DuPont, Standard Oil of New Jersey and Sears, Roebuck. Organizational structure, he argued, had been changed fittingly as new business strategies were adopted.

These giant corporations were like armies, and their corporate headquarters (a military term) housed general staff. Chandler advocated that there should be an 'administrator' at the top of the 'general office' to oversee strategic planning, which he defined as 'the determination of the basic long-term goals and objectives of an enterprise, and the adoption of courses of action and the allocation of resources necessary for carrying out these goals'. Chandler accepted that strategic planning could happen at various levels in the organizational hierarchy, but he reserved the prerogative of resource allocation to the 'general office' at the top. This general office, composed of 'general executives' and staff specialists, existed to 'coordinate, appraise and plan goals and policies and allocate resources for quasi-antonomous divisions' in order to meet short-term and long-term fluctuations and developments in the market. It is not hard to see here a reflection of the modern military model of strategic planning – as exemplified by the German General Staff in both the World Wars, but common to all armies. The Pentagon is the symbol of this model.

Mesmerized by the military model of *strategic planning*, the early business writers gave little or no attention to the processes of *strategic thinking*. Strategic planning was a corporate product, the new output of head office which largely justified the large general staff – Shell even called its executive restaurants 'messes' and they were graded by the rank of those who could use them. Meanwhile, in Russia, even vaster bureaucracies in the head offices of ministries and departments in Moscow were producing Twenty-, Ten- and Five-Year plans regulating the goals and objectives of an entire economy. This orthodox view of strategic planning, alias corporate strategy, was set out in an influential book by Professor Kenneth Andrews of Harvard Business School, entitled *The Concept of Corporate Strategy* (1971):

> Corporate strategy is the pattern of decisions in a company that determines and reveals its objectives, purposes, or goals, produces the principal policies and plans for achieving those goals, and defines the range of business the company is to pursue, the kind of economic and human organization it is or intends to be, and the nature of the economic and non-economic contribution it intends to make to its shareholders, employees, customers and communities.

The 'pattern of decisions' essentially means a plan. But Andrews did make an important contribution to understanding and improving the process of strategic thinking that precedes any form of planning. He advocated what became known as a SWOT analysis – that organizations should appraise carefully their Strengths, Weaknesses, Opportunities and Threats as a prelude to corporate strategy. He also stressed the importance of scanning the changing environment, using the ready-made headings of Political, Economic, Social and Technological (PEST) to consider the salient factors. These are now called 'tools' and are often no more than mental drills, substitutes for thinking rather than signposts for it. Eventually, in the field of business, the discussion of strategy has become dominated by the concept of *marketing* – the action, business or process of promoting and selling goods or services, including market research, choice of product, pricing and quality, advertising and distribution. A business strategic leader today is not short of advice – if he or she is prepared to pay for it – on what 'strategy' to adopt. The increased complexity of markets – now for most businesses a global one – has created another market for management consultants and business school gurus. The latter often sell strategic ideas which prove to be simplistic – like Dionysodurus (see page 13), they do not tell you how to adapt their 'strategies' to your unique circumstances; nor can you claim your money back if their nostrums don't work. The former – the management consultants – will even offer to do your strategic thinking for you, but is it all that difficult?

UNFREEZING YOUR STRATEGIC THINKING

The concept of a strategic leader takes us back to the origins of *strategia*, the art of being a leader-in-chief. Strategy is simply the thinking appropriate to someone at that level of leadership responsibility, and it embraces far more than military operations or marketing strategy. It is the product of an individual mind, not the output of a corporate staff at head office. So you do need to know how to think strategically, as distinct from the organizational process of setting goals and objectives, allocating resources and coordinating activities – a higher level of *planning*.

Divorcing strategic thinking from strategic planning is the first step to loosening up your mind. The next step is to rid yourself from the permafrost belief that strategy is somehow very difficult and complex, quite beyond your powers even if you could credit yourself with an average level of common sense or *phronesis*. In fact the *environment* in which you work as a strategic leader *is* complex, both for general reasons and reasons to do with our own time and age. But strategic thinking is always simple. The complexity lies more in execution than conception.

Some people seem to have strategic sense while others lack it. You can actually develop your strategic sense by reflecting on the adjective *strategic*. Why do we call something *strategic*? At the most general level it has two elements:

- IMPORTANCE   To be able to distinguish between the
                   important, the less important and the
                   unimportant, is the starting-point. If
                   it is important it is marked by or

possesses weight or consequence. It has evident value, either generally or in particular relation, and often by merely existing.

- LONGER TERM   How long is long? That all depends. But *strategic* implies a longer-term perspective rather than the short-term view. Indeed, to think strategically may mean trading short-term gain for long-term advantage.

People in any field who possess *phronesis* – intelligence, experience and goodness – tend to develop a strategic sense in general terms. In other words, by thought and experience, they evolve a *philosophy*, a mental framework of strategic ideas, which serves as the foundation for their strategic thinking in any aspect of their work. This philosophy is essentially the answer to the double question: What is really important for success in this field? What produces value in the longer term?

A philosophy of strategic leadership? That is what this book is all about. Call that your general philosophy if you like. But there is also a philosophy or relief map of what is strategic (of importance and longer-term value) in one's particular sphere of operations. Here are two examples.

THE CASE OF ERNEST ROBECK

Ernest Robeck, chairman and chief executive of a successful medium-sized Australian company, writing after thirty years' business experience, had this to say to his fellow members of the Australian Institute of Management (Victoria):

You make something, sell something or provide a service people want, and you charge a little more than it costs you. What could be simpler?

Maybe someone else is selling it at your cost? Then you must ask yourself a few awkward questions. Are they more efficient or effective? Do they have a genuine long-term advantage, like producing in a lower-cost environment? Can you match it? If not, how quickly can you get into something where you can compete against all-comers?

'SWOT' has become a word in our language – analysis of the Strengths, Weaknesses, Opportunities and Threats. I don't propose to regurgitate text book wisdom on the subject. But without it, it is hard to steer the boat in the right direction. The hardest thing is to get the facts. For that you need independent outsiders such as non-executive directors, because every organization has a 'company credo' and cannot see itself without distortion.

Again, I think it is simple common sense. It is the experts who make a science out of it. And, of course, the computer programmers make a feast of it. But remember, if the map is wrong or if the environment changes, extrapolating the wrong assumptions over ten years, to six decimal points, will make the story more impressive but it will be just as wrong as something written on the back of an envelope.

In today's usage 'products' can be goods or services. *The product we are selling is obviously the heart of our business*, and to forget that, even for a little while, is highly dangerous. Like any good heart, the *product should keep beating, needs exercising and continuous monitoring*. From time to time it will need surgery or even replacement and those events must not be delayed.

This does not mean that the positioning of the product in the market, the channels of distribution, market standing and promotion are not vital to success. However, they are the wrapping, the decoration and they cannot make up for deficiencies in *the basic product.*

The product's most important attribute is what we call 'quality', again a simple concept. *All it means is that the product should be completely fit for the use for which it is intended as seen by the user.* What could be simpler?

THE CASE OF WARREN BUFFETT

Warren Buffett, after sixty years as an investor, is widely regarded as the best in the world. Dubbed the Sage of Omaha, he is the legend who became extremely rich by investing his own money, bucking trends and identifying winning market niche opportunities. With a $40 billion personal fortune, his interests range from insurance and ice-cream parlours to shoe manufacturing and newspapers. Despite recording one of his worst performances in 1999, he can still make the extraordinary claim that, over the past thiry-five years, his company Berkshire Hathaway has achieved a massive 24 per cent annual return for its shareholders. It has never had a single down year and anyone who invested just $10,000 with Buffett in 1965 would now be sitting on $51 million. It was while studying at Columbia Graduate Business School that Buffett met the person who would provide him with the key to his success. Economic scholar Benjamin Graham quickly convinced Buffett of the merits of his unconventional theory that the best way to invest is to look for stocks of companies which are undervalued, but which will prosper in the long term. Such wisdom was to make Buffett richer than he could ever have dreamed.

His success has been based on three rules that are so simple it is amazing nobody else has been able to adopt them with the same results. He has always searched for fundamental values overlooked by the stock market, never invested unless he could find something worth buying and never put his money into anything he didn't understand. His high level of returns has demonstrated that common sense and consistent rationality win the day even in irrational markets.

This said, his whole career has in fact been built on the paradox that if everybody did search for and buy under-valued shares, their prices would rise rapidly until they were fully valued. Therefore, Buffett's unique success as an investor has depended on others not following his ideas.

Ernest Rodeck and Warren Buffet are strategic thinkers who, probably subconsciously, evolved a philosophy or map of their fields which marked out clearly what was *important* and *long-term*. They could see the wood for the trees. Their vision recalls Montgomery's theme (see page 99) that a strategic leader has to be able to separate out the essentials from the complex. Not only in terms of a given situation, we must now add, but in terms of the field as a whole.

EXERCISE

Take some paper and write down the five principles or essentials that anyone in your field has to get right if they are going to lead an organization within it to success.

ENDS AND MEANS

Strategy is customarily defined along the lines of the art or skill of carefully planning towards a goal. A simpler way of understanding strategic thinking is to see it as a form of ends-means thinking.

There are several basic relations in thinking. One is the relation of *cause* and *effect*, which is central, for example, in scientific thinking. The relation between the two terms is not arbitrary, for at all times and in all places *cause* must precede *effect*. That is why you can never be born before your own mother.

The relation between *means* and *ends* is a similar basic distinction. Strategic thinking is about relating means to ends, but the ends in question – be they organizational or individual – are *important* and *longer-term*. You may be considering how to cook your meat and vegetables (means) for a dinner-party (end) tonight, but you are not thinking strategically.

You can see why so much ink has been spilt in advising strategic leaders to be clear about the *end*, variously called vision, mission, purpose, Aim, goal or objective. The first Principle of War, you may recall, is Selection of Maintenance of the Aim. But what is the aim? What constitutes *means* and what *ends*? That is not always easy to determine, for what is an *end* at one level of thought is a *means* upon the next level up. Take the military as an example.

Ask most generals engaged in a war what the *end* is and they will reply in a word, 'Victory'. Understandably, for if you are in a competitive situation where one must either win or lose, obviously winning is the immediate end. Many a chief executive in business would echo the thought. 'We are in a fiercely competitive market', they would say. 'Our goal is to be the winner or one of the winners, and not to find ourselves the losers who go out of business.' As we have seen, business strategy theory focuses entirely on that end.

It was Carl von Clausewitz, a former Prussian officer with a philosophical mind, who left his mark in the voluminous and turgid *On War* with one simple and seminal principle. War, he declared, is always a *means* to a political *end*; in his famous phrase, it is 'politics carried on by other means'.

This relation of military strategy (ends and means) to the political level above it, so that military operations had significance only as means to a potential end or aim, had a profound influence on the military. As I discussed in Chapter 4, it meant that *strategia* as the art of a commander-in-chief now had to encompass the ability to work well with the 'political' master. Military commanders at all levels also needed to understand the political rationale of a military operation, or why they were being asked to carry it out.

The profound influence of Clausewitz's perception of *end* and *means* in war is reflected in this definition of strategic thinking and planning by Field Marshal Viscount Alan-brooke, who served as the head of the British Army, Churchill's chief-of-staff and his principal military adviser for most of the Second World War. The objects of strategy are :

to determine the aim, which should be political: to derive from that aim a series of military objectives to be achieved: to assess these objectives as to the military requirements they create, and the pre-conditions which the achievement of each is likely to necessitate: to measure available and potential resources against the requirements and to chart from this process a coherent pattern of priorities and a rational course of action.

In *The Art of Judgment* (1969), Sir Geoffrey Vickers made the seminal point that all the ends we pursue can be expressed in terms of changes in relation. To defeat an enemy, for example, if you happened to be a Roman general, meant that the vanquished entered into a new relation with you – slavery. The wealth and land you plundered and conquered gave you wealth, which changed your relation with others in a thousand direct or subtle ways. Or at least you might hope it would do so. Fame also changed your relative position in the list of those competing for high office in Rome.

The end of international diplomacy is for better relations between nations to mutual benefit. If the relation we call peace – however troubled and uneasy it may be – is lost, then the political end is to restore it as a step towards a better place, a better relation with that temporary enemy.

War is, of course, a bad means towards that end of a 'better peace', though in some circumstances it is a necessary evil in being the least worst option. For the nature of war is to arouse even deeper hostility, to exacerbate the latent aggression in all of us, and sow the seeds of hatred for generations to come. Clausewitz pointed out that the *means* politicians adopted when they went to war had its own inherent logic, and might well impose on them requirements or conditions that lay counter to the ultimate political end. This 'kick-back' factor is more significant in a nuclear age which has virtually abolished anything like the old large-scale conventional wars between nations. Civil wars or strife between rival groups claiming the same territory, sometimes with interventions from a third party to maintain or restore peace, are the order of the day.

THE CASE OF SIR WILLIAM WALLER

Most murders are family affairs, and civil wars can be murderous affairs. Yet one general in the English Civil War (1642–46) who always kept in mind the vision of a 'better peace' was Sir William Waller, subject of a biography by me entitled *Roundhead General* (1997).

Waller was an active, bold and valiant general who commanded Parliament's army in the west of England and then in the south, vigorously fighting battles, engaging in skirmishes and taking towns by siege. When his old and close friend Ralph Hopton, a Royalist general of the opposing army, wrote to suggest a meeting, Waller tactfully declined by letter adding:

> That great God, which is the searcher of my heart, knows with what a sad sense I go upon this service, and with what a perfect hatred I detest this war without an enemy . . . We are both upon the stage and must act those parts assigned us in this tragedy. Let us do it in the way of honour, and without personal animosities.

Waller won the ensuing battle. One Royalist prisoner, a young lieutenant, was captured unhurt, but was cruelly shot twice by a Scottish professional soldier. When he saw him Waller was exceedingly angry, sent for his own doctor immediately and did not leave the man until his wounds had been dressed. Waller also paid an innkeeper for the lieutenant's lodging, allowed him to send for a woman to care for him, and lastly gave him ten silver shillings for his personal expenses.

Waller would not have needed Clausewitz to tell him that the aim of the Civil War was political rather than military. He was a Member of Parliament and ranked among its political leaders. Although he had had some military experience when young (with Hopton), he had none of the assumptions of professional soldiers.

Waller always fought in the knowledge that one day Englishmen would live together again in harmony and peace, and – clear strategic thinker that he was – he avoided anything that would deepen rather than heal the division. He endured three years of imprisonment when Cromwell became military dictator. Upon his release, he worked secretly for a restoration of the old constitutional order which Charles I had destroyed through his deficiencies in practical wisdom. Waller lived to see a time once more 'when gardens only had their towers, and all the garrisons were flowers.'

The case study of Sir William Waller illustrates the importance of keeping the end of one's endeavours constantly in mind. In that context, the way Waller treated the maliciously wounded young lieutenant was not merely humane, it was *strategically* significant. For it was but one example of one of the *means* Waller deliberately adopted – a policy of being considerate and kind to prisoners – that contributed directly or indirectly towards his *end*, in the restoration of a true peace.

The first principle in strategic thinking, then, is to address the ends of your activities. What is the desired result? As specifically as possible, what do you have to achieve?

THE PRINCIPLE OF THINKING ONE LEVEL UP

Paradoxically, you will not understand your *end* until you see it as a *means* to another higher end. Therefore always think one level up.

You can always find that next level up by answering this question *why*. There are basically two ways of answering this question. One is related to *cause-and-effect*. '*Why* am I writing this book? *Because* someone asked me to do so a year ago.' Present activity is explained by something that happened in the past.

The other route belongs to the realm of *ends-and-means*. '*Why* am I writing this book? *In order to* help you, my reader, to be more effective as a strategic leader.' Here the orientation is to the future. For me, as I pen this page, the moment when you will read it is at least two years away.

EXERCISE

Identify and write down one target you have set for yourself in the next twelve months.

Beneath it complete this sentence. I hope to complete this objective *in order to* . . .

The more times you ask the *why* question in the context of *ends-and-means*, the higher you will go and the more general or abstract your answers will become. At a certain point – sooner rather than later! – you will cry halt. Unless, that is, your vocation is to be a philosopher. For we accept a lot of things as *ends-in-themselves*. They are striving for their own sake, and trying to see them as means to something else does not add to your understanding. The walk you take in the day is a means to the end of fitness or health, but there is little point in going on to ask *why* health? We all accept that as an *end-in-itself*, or, if you like, it has the end-value we call good.

Therefore where you choose to 'stick' in exploring the Chinese boxes of *ends* is where it seems natural for you to do so. For a general, for example, the political end he is given may be as far up the ladder he goes – for the military is a practical profession. Subject, of course, to the political end being a lawful and ethically defensible one, for the defence 'I was only obeying orders' is defective at any level of leadership responsibility.

What is the *end* a business strategy leader should have in mind? At one level it is clear enough, the business is manifestly the activity of producing and selling goods and services – now called product – at a profit. In a capitalistic economy, if you don't make a profit you tend to go out of business sooner or later. In a free society business is left with as much autonomy as possible to press on with this end, subject only to legalization to protect employees, investors, consumers and the environment – all part of the complexity which surrounds the strategic leader in business.

Although one school of thought tends to emphasize profits in the equation, while another school emphasizes the value of the product, both are strategically important of a business leader. The *end* that lies on the next level up – above the production and marketing of product at profit – is the *wealth of nations*, which is a key constituent – but not the only one – in a yet more abstract concept of a *better global society*.

THE END OF BUSINESS

When Alfred P. Sloan, one of the prime architects of
modern capitalism, published his autobiography, *My Years
with General Motors*, he gave a classic definition of the profit
motive and the way it works.

'We presumed', he wrote, 'that the first purpose in
making a capital investment is the establishment of a
business that will pay satisfactory dividends and preserve
and increase its capital value. The primary object of the
corporation, therefore, we declared, was to make money not
just motor cars.'

The end of business, then, is to make money. But Sloan
is talking about business here on one level of thought, like
a general stating that the end of his military operations is
victory. Yet, as Peter Drucker who knew him well told me
in conversation:

> Sloan had limitations. He lived entirely within the corporation.
> He had tunnel vision. In *My Years with General Motors*,
> Sloan has hardly any references to politics and none to the
> New Deal, the dominant social policy of the time. He had no
> concept of the relation of business and society. Born in 1876,
> he was essentially a nineteenth-century man. At work, totally
> aloof, yet a warm family man who loved his children. He
> was very keen on safety at work. A personally generous man,
> too, one who gave all his money away.

What Sloan lacked was the concept that, just as war (as
Clausewitz was the first to articulate conceptually) is a
means to a *political* end, so business is a means to a *social*
end. To make business a means to a *political* end —

communism, socialism, or imperialism – is to court economic disaster, because business (like war) has its own inherent logic that has to be respected if it is to fulfil its social functions.

One business strategic leader who saw clearly the *social* end of business was Konosuke Matsushita. Born in 1894, the youngest of eight children, he belonged to a well-off farming family who lived near Osaka. After his father's disastrous speculation in the rice market impoverished the family, the nine-year old Konosuke was sent off to Osaka as a live-in apprentice, first to a bicycle dealer. He then joined Osaka Electric and was eventually promoted to inspector, but decided to go off on his own at the age of twenty-three. Together with his wife and brother-in-law he started his own company, Matsushita Electric, in 1918.

From these humble beginnings the company grew into an international corporation of more than 200,000 employees, guided by the acumen and charismatic leadership of Konosuke Matsushita, first as president, then as chairman of the board, and finally as executive adviser. He died in 1989 at the age of ninety-four.

Because Matsushita's management philosophy was firmly rooted in his concern for people and his own experiences, his philosophy has had much influence in Japan; it particularly appealed to those in small businesses. So favourably were Matsushita's views received that he became popularly known in his lifetime as 'god of management'.

Matsushita was clear in his mind that corporations of all sizes are public institutions. Although corporations may legally be privately owned, their use of society's money, land and people makes them *de facto* public entities, obligated to society. When managers and employees come to the realization that a company is run not for private profit, but to improve the lives of everyone in society, including its own employees, they will have a heightened sense of mission that will lead to a stronger company.

It is tempting to polarize this division over the end of business between America and Japan (with Europe somewhere in the middle). But there have always been business leaders in the West who, in the final analysis, perceived that business needed an end beyond making profits – or 'increasing shareholder value' as it is now sometimes called. Henry Ford – a man who you might say personified cutthroat capitalism – once declared: 'A business that is in the business of making only money is a poor kind of business.'

The end of business can be qualified as *social* end but it is not necessary to define it any further in general terms. How a particular business acts as a means to achieving that social end depends on its changing circumstances which are as varied and unique as any general will encounter during a military operation. But having the 'next level up' end in clear view does enable a business strategic leader the better to balance the interests of the various 'stakeholders' in the enterprise: shareholders, staff, customers, suppliers, pensioners, local community, the natural environment and government as the elected leadership of the community-at-large.

As James Blyth, chairman and CEO of Boots, said, 'A sense of service is essential. It is one of the most indispensable of all the aspects of leadership. Customers, shareholders – there are many groups that are served. True leadership is the greatest service anyone can perform. My job is to inspire people in the organization about how *good we can be*, not how good we are.'

CREATIVE STRATEGIC THINKING

The natural way to think strategically is to identify your *important* and *longer-term* ends and then deploy your *means* – resources, capabilities, time and energy – to achieve the objectives that lead you like stepping-stones towards the desired result. You will notice that the setting of these intermediate targets, objectives or goals signifies that you have moved beyond strategic thinking and into strategic planning.

There is, however, a creative alternative. A cause *must* come before an effect, but there is no similar logic that says an end must come before the means. By creatively thinking about your resources and capabilities – using not just your own imagination but that of others in the organization – new intermediate ends can hatch out from the means at your disposal. But the process does take some creative thinking.

An obvious example in the business context is the development of new products from one's existing resources, which are strategic in the sense that they create *important* and *long-term* value businesses within the overall business. In time these can be hived off to form self-standing product/profit centres.

NEW USES FOR DISNEY CHARACTERS

Walt Disney's vision to create what eventually became Disneyland grew from visits to amusement parks with his own daughters. He observed the parks' run-down squalor, litter and unfriendly employees, and the boredom of the parents. Furthermore, he sensed a need among tourists for something to see when they visited Hollywood. In a 1948 memo, he sketched out plans for what he tentatively called Mickey Mouse Park:

> The Main Village, which includes the Railroad Station, is built around a village green or informal park. In the park will be benches, a bandstand, drinking fountain, trees and shrubs. It will be a place for people to sit and rest; mothers and grandmothers can watch over small children at play. I want it to be very relaxing, cool and inviting.

Disney had a *means* at his disposal – the Disney characters and their fantastic worlds as created in the films. What he came up with was a new *end* to which they could be profitably put – entertaining visits in Disneyland theme parks.

Source: J. A. Conger, *The Charismatic Leader* (San Francisco: Jossey-Bass, 1989), and B. Thomas, *Walt Disney* (New York: Simon & Schuster, 1976).

With creative strategic thinking it is essential to draw upon the whole 'collective wisdom' of the organization, which is not confined to those in operational or team leadership roles. Here you can use the internet or intranet system to good advantage. As one CEO said, 'Information technology is wonderful because it makes rich exchanges possible without formal structures'. When Sir Peter Davies took over as chairman and chief executive of Sainsbury's he invited everyone in the company to e-mail him with suggestions for the strategy that the company should adopt in order to regain its premier position in the UK food retailing industry. The response from staff of all levels and responsibilities was so great that he had to abandon his original intention to reply personally to each e-mail, though he renewed his pledge to read every one himself.

HOW TO SET ACHIEVABLE AIMS

Strategic thinking has to issue in a strategic *plan* which clears the desk for action, otherwise it degenerates into strategic day-dreaming. The process of strategic planning is a two-way and highly interactive one between you as the strategic leader and the operational leaders who head up the 'strategic business units' (as they were first called in General Electric) or their equivalents. What is critically important is the 'one-liner' directive from the top which points the 'part' to an achievable mission which is coherent with, and contributing towards, the overall strategy.

The austere Swede Percy Barnevik welded together in secrecy and at great speed two 'national monuments' (his phrase), Asea of Sweden and Brown Boveri of Switzerland, to form the 1,200-company ABB group that is now the world's largest single supplier to the electricity industry. Barnevik's achievement in creating the paradigm of a global company in thee years – 215,000 employees around the world, with half its $27 billion sales in Europe, one-quarter in North America and the rest in Asia-Pacific and developing countries – made him a business legend. In 1992 he gave this example of a 'one-liner' strategic directive:

> Stromberg of Finland, for example, couldn't be a broad-based electrical engineering company working out of Finland for the whole world. So we had to give them a new mission – to provide the world's biggest, most profitable, most successful

technology in a particular field. Better to be the king of AC drives than be a peasant in generators and transformers.

Now ABB Stromberg is one of the group's most profitable companies and a world leader in drives. Barnevik provided Stromberg of Finland with a strategic *aim* – not open-ended and directional – not a (closed-end) *objective* or *goal*. You should not confuse the two. The problems of setting a *goal* as opposed to defining an *aim* and then breaking it down into *goals*, *targets* and *objectives* (all specific and time-bounded) are well explored by Sir John Harvey-Jones in the following case study, drawn from *Management Week* (2 October 1991).

CASE STUDY: SETTING A GOAL IN ICI

The task of leadership is really to make the *status quo* more dangerous than launching into the unknown. Target-setting helps in these areas, but the problem with target-setting is that it is a very difficult art. Set targets which are impossible to achieve and you switch your people off. Set targets which are too easy and you also switch them off. Set targets which are difficult but just achievable, and then ensure that you achieve them, and you will switch people on. One of the difficulties that we all face is that the sale of possible and necessary achievement is so far beyond what most of us normally manage. We have estimated for many years that in industry we get about 30 to 40 per cent of what people are actually capable of. Probably the absolute optimum would be around about 60 or maybe 70 per cent, so there is plenty of scope for improvement.

Moreover, living with success has all sorts of dangers and

makes even these targets difficult to attain. Nevertheless, the targets have to be related to what is necessary and what our competitors can achieve, and this in itself contains all sorts of other problems.

I remember when I set the aim of a thousand million pounds' profit for 1984 at ICI it was not a particularly sophisticated exercise, and not one which was the result of enormous amounts of staff work or even very large amounts of consultation. The figure was provable in all sorts of ways as being the sort of minimum continuous target number that was necessary if the group was to continue in the way which all of us wished to see. The thousand million represented 10 per cent on our probable sales at that time, not by any means an unreasonable return, bearing in mind that we were a high-technology company. It represented the sort of profit that my company had made in two previous high-earning years, adjusted for inflation. It also represented the level of profits which would enable us to increase our dividends to shareholders, which we had set as a major aim, and was also plainly the minimum consistent earning pattern to enable us to sustain the size and power of the company in its present form. But when it was produced as a target it seemed, and indeed I personally believed it to be, totally unattainable. I produced it as a result of a question at central council, when I was asked when I would be satisfied with the profits that we were making, which admittedly had shown a sharp recovery from the appalling levels which we had been achieving in 1980 and 1981, levels which would have led the group inexorably to a steady reduction in its size. Once the thousand million was expressed, even from such 'back of the envelope' calculations, it became a target, not only in the minds of our people but in the minds of the press, the analysts, and the leadership. But I have to say that it became such a target partly at least because of its apparent unattainability

By a happy concatenation of circumstances we achieved the target in 1984, and in some ways I wished we had not, because the actual numerical figure was achieved at least as much by a set of favourable external circumstances as by our own efforts. Because the target had seemed to be so unattainable its achievement seemed to mean that we had entered the promised world where we were masters of our own destiny. Would that were true because yesterday's one thousand million is tomorrow's one thousand one hundred million. Yesterday's favourable circumstances are tomorrow's unfavourable ones, which lead us in turn to struggle more and more to stay in the same place. The fact is that very large numbers like these are beyond the comprehension of the people that we try to motivate. Even one hundred million pounds appear to be riches beyond the dreams of Croesus, and a thousand million pounds seems just plain greedy.

No matter how much we tried over the years to communicate with our people and to teach business realities, I find that the scale of the numbers blinds one to their relativity. This is made even worse when apparently one's own profit performance exceeds that of one's competitors, and increasingly we are asked, and indeed ask ourselves, how much we need before we will be satisfied. The answer is, of course, that the industrial manager will never be satisfied, and should not be, because the more money that is earned the more opportunities are open to one. The more chance of creating an uncatchable lead over the competition, of developing tomorrow's world and managing our own future for ourselves, our shareholders and our people. This may sound like the philosopher's stone but it certainly is something which will switch most of us on and is worth continuing to hunt for.

THE NEED FOR FLEXIBILITY

It is not enough just to have vision – to see the end or desired result clearly. This must be translated into all the specific statements of long-term goals and medium-term objectives, strategic options, detailed plans, action programmes and budgets that are necessary to make the vision a living reality which is 'owned' at every level of the organization.

This strategic planning process is done differently in every organization and, in large multi-product multinational companies, it still tends to be an immensely complex and time-consuming process involving managers at every level of the organization.

The best course for a strategic leader today is to delegate as much as possible of this process to the operational leaders – the heads of the chief parts that make up the whole. Be an architect rather than a master builder. You should always be able to write your strategic directions in the format of a few broad goals on a piece of paper the size of this page. Encourage others further down the organization to propose other objectives, while creating an expectation that more should be allowed to emerge as things progress.

What your broad goals should do is to define the strategic direction of the organization, so that operational leaders work out their own plans and objectives – and propose others – in the light of that flight path. Some 'one-liners', as Sir John Harvey-Jones calls them – simple directives to particular parts of the organization or, in a federal set-up, to organizations within the group – may provide all the focus that an operational leader with vision, *phronesis*, creativity and an entrepreneurial spirit needs. If he or she just cannot translate the score into great music, they should not be heading up the strings or woodwinds. Look for replacements. It is not your job to lead the violins.

Actually, immensely complex strategic plans are not a good idea, because they offend the principle of flexibility. Here is a parable:

> Von Schlieffen was a Prussian Chief of General Staff who died in 1913, but his eponymous plan, revised and updated by his successor, lived on after him. It was an elaborate plan for mobilizing and deploying great armies against France and Russia, using the railway network. France would be knocked out first in a lightning campaign through neutral Belgium to outflank the Maginot Line. Then reinforcements would be sent by train to apply decisive force against Russia. At the eleventh hour in 1914, however, the autocrat of Germany, Kaiser Wilhelm, decided that he only wanted a war against Russia, not France or its ally Britain. His Prussian Chief-of-Staff, von Moltke, declared that it was now quite impossible to change the plan. All the railway timetables were fixed towards a war against either France and Russia, or no war at all. The Kaiser eventually gave in. By 1918 over 20 million people had lost their lives as a result.

The trouble with the Schlieffen Plan was that it lacked flexibility. Strategy, as the *product* of a mind or minds, once incarnated as a plan, is like any other artistic product – a book, or poem, a musical composition – in that it can take on a life of its own quite independent of its creator. If the umbilical cord of strategic thinking is cut, the strategic *plan* may soon become out of date or inappropriate in some form or another.

As an Israeli general once said, 'A plan is a very good

basis for changing your mind.' When it comes to strategic planning, keep the plan as simple as possible, so that it can easily be modified if circumstances demand it. Second, if there are obvious contingencies – something liable to happen as an adjunct to the planned course of action or a possible situation that can be foreseen – build them into the plan. For unforeseen contingencies make sure that you have something in reserve, just as a wise general always keeps some units out of the first encounter. If the plan itself proves unworkable for really unforeseeable reasons – not the ones you should have foreseen but overlooked or ignored – have a Plan B ready to fall back on.

Flexibility begins in the mind. It should characterize the way you think strategically, not merely the down-stream activity of drawing up plans. There is a balance to be struck between flexibility and not abandoning carefully thought out plans or courses of action lightly. It is a matter of judgement. But it helps to remember that flexibility is essentially about *means* and not about the *end* in view. You should be flexible about means, especially if the differences between them are inconsequential. As the Chinese proverb says, '*It matters not if a cat is black or white as long as it catches mice*'.

Some people confuse flexibility with weakness. There is a tradition which emphasizes the strength and indomitable willpower of the individual leader. A strong leader who perseveres without a second thought down the path he or she is committed to after the course has changed is perceived as weak. Even if compelled to change course, a 'strong' leader denies it has happened to avoid the feared accusation of weakness. But such thinking betrays a misconception of strength. It is quite possible to be both flexible and firm.

Field Marshal Slim in his Sheffield lecture on leadership (1948) emphasized the quality of *flexibility of mind* as 'more and more important to leadership'. He continued:

> We have found that tremendously so in the Army, because the world in material and scientific matters has advanced so much. As soon as you get into any position of command, you find yourself surrounded by new and changing factors. What it was right to do yesterday may well be wrong today; some scientific invention, some new process or political change may have come along overnight and you have got to adjust yourself and your organization to it. After all, it is the organism which can adjust itself to changed conditions which survives. This quality of flexibility of mind is increasingly vital. Time and again you will see in leaders a conflict between flexibility of mind and strength of will. I have known fellows who were very good commanders in many ways – I have served with them and under them – who had strength of will but who translated it into refusal to change their minds or to receive suggestions from outside, whether from above or below. I have seen commanders who had such flexibility of mind that they always agreed with the chap they spoke to last. You have to hold this balance between flexibility of mind and strength of will, to watch that your strength of will does not become just obstinacy, that your flexibility of mind does not become vacillation. Every man must work this balance out for himself. One word of warning: if you go about reminding yourself that you are a strong man you'd better take a good look at yourself; there's something wrong.

One of the strengths of Japanese management has been broadbrush and long-term thinking, matched with considerable flexibility over means. Richard Pascale and a co-author touched on this theme in *The Art of Japanese Management* (1981). In it they quote Takeo Fujisawa, co-founder of Honda, who said that: 'Japanese and American management is 95 per cent the same and differs in all important respects.' As one part of uncovering these differences, they look at Japanese decision-taking. 'Whereas Western management beliefs tend to portray a decision as fixed and final, Eastern philosophical tradition emphasizes individual accommodation to a continuously unfolding set of events.' Indeed, faced with an obstruction, the Japanese often see the best solution as being 'to trace a way around it with a light touch, enough to get a trickle flowing. Let the flow of events do the rest of the work.

Yet it is important that a strategic plan should not be too formless or inchoate. It has to be explicit to be effective and specific enough to require some actions and exclude others.

CASE STUDY: PAUL SEVERINO, FOUNDER OF WELLFLEET COMMUNICATIONS

Paul Severino and a team of four founded Wellfleet in 1986; in 1998 it announced a merger with SynOptics Communications, creating a $1 billion networking business that ranked about 350 in the Fortune 500. Here is his advice on strategic leadership given in a newspaper interview:

> We have always run our business according to very specific business plans. Before we start a new operating year we have a complete, well-documented plan . . .

Building plans forces us to make decisions about what business we're in, what business we're not in, where we compete, where we don't compete. It sends a clear message to the organization so they don't spend their time doing things they shouldn't be doing. It's the only way I know to run a company. And it takes a lot of effort . . .

I never say to my people, 'Next year I want to grow by 200 per cent.' What I say is, 'Okay, we need to figure out and develop our forecasts for the next fiscal year.

'This is how much we're going to grow next year. That's our number. Forget about how fast the market or the competition are growing. Don't try to chase anybody else.' That's a number our organization feels good about going out and winning with . . .

You can really manage growth if you understand it, where it's coming from, what's driving it, and if you have faith in your forecasts. The key thing is to build a sales channel that gives you good information and is responsible.

I consider myself a technical person, but what I do now is look at the architectural aspects of what we're doing. I match that with the market needs and the sales organization and what I think is the right business direction for the company. Having the technical and the product architectural background have been a real help. I can say, 'If we build this product capability – if it has these characteristics – then we can bring it to market and make a success out of it'. But I don't develop the product.

'Paul Severino actually works for me,' says Steve Jenkins, managing director of Wellfleet Communications UK which has expanded to a turnover of £27 million in three years, selling network components through resellers. 'If I need to get something done or I need him to close some business or get him to a customer, I ring him and say, "I need you in the UK next week."'

Severino agreed:

The only way you can build a major company is by hiring good people and saying to them, 'This is what you've got to do. It's your job. I'm here to help you, I'm here to knock down walls if you need me to, but this is what *we* have to accomplish.'

Don't treat your employees like criminals.

There are two ways you can think about your company and your employees. One is that you put all sorts of controls and procedures on them because you don't trust them. The other is to give them the opportunity to do what they need to do . . . I don't sign any company cheque under $250,000. I don't even want to sign that.

SUMMARY OF KEY POINTS

- Strategy is a military concept by origin. Its transfer to the business field – and to organizational life more generally – was attended by much muddled thinking and misconception about it.

- *Strategia* or strategy is the art of the leader-in-chief. Strategy in the narrower sense is the thinking appropriate to the strategic leader and applies to all aspects of his or her responsibility. As it calls for above-average *phronesis* or practical wisdom – intelligence, experience and goodness – it cannot be taught like a science or skill, but like any art it can be learned by those who have an aptitude for it.

- Strategic thinking should be distinguished from strategic planning. It is essentially one form of *end-and-means* (as opposed, for example, to *cause-and-effect*). The only differences from daily common-sense considerations of end-and-means ('Shall I catch the train or fly to Paris?') is that the ends in question are *important* and *longer-term*.

- Strategy as a thing (or set of things) you can be taught to implement in generic situations does not exist. But there are *strategic ideas* in any field which are worth learning, together with historical studies of how they were applied.

- Some of these strategic ideas are fashions, but others survive the tests of time and become *principles* in their fields. The wisest strategic leaders often have a philosophy, a sketch map which helps them to identify rapidly the essentials in a very complex situation. They know what are the simple questions to ask.

- You should always be able to think one level up from a strategic *end* – which is the next higher level to which it is a *means*? Generals, for example, pursue military ends which are means to a political end. Business leaders serve ends (profitable growth, etc.) which are means to a *social* end.

- Means can be seen as creative resources and capabilities, throwing up new ends. In creative strategic thinking of this kind, it is essential that members of an organization, not just those in senior leadership roles, can themselves think creatively and strategically.

- Strategic thinking leads to strategic planning. At corporate level, the key step is to identify and communicate the 'one-liner' directives. Then it's a two-way interaction – top down and bottom out – to thrash out the actual strategic plan.

- Planning is a process not a destination. The golden rule is flexibility of mind, so that you can adapt after the plan but *still make forward progress* as circumstances unfold.

- Therefore it makes sense to keep your plans as simple as

possible. Be as clear as possible about the direction that is forward or progressive. For complex plans are difficult to change at short notice. See yourself more as an architect now than a master builder.

- Your essential function here is to determine with others the direction the organization takes. The measure of your strategic thinking is whether or not it influences the way people think about what is possible, desirable and necessary.

Vision is the art of seeing things invisible.
Jonathan Swift

8

CHANGING THE ORGANIZATIONAL CULTURE

Changing things is central to leadership. Changing them before anyone else is creative leadership.
Ordway Tead

Organizational culture is strategically important, partly as the end in itself and partly as the means to an end – your overall success strategy. What is certain is that it will need to be changed, for a culture that is static is already moribund.

Change, however, is a very broad concept. It embraces any variation, whether affecting a thing superficially or essentially. It covers in the same word a loss of original identity or a substitution of one thing for another and quite trivial alterations. Indeed, *any* process of variation, slight or great, in appearance or essence, in quality or quantity, is signified by change.

After your First Hundred Days you should have a good idea of what differences you want to make – the changes that are, in your view, necessary or desirable. If you are involved in a business organization, these may include changes in products and marketing strategy, in the organizational structure that balances the parts and the whole, and in the composition of the top team. But, with the fresh eye of a newcomer, you may sense the need for a deeper change, a change in 'the way we do things', and consequently in the way the organization thinks. You are now on the borders of the organizational culture, which may well be marked by KEEP OUT signs.

Earlier in this book I compared an organization to an individual person. Each organization has a set of *generic* needs – task, team and individual – whose properties and interactions I have discovered and explored over the last fifty years. Each one, however, also has a *generic* group personality, a corporate identity often traceable back to the founder-ancestor, which is as unique as an individual's DNA or fingerprints.

The John Lewis Partnership still follows the basic values of its founder, John Speedon Lewis. McDonalds base their operation on the explicit values of Ray Kroc. Sam Walton built Wal-Mart into the world's largest retailer from a single discount store. His values still dominate the business: frugality, hands-on management, value for money and an unswerving dedication to his staff. 'If you want the people in the stores to take care of the customers, you have to make sure you're taking care of the people in the stores. That's the most important single ingredient of Wal-Mart's success.'

Have you ever tried to change your own temperament or personality? If so, you will have found you cannot do it. They can be controlled or modified, but not changed essentially. Because you are you. And you always will be you.

But in the case of organizations, the analogy with an individual's personality breaks down. A better one is that of a *family*. Although some genes are passed down, each generation is different. The less inbred the family, the wider this genetic variation. A family likeness may persist, at least from parents to children, but beliefs, attitudes and values may change radically even in the short span between those two generations. The family *culture*, as we might call it, will probably have some continuities but it is also something that changes organically.

The metaphor behind *culture* is the agrarian one of preparing or cultivating soil and raising crops. On that analogy, it means the act of developing the intellectual and moral faculties, and especially improvement by education. By extension it also applies to a particular stage of advancement in civilization, and the characteristic features of such a form, state or type. We use it more loosely to describe the behaviour typical of an organization, group or task. In fact, culture is wider than behaviour: it embraces the distinctive customs, achievements, products, outlook, values, and beliefs of a society or group – its way of life.

Going back to the agrarian metaphor, the organizational field you are contemplating has wheat and tares growing it. The art of changing the culture is to keep the wheat and encourage its growth while rooting out the weeds. When you take charge of an organization, you may notice a 'weed' in the culture which needs to be addressed immediately as it could jeopardize the organization's very survival if it is in a crisis situation.

UNDERSTANDING VALUES

In the case study on page 47, Field Marshal Montgomery was addressing one aspect of organizational culture – what he called *atmosphere*. He could equally have described it as *morale*, the attitude of the army to the task in hand. Morale can fluctuate like the weather, and an effective strategic leader knows how to restore and build it up. But *climate*, as opposed to *atmosphere*, is a much more deep-seated pattern of weather. It can be changed, as we know to our cost in the phenomenon of global warming, but it is a taller order. Climate is much more akin to what is now commonly called organizational culture.

One tool you have as a strategic leader is the concept of *values*. Originally the concept of value came from the market place and meant a fair or satisfactory equivalent or return. In the plural, *values* signify the principles or moral standards of a person, group or organization: what is considered to be valuable or important. The assumption is that these are basic beliefs and convictions which govern behaviour.

Values are abstract – you cannot see them and it is sometimes tempting to believe (or act) as if they do not exist until the keel of your ship strikes a submerged iceberg of a neglected value.

A key distinction must be made between *espoused* and *real* values. An individual or an organization may profess values as beliefs, but not live them. Actual behaviour does not match up to the espoused values. As T. S. Eliot wrote, 'Between the idea and the reality, there falls a shadow.'

The dissonance between theory and practice should not be lightly interpreted as hypocrisy – play-acting – although it could well prove to be that. Hypocrisy is the robe which vice steals from virtue to mask its true nature. The test is what action the individual or organization takes when the shortfall is pointed out. Integrity will acknowledge the fault and put it right.

Apart from acting as standards and criteria for evaluating our own behaviour and that of others, values serve to stimulate or discourage certain ways of behaving. Moreover, values held in common among people provide an enduring bond, forming them into teams and communities. These values will find many expressions in the common life – political, social, economic and legal attitudes, traditions, customs, conventions and laws. Values therefore underlie our everyday relationships with each other.

'THE HP WAY'

In 1939 two young engineers set up shop in a small rented garage, just big enough to hold a single car. William Hewlett and David Packard had a combined capital of $538. They had not formulated a grand vision or a Five Year plan, nor did they have any inkling of the Silicon Valley they were eventually to pioneer. 'We just took on odd jobs,' recalled Hewlett a few years ago.

Some of those jobs were odd indeed. They included developing an optical device to flush a urinal automatically, a shock machine to help people lose weight and an automatic lettuce thinner, designed to thin out rows of seedlings.

So was born Hewlett–Packard, one of the giants of the electronics and computer industry, a company that today is worth $61 billion and has 88,500 employees. At business schools across the world, 'the HP way' is studied and analysed by putative managers of the future, anxious to square the circle of being good employers while maximizing profits for shareholders.

Hewlett and Packard rewrote the rulebook as far as employee relations were concerned. They introduced 'management by walk-about', wrote a corporate philosophy based on openness and respect for the individual, and in 1967 introduced what was then the radical idea – and in some places still is – of flexible working hours.

'We didn't want to have a hire-and-fire company,' Hewlett explained. 'Both Dave and I were products of the Great Depression. We had observed its effects on all sides, and of course it had a strong effect on us. It could not help but influence our decisions on how a company should be run.' From the earliest days Hewlett–Packard paid a production bonus to all its staff. 'The same percentage was paid to the janitor as to the top man,' said Hewlett.

The company introduced telecommuting and home working policies in 1994. The resulting reduction in commuting time, increased flexibility about personal and work schedules and lower levels of stress meant that the offices could be smaller and fewer employees resigned and had to be replaced.

Stemming from an overriding trust in the employees – which was generally repaid – the company's philosophy came to be known as 'the HP way'. On one occasion Hewlett came in to work at the weekend and found the equipment storeroom locked. He immediately broke it open and left a note insisting that it should not be locked again because HP trusted its people.

This approach extended to dealings with competitors, whom Hewlett willingly showed round his plant. 'You show competitors what you are doing – they will learn soon enough,' he explained. 'Just don't tell them what you are thinking.' On another occasion the shirt-sleeved Hewlett, who was prone to answer the telephone himself, took a call from a twelve-year-old looking for spare parts and ended up offering the youngster some vacation work. The boy in question was Steve Jobs, who is today chief executive of Apple Computers.

The company celebrated its fiftieth anniversary in 1989. By this time Silicon Valley, home to much of the world's computer development, had grown up around them. The garage where Hewlett and Packard began their business, regarded as the birthplace of the Valley, is today protected as a California State historical landmark.

While the company's name appears in numerous business school case studies, many of them no doubt apocryphal, Hewlett maintained that the only approach to planning the future of computing and electronics was innovation and a willingness to adapt. 'It's not like making a railroad,' he opined. 'You have to be flexible.'

The Times, 15 January 2001

Almost everything can be expressed in terms of values. For example, the relations between parts and whole in an organization – decentralization versus centralization – can reflect the values of *freedom* and *order*.

One advantage of thinking about values is that it helps to simplify the complexity of life. The Greek mind searched for the simple and generic amidst complexity – the search for the elements that make up nature illustrate that tendency. They thought there were four – earth, fire, air and water – but we know there to be not less than 100 elements. But the Greeks introduced the key concept of an element. In the field of values, we owe them the identification and naming some of the 'elements' or basic values we know today, not least the trinity of *good*, *truth* and *beauty*.

The source of these essential values, and how they relate to each other, are metaphysical issues. Strategic leaders aim to be pragmatists – their vocation is *practical* wisdom. For a leader, what matters most about values is that they function like stars in our lives, individually or corporately, providing a guidance which is qualitatively different from the direction we gain from maps, charts or sets of rules. By values, whether consciously or on automatic pilot, we navigate ourselves through life.

PROVIDING DIRECTION THROUGH VISION AND VALUES

Values is a term that works well in everyday life without definition, for we all know what it means. But if you think a significant change of culture is called for, you have to examine your organization's values. Or, more precisely, invite the organization to do it. There are two questions that you need to ask:

> What are our values now?
> What should our values be in x years' time?

(What x equals depends upon a variety of factors, such as the degree of crisis, the size and history of the organization in question. It must be far enough away to be realistic in terms of cultural change and near enough to be real, exciting and challenging.)

With e-mail, technology can give everyone in the organization the opportunity to contribute to the discussions. You should personally lead the discussion of these questions at board and top executive team levels, and expect the operational leaders to do the same with their senior teams.

What should emerge is a profile of about ten dominant *characteristics* which govern the present culture, unerringly reflecting its underlying values. You should also have a list of the characteristics of tomorrow's organization, the fruits of the practical wisdom which all staff (not just leaders) possess in more abundance than many so-called strategic leaders conceive. It is the one resource that managers neglect at their peril.

When you and your colleagues compare the two lists you may notice that some characteristics – for example, a *reputation for excellent craftsmanship* – appears on both lists. These characteristics or values are the pearls on the necklace of continuity. Other characteristics – for instance, *over-cautious and risk-adverse* or *conservative and hostile to change* – have mysteriously disappeared. Well, disappeared on the list. But how do you actually substitute a new value, behaviour and attitude, such as *bold but prudent entrepreneurial spirit*, or *a positive willingness to change*, in place of these tired and due-for-retirement characteristics?

There are three courses open to you, and you should follow them all: communication, example and system. Let us consider each in turn.

If you have conducted an exercise along the lines of the one I have sketched immediately above, you have already begun not only that process, but also the equally important one of getting commitment to change and 'ownership' of it. The next obvious step is to write down and circulate throughout the organization a statement of the *vision* of tomorrow's organization that has emerged, together with the consistent *values* which give it body, colour and shape.

Common sense supports you in taking this step, but do not expect too much of it. First, whatever you write down is a snapshot photograph of your thinking today – it will evolve and change. The remedy for that potential objection is to build in a review date. Second, the chief benefit is derived to those who actually *write* the statement of vision and values, for writing does involve thinking. Receiving a paper, perusing it or even reading it, doesn't necessarily involve the thought process. The fate of many organizational 'mission statements' is to be filed a way and eventually forgotten. How do you write the vision and values on people's hearts?

Granted that a written summary is part of your strategy, there is an art in doing it. Here are the principles:

- The statement should be brief but specific. Ideally it should be contained upon one side of A4 paper. Such a succinct statement can then be better communicated with the various intended audiences, through such means as inclusion in company reports or plastic cards that people can keep in their pockets.
- It should contain a clear vision of what type of organization is being created for the future. A short, clear, sentence encapsulating the essence of the organization should head the page.
- This unifying vision of what the organization is being built for tomorrow should be creative, exciting and achievable so as to gain commitment from all its members. Dreams should be excluded.
- The more detailed sections should spell out how this is going to be achieved. These will include some broad strategic directions, such as a definition of the business the company *will be in* (not necessarily *is in*).
- The body of the statement should always contain a section that sets out clearly the moral or ethical values that *will* guide the organization in the future, whatever may have been the case in the past.

You will notice that touches of strategic thinking come into an effective statement of vision and values. The reason is that purpose and organization in their broadest senses cannot be divorced (as the three-circle model reminds us). The vision of what kind of organization is being built, and what its key values are, is inextricably interwoven with its core purpose and the strategy that will thereby be more effectively fulfilled. Each of the values or characteristics listed should be justifiable in terms of the reason why the organization exists and where it intends to position itself within its field. That is not to say that some values – for example, the value of the individual person or of the environment – may not be ends in themselves, but they are also means to ends as well, as far as creating a better organization is concerned.

THE JAPANESE WAY

Japanese companies have worked best by establishing broad direction. Writing in *Director* (February 1992), Bob Tricker considered this feature among others that make them so effective:

> Top management creates the broad, long-term vision for the enterprise as a whole. This is not strategic planning in the sense that it is known and practised in the West. In major Japanese firms, the business leaders share a view of the development of their sectors, and have a vision of their company's place in it, often well into the next century. This perspective on strategy emphasizes corporate values – what the leaders believe is important. It may be captured in a simple, mind-focusing sense of mission – as in NEC's strategic decision to be in the business of 'computers and communications', recognizing the convergence of these sectors long

before it had become conventional wisdom, or Fujitsu's corporate mission to 'catch IBM' or Komatsu's to 'encircle Caterpillar'. In this way a sense of purpose and commitment is created for everyone in the organization.

Then medium-term plans are created for each business, sector by sector, typically with a three- to five-year focus, complete with competitive, technological and socio-political analysis, and their strategic implications. The process tends to be informal, involving much sharing of information, rather than a formal planning exercise.

Even in the one-year performance budgets, which are the responsibility of middle rather than senior management, the focus seems to be on operational issues, such as requirements for people and funds, rather than on detailed financial analysis. The emphasis is on obtaining commitment to the results rather than creating a basis for control.

Kunosuke Matsushita exemplified this approach. A sound leadership vision in terms of broad direction and values was the chief article in his philosophy of management. Manpower, technology, funding, plant and equipment are important to management, but it is even more important, Matsushita believed, that the chief executive should set up sound company goals and ideas and make sure that all his employees are thoroughly acquainted and in agreement with them. Such a philosophy is the foundation on which all other elements can be made to work.

The key to the Japanese success was 'management by collective wisdom'. Matsushita and his contemporaries in such firms as Sony, Toyota and Mitsubishi held that no matter how good a manager is, his knowledge and abilities are limited. Every employee actively involved in management, freely giving of his or her ideas and innovations, is an indispensable factor in the corporate process.

To that end of involving the hearts and minds of all to achieve the corporate vision, most Japanese companies have either a *shaze* or a *shakun* – or both. *Sha* means company, *ze* means what is right or justified, *kun* means precept. Therefore *shaze* is a tersely expressed statement, in lofty, high-sounding, formalized language, of corporate ideals and principles, whereas *shakun* is in the same form but, directed at a company employee, tends to be expressed in ordinary language.

The original is usually written in brush calligraphy, framed and hung up in the president's office or the board conference room. In some Japanese companies it is still customary to recite in unison the *shaze* or *shakun* every morning before starting work, as part of the *chorei* – the inspirational briefing which often begins the week or even the working day. It may last only a few minutes but it helps to create a 'let's go' state of mind and a feeling of identity with the team.

CASE STUDY: THE BANK OF CREDIT AND COMMERCE (BCCI)

The mission was to create the largest bank in the world by the turn of the century; the vision, massive aid to the poor of the Third World; and the corporate values were all spiritual ones. Never having read anything quite like it before in a corporate statement of values, I telephoned for more information. As a result I was invited to BCCI's sumptuous offices in Leadenhall Street in the City of

London, both for an in-depth briefing and to meet the founder himself, Agha Hasan Abedi.

Abedi was born into a Muslim family in Lucknow and educated in law and English literature at Lucknow University. At Partition his family moved to the newly created Pakistan. Abedi had already begun a career in banking with the Habib Bank in India and when it moved to Pakistan he went with it. He later moved to the United Bank of Pakistan, which was noted for its progressive methods and its drive for constant expansion. It was the first company in Pakistan to use computers and, with Abedi as managing director, it opened branches across the country.

While at the United Bank, Abedi met Sheikh Zayed bin Sultan al-Nahyan, ruler of Abu Dhabi, who was on a visit to Baluchistan to hunt the rare sand bustard. As a result of a friendship which developed between the two men, Abedi became host to many United Arab Emirates sheikhs. With the threat of nationalization hanging over the United Bank of Pakistan, Abedi set up BCCI with $2.5 million of Abu Dhabi funding, opening its headquarters in Luxembourg in 1972.

Taking with him some of his most talented colleagues from the United Bank, Abedi attracted more than a million depositors and built an empire of 400 branches in seventy-two countries. A rich source of cash was the flood of Pakistani immigrants working in the Gulf who, at the height of the oil boom, were saving $3,000 million a year.

But this headlong rush for deposits inevitably led to a carelessness about what the source of the case might be. The mystical-sounding Abedi manifesto — 'Western banks concentrate on the visible, whereas we stress the invisible' — was capable of a very different interpretation when applied cynically. BCCI became the bank to bank with if you had something to hide. Drug smugglers and terrorist groups were given unregistered accounts. As the books were adjusted to show ever spiralling growth it was these unregistered deposits that were used to plug holes in the balance sheet.

Part of the bank's problem was that it never really had a home base. It was decentralized to the point of having no centre. With its HQ nominally in Luxembourg, it was effectively run from Leadenhall street, London and Abu Dhabi.

Nor did it ever really break into the Saudi or American markets. When it attempted the latter, it tied itself in with dubious characters in the intelligence and business worlds. Important clients could be granted large loans without collateral.

In 1988, after a series of heart attacks and a heart transplant, Abedi stood down as head of BCCI and later sold his interest to his first backer. It was to be another three years before international banking regulators closed in and shut the institution down amidst a plethora of charges ranging from theft, bribery and corruption to laundering drug money and financing international terrorism. Abedi had retired from the chairmanship, suffering from acute heart problems. But at the time of his death he had been convicted of fraud and sentenced *in absentia* to eight years' imprisonment by a United Arab Emirates court.

Depositors, including many British Asians, lost millions of dollars as international banking regulators seized BCCI's assets. Yet in Pakistan Abedi was admired to the end for his attempt to build a Third World bank large enough to compete with the financial giants of the developed countries. And, in spite of the fact that he was wanted in the United States as well as in the United Arab Emirates, the Pakistan Government persistently refused to extradite him.

In inspirational terms the vision-and-values statement of BCCI was in a class of its own. Nor has any business leader in modern times outstripped Agha Hasan Abedi in his sense of the social end of business. But, despite his undoubted talents as a banker, Abedi lacked the *phronesis*, practical wisdom – intelligence, experience and goodness – to be an effective business strategic leader. For he failed to design an organization that had a controlling centre (or whole) as well as autonomous parts. Nor did he imprint in the culture where there were moral or standards governing the *means* – the tactics of banking – to match the social and spiritual *ends*, the vision. The end sometimes justifies the means, but not in this case.

Visiting the Leaderhall Street offices of BCCI in 1987 was like visiting the head offices of a religious cult: all vision, rhetoric, soft lights and acolytes, yet feeling strangely unreal and out of touch with the real world outside. Mr Abedi was delayed on his flight from Luxembourg, so we never met. Having had my briefing and been shown around the place, I left with an uneasy feeling that it was all show and no substance.

LIVING THE VISION AND VALUES

The *Herald of Free Enterprise* disaster was a tragic example of a situation where values and reality find themselves in conflict. On 6 March 1987 a modern British cross-Channel ferry suddenly rolled on to its side in calm, shallow water off the Belgian coast and 192 people lost their lives. The central value of *safety* was accepted in principle by the company: 'The first consideration of the Master and of every Officer and Rating must be the safety of the ship and the lives of the people on board,' says P&O Fleet Regulations. Yet inquiries revealed fundamental concerns about the designs of the *Herald of Free Enterprise*'s bow doors, the communication system on board, and on-shore and other management issues. The lesson is that at the end of the day management is accountable for ensuring that central values are converted into operational reality.

No matter how relevant to vision and strategy the corporate values may be, and no matter how clearly they are communicated and discussed, the real test is simple. *Do they substantially influence the day-to-day behaviour of people at work?*

LIVING THE VISION

Because example is so integral to leadership at any level, it crops up in every chapter of this book! Here it is again: it is no good just sending out a piece of paper with your corporate vision and values inscribed on it – you and your colleagues in leadership roles must *live the vision and the values*. That doesn't imply that you should be perfect – shortcomings and shortfalls are human and inevitable. But acknowledge conduct or behaviour that falls below the standards you have incised with lapidary clarity on the corporate tablets of stone, make amends *and try again*. It is only by making real in your own life what you and the top team expect from others, that they will be able to *see* the new order and not merely *read* it.

Make sure, too, that the systems in the organization that have to do with the selecting and training of people, how their objectives are set and their performance appraised, reinforce the communication of vision and values. If your organization *rewards* people for being over-cautious, don't expect them to become bolder and more innovative. If the system decapitates those who make errors, don't be surprised if people never stick their necks out – even if great opportunities float by.

'We acknowledge that *failure is part of life*,' Dr William Coyne, senior vice-president for research and development at 3M, said at the 1996 UK Innovation Lecture. 'And we expect failure on a grand scale. For every 1,000 raw ideas, only 100 are written up as formal proposals. Only a fraction of these become new product ventures and more than half of our new product ventures fail.' 3M allow their researchers to spend 15 per cent of their time on projects of their own invention. The '15 per cent rule' has been the midwife for some of the company's most important launches, including Post-it notes.

Clearly 3M has a culture that does not punish errors and encourages innovation. You do not get creativity, however, without individuality, and that in turn means resolutely giving people the licence of *freedom* within the broad framework of *order*. To be deviants – to be those who differ markedly from the group norms, the established ways, the ideas and assumptions that govern the majority – is often a necessary condition for being creative (not a sufficient one, however, for many deviants are disruptive, antisocial and unconstructive).

There is an analogy here with how a beehive operates, as

J. William Pfeiffer pointed out in *Shaping Strategic Planning* (1989):

> A worker finds a major source of pollen, flies back to the hive, and performs a dance that shows the other bees the direction of the pollen source. Then out of the hive fly the workers directly to a newly found pollen. At least, 85 per cent of them do. The other 15 per cent don't follow the swarm. They appear not to have comprehended the message and go wandering off in other directions. And what happens to this 15 per cent? They look for other sources of pollen, and when they find it the story starts all over again.
>
> Someone once asked, 'Did you know that the mortality rate is higher for the 15 per cent?' Being part of that 15 per cent in human organizations may mean that the 85 per cent try to hammer you into shape. However, for an organization to be effective and survive, it must recognize the value of the behaviour of the 15 per cent and, in fact, reward that type of behaviour. If you look for common denominators in successful organizations, you will see that a strong one is to find a way to get some of the people to do a deviant thing. If a system is too tight for this, if every bee is required to go to a particular source of pollen, there will be no research and development.

There must be something about this 15 per cent figure. Perhaps we should invent the '15/85 Innovation Principle' to accompany the well-known 80/20 Pareto Principle!

GETTING THE PACE OF CHANGE RIGHT

Changing the organizational culture is a very slow business in an organization which has a culture adverse to change. 'Do I really *have* to change?' is the silent cry. Of course, if an organization *has* to change it will – at the last minute, truculently and with many a complaint. When panic really sets in, the response to change suddenly switches from '*Over my dead body*' to '*Let's do it overnight*'.

Abraham Lincoln used to tell a story about a frog that fell into a deep, muddy wagon track. A couple of days later, he was still there. Frog friends found him and urged him to get out of his predicament. He made a few feeble efforts, but remained mired in his rut.

For the next few days, his friends kept encouraging him to try harder, but they finally gave up and went back to their pond.

The next day the frog was seen sunning himself content-edly beside the edge of the pond.

'How did you get out of the rut?' his friends asked.

'Well, as you know,' said the frog, 'I couldn't, but a wagon came along and I *had* to.'

The problem with Lincoln's Frog is that inordinate delay in changing left him only one option. As a general prin-ciple, the sooner an organization is willing to change – ahead, that is, of the time that it *has* to change – the more options it has open to it. Instead of being forced, change becomes proactive in nature and aimed at securing the heights of advantage.

By changing *ahead of time* you gain some solid advan-tages. Most organizations in any field have a herd instinct: they stick close together and only change when they are

Planned change   Change forced by external factors

Proactive	Sense of Urgency	Reactive
• Good communication	• Have to focus – can't do all the good things you would like	• 'Catch-up'
• Involvement	• Trying to keep up with competition	• Trying to do too many things at once
• Training for new ways	• Doing the same things everybody else is doing	• Falling behind the competition
• Anticipating customer needs		• Driven by short-term, crisis decisions which change frequently
• Staying ahead of competition		

Figure 8.1 *Planned Change versus Change Forced by External Factors*

following suit or catching up. Organizations that are leaders in their field (is that not in *your* vision?) are pioneers – they change first before necessity or competitive interest compels them to do so in varying degrees of reluctance. It is always better to take change by the hand and lead it where you want it to go before it takes you by the throat and drags you in any direction.

WHAT REALLY MOTIVATES THE BEST PEOPLE

A recent survey published in the McKinsey Quarterly showed that what really motivated executives and caused them to stay loyal, was *their job* and the respect they had for the companies they did it for. That meant jobs where they had freedom, autonomy, exciting personal challenges and where they could advance their careers. Above all, they wanted to work for bosses they admired and respected.

As for their employers, they wanted to work for companies whose values and cultures they admired, which were well managed and faced exciting challenges. What's more, they wanted to work with other talented people, 'have fun with colleagues' (there goes the literalism again) and be inspired by the business mission.

So perhaps employers should think less about building fences to keep people in, and more about how they can be magnets, so that people stay because they respect the companies they work for and love their jobs.

The necessity to change ahead of a Lincoln's Frog Jump, and the change that is both necessary or desirable in terms of vision and values, should form your major theme as a communicator.

Standing up and addressing meetings as Montgomery did before Alamein, issuing short statements on paper, talking informally with groups, having conversations with individuals – these are all 'moments of truth' when you can share your message and listen, as part of your overall strategy of communication.

CASE STUDY: JACK WELCH

Jack Welch, who became CEO of General Electric (GE) in 1981, became America's most admired business leader. Twenty years after he took the helm, GE's market value had soared from $14 billion to $566 billion. Sales had quadrupled to $112 billion and profits had grown sixfold to £10.7 billion. GE, which makes everything from jet engines to washing machines and runs financial service companies and the NBC television network, continued to improve its efficiency. Operating margins rose from 15.7 per cent in 1997 to 16.7 per cent in 1998 and hit 17.8 per cent in 2000.

Welch galvanized his staff with creative ideas and deeply personal leadership. An armful of books have been written on his management style. He was paid $7.1 million to spell out his secrets in an autobiography.

Some foretastes of his philosophy appeared over the years. In *Control Your Destiny*, by Noël M. Ticky and Stratford Sherman, Welch set out both his perception of the business environment and his views on the priorities of business strategic leadership:

- 'Only the most productive companies are going to win. If you can't sell a top-quality product at the world's lowest price, you're going to be out of the game . . . in business after business, wherever you look, value is what people are buying. With a few exceptions such as pharmaceuticals, the demand for the newest, most expensive, fanciest products is not booming. Look at the sales of European luxury cars – or super-computers for that matter. That's not what people want any more.'

- 'I think any company has got to find a way to engage the mind of every single employee . . . if you're not thinking all the time about making every single person more valuable, you don't have a chance.'

- 'If you have a simple, consistent message, and you keep on repeating it, eventually that's what happens. Simplicity, consistency and repetition – that's how you get through. It's a steady continuum that finally reaches a critical mass.'

- 'Trying to define what will happen three to five years out, in specific quantitative terms, is a futile exercise. The world is moving too fast for that. What should a company do instead? First of all, define its vision and its destiny in clear, broad terms. Second, maximize its own productivity. Finally, be organizationally and culturally flexible enough to meet massive change. The way to control your destiny in a global environment of change and uncertainty is simple: Be the highest value supplier in your market-place.'

And Welch's six rules for every CEO, published by *Fortune* in 1989:

- Control your destiny, or someone else will.
- Face reality as it is, not as you wish it were.
- Be candid with everyone.
- Don't manage, lead.
- Change before you have to.
- If you don't have a competitive advantage, don't compete.

One analyst wrote of Jack Welch as he was nearing retirement: 'He cares more about how he is judged on the succession than on almost anything else he has done. He has spent 50 per cent of his time in the past ten years on human resources, on getting to know his people and picking leaders. He has spent a huge amount of time in the last three years trying to find this guy. He doesn't want him to stumble like the people who have taken over so many other big companies.'

Failing to find the right successor has proved disastrous for many a large company. At least GE under Jack Welch, had the advantage of knowing what it was looking for in his successor – an outstandingly *effective strategic leader*. As Tichy says: 'Leadership is the head, heart and guts of it. This is someone who has demonstrated, through all the ups and downs (of business cycles), his leadership abilities. They must also be able to manage the world's most complex portfolio (of different businesses). All (the contenders) have to pass that test.'

One common mistake is to believe that communicating the broad aims, values or ideals of the organization can be done on video or down-line. Research confirms that tele-communication of this sort is rarely effective except as a back-up. Face-to-face communication, preferably in small groups, cannot be beaten when it comes to changing the organizational culture.

When Jack Welch set out to improve productivity by rebasing and harnessing the full energies of each of GE's 300,000 employees he did all the things I am advocating in this chapter. Rules and responsibilities were made clear and related to the company vision. The reward system was altered so that it encouraged boldness, risk-taking and innovation. The speed of change was altered from 'Reactive' to 'Proactive'. He dismantled 'the endless paper that flowed like lava from the upper levels of the company' and endless time-wasting meetings, both symptoms of the old corporate bureaucratic culture. Releasing people from a 'box on the organizational chart', so that status derived more from achievement than position, sprang from a belief that self-confidence and simplicity in organizational roles and structures are linked. Free people to achieve and they will grow in self-confidence.

Of course, Jack Welch could not do it alone. Communication *in small groups* formed the key which unlocked the door to the desired new culture. GE's leaders met on a monthly basis to exchange views about the business and dismantle hierarchical and bureaucratic barriers to communication. 'Town meetings' were also set up.

These meetings were based on the local governance system used in colonial New England where citizens met as a total community to make decisions about laws and policies. It was an innovation introduced by the early Puritan leaders on the inspirational model of the assembly in ancient Athens, where democracy made its first appearance in the world. In GE's town meetings, employees from all levels came together in large groups to discuss improvements to the business and reach specific decisions about ways to break down boundaries, cut out duplication and change bureaucratic processes.

Perhaps the most important change agent of all, however, was redefining management as business leadership. For Welch also defined the types of leader who would succeed in GE as those who both delivered on commitments and shared GE's core values. Those who did not share such values would not last long: 'In an environment where we must have every good idea from every man and woman in the organization, we cannot afford management styles that suppress and intimidate.'

This transformation of managers into business leaders constitutes every success story in bringing about organizational change – *there are no exceptions*. There is no other way to lead a global organization except by the leadership of a vision and values which all serve, including the chief executives. Self-discipline is the only way to reconcile those two apparent opposites, *order* and *freedom*. If I freely and willingly accept *order*, I remain *free*. Offering a person a vision and a set of values which reason accepts and heart affirms, is now the best way to provide strategic direction.

'People think I am some kind of giant who is everywhere,' said Percy Barnevik of ABB. 'Not so, it's a question of making values known and accepted by hundreds of managers who reach down ultimately to 25,000 more. This is also important when it comes to recruiting, keeping and promoting talented people. I have to convince them to be managers, to be leaders. We are in an industry with a good population of bright people, at least 25,000 to 30,000 with academic degrees. You have to bring the right people in, give them the mission, then mobilize them.'

Jack Welch reinforces this message of 'leadership through values' in large and geographically widespread global organizations. He identified his major personal priority as making sure corporate values are implemented. 'Every organization needs values, but a lean organization needs them even more. When you strip away the support system of staffs and layers, people need to change their habits and expectations or else the stress will just overwhelm them . . . *values are what enable people to guide through that kind of change.*'

Leaders at all levels must therefore live the values. Welch once described four kinds of executive leader in GE. The first delivers on commitments and shares GE's values: 'His or her future is an easy call. Onward and upward.' The second category doesn't meet the commitments and doesn't share the values. 'Not as pleasant a call but equally easy.' The third type *misses commitments but shares the values*. Of these Welch says, 'He or she usually gets a second chance, preferably in a different environment.' It is the fourth group which represents the real difficulty, delivering against commitments but fundamentally breaching GE values with tyrannical behaviour, absence of teamwork and the like. The conclusion of Jack Welch here is that 'we cannot afford management styles which suppress and intimidate. Whether we can convince and help these managers to change – recognizing how difficult this can be – or part company with them if they cannot, will be the ultimate test of our commitment to the transformation of this company and will determine the mutual trust and respect we are building.'

SUMMARY OF KEY POINTS

- Few strategic leaders will not be faced with the challenge of changing the corporate culture of the organization they head. Culture is not the same as structure, which is relatively easy to change. It is the deeper-seated pattern – unique to every organization – of assumptions, beliefs, attitudes, habit, customs.
- The concept of *values*, which came into wider currency as a substitute for *ideals* some forty years ago, is a useful way of expressing a culture. 'An institution is the lengthened shadow of one man,' said Emerson. Values are often the cultural genes of the founder.
- One proven way to initiate or further corporate change is

to list the ten adjectives that *characterize* the organization now, and the ten that should characterize it in x years' time. The values which appear on both lists is your *continuity*; the new arrivals are indicators of change.

- As part of a strategy for change, it makes sense more often than not to produce a short written statement of vision and values. Together they should provide all members and stakeholders with a clear and consistent picture of the longer-term state and the character of the organization.

- Do not expect such a statement to be effective by itself. It needs to be communicated and discussed in small group meetings at every level. Not just by words – live the vision and values yourself and expect your colleagues to do the same.

- The cluster of beliefs and attitudes that facilitate or retard change is critical in any corporate culture. In any age where the accelerating pace of change calls for speedier response times, organizations that are changing 'proactively' rather than 'reactively' will always have a competitive advantage.

- Central to all corporate renewal is one necessity: you have to transform your managers into business leaders at all operational and team levels. For only leadership by example – leaders who lead the way instead of talking about it – can unlock the hidden greatness in the organization.

Do not like some ungracious pastors do,
Show us the steep and thorny way to heaven,
While they the primrose path of dalliance tread
And reck not their own rede [advice].
                                        William Shakespeare

9

FINDING TIME FOR INDIVIDUALS

*Not geniuses, but average men require profound
stimulation, incentive towards creative effort,
and the nurture of great hopes.*

John Collier

However great their responsibilities, strategic leaders only
have twenty-four hours in a day like everyone else. 'If only
I had more time' is a natural feeling which besets all busy
people, and who in these days is not busy? Yet we shall
never have any more time. We have, and we have always
had, all the time there is. 'Those who make the worst use
of their time are the first to complain of its brevity,' said
the French seventeenth-century moralist Jean de la Bruyère.

Time, then, is your scarcest resource. It is irreplaceable
and irreversible. Few things are more important to a
strategic leader than learning how to save time and how to
spend it wisely. For the 'time bill' of strategic leadership
within the organization is a high one. Each of the four
preceding chapters will have carried that message home.
Moreover, on becoming a strategic leader you move out of
the engine room and on to the bridge. A large amount of
your time will be spent 'outside the egg' of the organization
as such. That may entail travelling to meet major customers, relating to major allies, or being away in connection
with mergers or acquisitions. Then you need to spend time

out of the organization, keeping up to speed on what's going on in your own field, or investing time in growing in stature as a strategic leader. For many shrink while in office as strategic leaders. As Dag Hammarskjöld, Swedish statesman and Secretary-General of the United Nations put it: 'Time goes by; reputation increases, ability declines.'

To these time-calls we must add any strategic leader's core or generic function (see page 95) of managing the interface of the organization with society as a whole – the sea on which the organization moves. It's a two-way process: society impacts with fresh demands, expectations and values on the organization; the organization has a potentially positive or negative effect on society.

To these work-related demands must be added the modern expectation (and desire) to spend much more time with one's family than earlier generations of corporate leaders. Duty, yes, but let it not eclipse the values of family life. It is a balance that, in effect, does cut down *some* of the time we are prepared to devote to work.

The strategic leader who allows himself or herself to be overwhelmed by the sheer avalanche of demands on their time soon ceases to be a leader and resorts to being a manager, executive or administrator. The urgent drives out the important, the short term triumphs over the long term, and so strategic thinking goes out of the window. The vision and values which shone before you like stars at the end of the First Hundred Days' honeymoon, are now merely words on paper, filed away for attention at some further date 'when we have more time'. You are too busy to spend time – real time – with individuals, even key operational leaders.

How do you avoid this common fate? You can start with either the 'supply' side or the 'demand' side of the equation.

On the 'supply' side, the key question is: how can you release as much discretionary time as possible – that is, time that you can choose to spend as you wish? On the 'demand' side, the matching question is really about what you are being paid to do:

- *Achieving the task*   Strategic thinking, planning and implementation – making it happen.

- *Building the team*   Not just the top team but teamwork – based on a just balance of whole and parts – as the other face of the coin of organization.

- *Developing the individual*   Helping individuals to grow and to make their maximum contribution.

As I have already written fully on the *task* and *team* broad functional circles of responsibility, I shall focus in this chapter on the *individual* one – your function as a leader in that key area. But first there is the issue of how to make the time available for all those key responsibilities, not least time for individuals – so often at the bottom of the manager's list of priorities. That takes us to the 'supply' side – the call to become an excellent manager of your time.

THE TEN PRINCIPLES OF TIME MANAGEMENT

In a companion book to this one – *Effective Time Management* – I suggested that there are ten key principles of time management. Under each heading I explored the 'how-to-do-it' aspects of the subject. Rather than going over the same ground here, I shall use the framework to remind you of what you as a chief executive should be doing strategically to make the best use of your time. For I am assuming that you have long since mastered the tactics of the subject.

- *Develop a personal sense of time*

> But at my back I always hear
> Time's wingèd chariot hurrying near.

Like Andrew Marvell in these words from 'To His Coy Mistress' (1650), you should remind yourself and your 'mistress' – the organization – that your days as a strategic leader are numbered. You cannot afford to waste your own time or allow others to waste it, wittingly or unwittingly.

That doesn't mean, however, that you become a kind of time miser, grudging every minute. The object is to be able to spend time freely, generously and spontaneously. You have heard of 'value for money' – get 'value for time'.

- *Identify long-term goals*
  Your work of identifying the *ends* of your strategic thinking and expressing them in simple terms of vision, four or five open-ended aims and a set of defining values – all in a single unified concept of the kind of organization you are there to bring into being during your term of stewardship – is immensely important as a guiding principle for how you should be spending your own time.

- *Make middle-term plans*
  Organizationally, this is the realm of strategic planning: establishing the goals and objectives – specific, time-

bounded, realistic, stretching and exciting – which are the concrete destinations, like towns and cities, the chief parts of the organization need to achieve on the road forwards that your long-term thinking has identified.

On the personal level, you can apply this principle by setting yourself five or six (not more) goals or objectives as part of the agreed general strategy and distinct from what the operational leaders have committed themselves to achieving. This personal profile of objectives for completion in three to five years may well become clear to you during the First Hundred Days. For example, like Sir John Harvey-Jones at ICI or Sir Peter Davies at the Prudential (and again at Sainsbury's), you may decide to sell the corporate head office as part of changing the culture. Another example of a common personal objective, as one's time for moving on draws near, is to identify the right successor, from within or outside the organization, to take over the helm.

- *Plan the day*
  An excellent personal assistant (and supporting staff in a large organization) is essential for any strategic leader. With such a PA it is comparatively easy to work out a system for managing the diary. Reviewing the week ahead together makes sense at any level of time management.

  Like any plan, flexibility is essential. If you have to make changes, remember that it is essential that you personally, or your PA, explain to those affected the reasons for doing so, and of course make the necessary arrangements.

- *Make the best use of your best time*
  Reserve high-quality time – usually early in the morning

– for thinking time. By that I don't mean necessarily
being on your own. Solitude and thinking are linked, but
you will have plenty of solitude while travelling, for
example, or at odd times of the day like a free lunch hour,
or at home during the weekends, doing some gardening or
driving about. Thinking time in strategic leadership
involves others, either a small group or individuals. What
matters, however, is that subjects which demand
creativity, wisdom or imagination are not left as an after-
thought at the end of a gruelling ten-hour day, or just
before you are leaving for an airport.

- *Organize office work*
You need an office staff to handle your affairs, and a room
where you can work quietly on your own and hold
meetings with small groups (round table to be preferred)
or individuals (comfortable chairs round a coffee table).
But the less time you spend in your office the better.
When asked why he was so rarely behind his desk, the
president of Toyota replied, 'We do not make cars in my
office.'

The skills of handling the inevitable paperwork and e-
mails, filtered and placed in simple categories by your PA,
are covered in *Effective Time Management*. The key is to be
able to spot the simple issues in the complexity of the
written word. It is a matter of isolating the essentials.

As a general policy, if a paper requires a decision from
you the relevant issues, features or information should be
set out and the person or committee submitting the paper
– having identified the courses of action open – should
make their recommendation. In other words, get them to
bring you solutions rather than naked problems.

- *Manage meetings*

  Meetings should begin on time and end on time. Your
  skills as a leader of meetings need to be well honed, for
  you will find yourself chairing plenty of them. If you
  can be brisk and businesslike, yet gracious and courteous,
  the business gets done and people will look forward to
  your meetings. There is no rule that says meetings
  should be unenjoyable, but hilarious ones are usually
  unproductive.

    Your main concern at a meeting should be for the
  quality of the thinking displayed there. For the process of
  gathering and sifting the collective wisdom – the
  leadership of ideas – creates judgement. Only decisions
  based on sound judgement are likely to be good ones, and
  so the preliminary thinking needs to be as rigorous as you
  can make it.

- *Delegate effectively*

  The Golden Rule of time management for strategic
  leaders! The main candidates for delegation are the
  managerial parts of the role. You may recall from chapter
  4 that *strategia*, the art of being a commander-in-chief or
  equivalent, includes responsibility for the day-to-day
  operations of an organization and its sustainability in
  terms of logistics and administration. As there are plenty
  of people who both like doing this sort of work and are
  better at doing it than you are, why not let them do it?
  That frees you up for what you are being paid for –
  strategic leadership.

    Yet delegation should never generate into abdication,
  the vice of mentally slothful senior managers. You should
  have a passion for good administration and really value

those who deliver it, just as Abraham Lincoln esteemed Stanton for doing so (see page 148).

The mistake some strategic leaders make is to delegate only what they don't want to do themselves! If you see delegation as a means of developing your colleagues and not merely as a way of reducing your own workload, offer them some demanding and challenging tasks – things you would really like to do yourself if time allowed.

- *Make use of committed time*
  Julius Caesar dictated to five secretaries who accompanied him on horseback as he rode on his campaigns – his equivalent of a mobile phone. Travel time is especially useful to a strategic leader because it does allow time to think. Nowadays, however, the mobile phone, useful tool as it is, brings interruptions even into travel time, unless you are minded to switch it off.

  Waiting time – for example, when someone is unavoidably late for a meeting in your room – gives you some minutes to check a letter or read a paper. During a busy day, committed time does yield these pockets – five minutes here, ten minutes there – which can all be put to use. *Look after the minutes and the hours will look after themselves.*

- *Manage your health*
  Being a strategic leader in today's changing world is a demanding role: you need to be mentally and physically fit. Energy, vitality and resilience can only be sustained by adequate sleep, temperance and taking sensible exercise.

  How do you stay *mentally* fit? Use your brain in spheres outside the organization, in related or unrelated interests which call for the exercise of the mind. The simplest and most time-efficient way of doing that is to read books. Not for information – use the internet for that – but because they invite you to think, reflect and keep things in perspective.

CASE STUDY:

LIEUTENANT-GENERAL SIR BRIAN HORROCKS

Lieutenant-General Sir Brian Horrocks commanded 13 Corps, a group of armoured divisions, under Montgomery at the crucial battle of Alam Halfa on 31 August 1942, when Rommel made his final attempt to win Egypt. Horrocks's troops took the brunt of the attack and within three days the thrust had been defeated. In his memoirs, *A Full Life* (1960), he recounted this sequel:

On the day after the battle (Alam Halfa) I was sitting in my headquarters purring with satisfaction. The battle had been won and I had not been mauled in the process. What could be better? Then in came a liaison officer from Eighth Army headquarters bringing me a letter in Monty's even hand. This is what he said:

Dear Horrocks,
    Well done – but you must remember that you are now a corps commander and not a divisional commander . . .

He went on to list four or five things which I had done wrong, mainly because I had interfered too much with the tasks of my subordinate commanders. The purring stopped abruptly. Perhaps I wasn't quite such a heaven-sent general after all. But the more I thought over the battle, the more I realized that Monty was right. So I rang him up and said, 'Thank you very much.'

I mention this because Montgomery was one of the few commanders who tried to train the people who worked under him. Who else, on the day after his first major victory, which had altered the whole complexion of the war in the Middle East, would have taken the trouble to write a letter like this in his own hand to one of his subordinate commanders?

Not long after the following battle at Alamein, while preparing for the final offensive in Tunisia, Horrocks was gravely wounded while in the forward area. After a year in hospital, soon after D-Day, he took command of 30 corps on the Normandy beaches – once more under Montgomery – and put into practice the lessons he had learned at Alam Halfa.

A LEADER OF LEADERS

What Montgomery was doing, as we can all recognize, amounted to 'on-the-job' training in strategic leadership for one of his senior operational leaders now in a strategic leadership role. Hedged between two great battles only days apart, Montgomery both found the time to do it – time management – and did so directly and effectively. Horrocks, for his part, had great respect for Montgomery – 'He was obviously a complete master of his craft, the craft of war' – and he had the humility to see that he had much to learn about giving his divisional commanders direction and freedom.

The same theatre of operations in the Second World War

gives us another compelling example of an exceptionally burdened strategic leader finding time to teach leadership on a one-to-one basis and in the context of an actual situation. Auchinleck, who had succeeded Wavell as Middle East Commander-in-Chief, was a diffident, reserved and rather remote man. In a memo dated 29 November 1941 and headed 'Personal and Secret', Churchill urged Auchinleck to 'visit the battlefield. Coming fresh to the scene with your drive and full knowledge of the situation you will put new vigour into the troops and inspire everyone to a supreme effort . . .' This memo did the trick, as history relates. For it was Auchinleck's visit to the front that restored confidence when the offensive against Rommel was on the point of being abandoned, and led to the stopping of Rommel's army south of Tobruk: 'the end of the beginning'.

Yet Auchinleck could not grasp the principle of why these forward visits had worked. As the war in the desert fell into the doldrums, Churchill flew out to meet him and assess the situation for himself. He sensed the morale problem in the Eighth Army, and once more urged Auchinleck to make himself familiar to the troops. The general replied that in his experience familiarity only bred contempt. 'In *my* experience,' replied Churchill, 'you cannot breed anything without familiarity.' Alexander was brought in to replace Auchinleck, and Montgomery took over the Eighth Army: 'Everyone felt that new dynamic force had entered into the tired, rather stale old body of the Eighth Army.'

The selection, support, encouragement and development of your key operational leaders – balanced by the capacity to stand back and give them the maximum freedom to achieve objectives in their own way and in their own personal style – is a core requirement in a strategic leader. You are 'a leader of leaders', as was said of Alexander the Great.

Essentially what is happening here is that you are finding time for individuals. At the core of these conversations and interchanges are the *agreeing of objectives* and the *appraising of performance*. At this level – indeed at all levels of leadership – communication is two-way. Nor is it a question of a formal interview to agree objectives and another, six months later, to do a 'performance appraisal', filling in forms and all that sort of thing. You should leave all that for the management textbooks. You should establish close and continuing contact, but on a non-interference basis. Progress-reviewing is the natural theme for these separate conversations with the chief operational leaders, but they will include a wider range of subjects – not least the ever-changing situation of the business and the field as a whole.

'A good shepherd knows his sheep.' In this way, the members of the top team get to know your mind well, just as Nelson's captains came to understand his views on the tactics to be employed in all the conceivable situations they might face. Equally, your knowledge of each individual slowly builds up, so that you are aware of each person's uniqueness – what they can do and how they choose to do it.

As Napoleon said, because of the variety of individual qualities 'in the profession of war, like that of letters, each man has his style'. Of his own generals, for example, he knew that Messena excelled in vigorous attacks, but Jourdan would be preferable in defence. Reynier, a topographical engineer, always offered sound advice, but his personality was incommunicative, cold and taciturn. Lannes was 'wise, prudent and bold', ill-educated but with natural talent and imperturbable sang-froid. Moreau was useless at *la grande guerre* but always led from the front. And so on. Napoleon knew his marshals and generals thoroughly. He did not treat them as being interchangeable, for each one was particularly suited for a certain kind of task. But, he added, a complete general – fit for all situations – 'is no common thing'.

It follows that your relationship with each individual in your team will be different. For each person will evoke a fact of your own personality which may not be touched by others. Like a parent, however, you should ensure that these relationships are essentially professional, not to be confused with friendships. For friendships grow from liking some individuals more than others, which has the corollary that you like others less. And people, not being short on discernment, will soon sense where your personal preferences lie. Who are the favoured sheep and who the unattractive goats? Avoid giving any the impression that some operational leaders are your personal friends, while others are not. That kind of perception is divisive in a team, whereas you are there to build the relationships *between* these individuals as members of a team, not merely to relate to them on a one-to-one basis like spokes on a wheel-hub. Even worse, these chief executives who indulge in 'divide-and-rule' tactics have lost touch completely with the spirit and practice of strategic leadership.

EACH INDIVIDUAL COUNTS

Field Marshal Montgomery exemplifies the strategic leader who knows how to make time to think. 'When all was confusing,' said Sir Brian Horrocks, who as one of his chief operational leaders knew Montgomery well, 'he had the supreme gift of reducing the most complex situation to simplicity. More than any other man I have ever met he was able to sit back and *think*, with the result that he was never deluded by "the trees".'

Montgomery's second great priority, as he once told me in the boardroom of St Paul's School (see page 63), was to make the soldiers in the Eighth Army 'partners with me in the battle' – not just the headquarters staff or the unit commanders but *each* soldier. Each individual needed to know the strategic importance of what they were being asked to do and their precise part in the drama that was unfolding. By word of mouth and in writing, Montgomery used the time he had created by ruthless delegation to get across that simple message – both personally and by insuring that commanders briefed their troops properly on the strategy and tactics. As Horrocks said, speaking of the main qualities of leadership which bound the Eighth Army to its commander-in-chief, 'He took infinite pains to explain to every man in the Army exactly what was required of him.'

IT ALL COMES DOWN TO THE INDIVIDUAL

' . . . And they said he's a skilful commander,' rejoined Pierre.

'I don't understand what is meant by "a skilful commander",' replied Prince Andrew ironically.

'A skilful commander?' replied Pierre. 'Why, one who foresees all contingencies . . . and foresees the adversary's intentions.'

'But that's impossible,' said Prince Andrew as if it were a matter settled long ago.

Pierre looked at him in surprise.

'And yet they say that war is like a game of chess?' he remarked.

'Yes,' replied Prince Andrew, 'but with this little difference, that in chess you may think over each move as long as you please and are not limited for time, and with this difference too, that a knight is always stronger than a pawn, and two pawns are always stronger than one, while in war a battalion is sometimes weaker than a company. The relative strength of bodies of troops can never be known to anyone. Believe me,' he went on, 'if things depended on arrangements made by the staff, I should be there making arrangements, but instead of that I have the honour to serve here in the regiment with these gentlemen, and I consider that on us tomorrow's battle will depend, not on those others . . . Success never depends, and never will depend, on position, or equipment or even on numbers, and least of all on position.'

'But on what then?'

'On the feeling that is in me and in him,' he pointed to Timokhin, 'and each soldier . . .'

Leo Tolstoy, *War and Peace* (1866)

In Tripoli, after the successful 'break-through' in Alamein, Horrocks witnessed an example of the Army's affection for its commander — a standing ovation by all ranks before and after a concert party's performance.

And here in the Eighth Army was the same outward and visible sign of the greatest battle-winning factor of all — a spirit of complete trust, confidence and affection within a formation. This sort of happy family atmosphere is common enough in divisions which have lived, trained and grown up together, but it is comparatively rare in higher formations. I know of only two in our army where it existed strongly during the last war —

Montgomery's Eighth Army and Slim's Fourteenth Army. And it is significant that both men took over their commands at a time when things were going badly and morale was low.

If such strategic leadership – one that touches each individual – is rare in very large formations like armies, it is not surprising that it is so uncommon in peacetime. Size is often given as the reason by less than excellent strategic leaders. How can you communicate in Montgomery's way with each individual when, as for instance in Britain's National Health Service, there are almost one million employees? Yet Slim's Fourteenth Army was also composed of more than a million employees. If Slim could do it, why not you?

CARING FOR EACH INDIVIDUAL

As individuals we respond to those who care for us, who meet our individual needs. It is futile to expect individuals in any organization to respond by giving their best unless the organization – the leadership at all levels – demonstrates in the most practical way *that each individual matters*.

In a large organization like an army it is, of course, impossible that the strategic leader should personally care for the individual, although it is not unknown and when it happens the effect is always powerful.

WU CH'I

Regard your soldiers as your children, and they will follow you into the deepest valleys; look on them as your own beloved sons, and they will stand by you even unto death.

Tu Mu drew an engaging picture of the famous general Wu Ch'i:

> He wore the same clothes and ate the same food as the meanest of his soldiers, refused to have either a horse to ride or a mat to sleep on, carried his own surplus rations wrapped in a parcel, and shared every hardship with his men. One of his soldiers was suffering from an abscess, and Wu Ch'i himself sucked out the virus. The soldier's mother, hearing this, began wailing and lamenting. Somebody asked her, saying: 'Why do you cry? Your son is only a common soldier, and yet the commander-in-chief himself has sucked the poison from his sore.' The woman replied: 'Many years ago, Lord Wu performed a similar service for my husband, who never left him afterwards, and finally met his death at the hands of the enemy. And now that he has done the same for my son, he too will fall fighting I know not where.'
>
> If, however, you are indulgent, but unable to make your authority felt; kind-hearted, but unable to enforce your commands; and incapable, moreover, of quelling disorder: then your soldiers must be likened to spoilt children; they are useless for any practical purpose.
>
> Sun Tzu, *The Art of War* (c. 500 BC)

Although it is the role of operation and team leaders to care for the individual, the strategic leader still 'owns' the third circle – 'meeting individual needs' and it is strategically important that lower levels of leaders do actually lead in this respect. The strategic leader should be watchful and observant, falling like a ton of bricks on those who fall short of this basic requirement. Here are two brief examples of strategic leaders who did just that.

Wellington

Wellington appeared to be rather remote. But he showed a real concern for the individual well-being of his men.

During the Peninsular War in Spain, a guest at dinner one evening mentioned that he had just come from a place where a number of sick and wounded soldiers lay without shelter, exposed to the cold.

Immediately after dinner Wellington ordered his horse. With his ADC he rode thirty miles, arriving at midnight to find officers comfortably installed in warm quarters on a bitterly cold night, while the sick and wounded lay outside exposed to the elements. He ordered the sick and wounded to be housed and the officers to sleep outdoors. He returned to his own headquarters before dawn.

The following evening he told his ADC that he had the nagging suspicion that the surly officers might have disobeyed his orders when his back had turned. So Wellington again rode thirty miles at night to find that the sick were indeed still in the open and the officers sleeping in warm beds in their quarters. He had the officers arrested for disobedience and cashiered.

Slim

Slim linked unselfish care for others, which he expected from his officers, with that overarching leadership virtue – integrity. It combined 'being honest with all men' and not putting self first. Integrity means 'thinking of others, the people we head, before ourselves. Moral reasons are, strangely enough, the ones that both in war and commerce tell most in the long run, but apart from its spiritual aspect this attitude – and there need be nothing soft or sloppy about it – has a practical material value. The real test of leadership is not if your men will follow you in success but if they will stick by you in defeat and hardship. They won't do that unless they believe you to be honest and to have care for them.

'I once had under me a battalion that had not done well in a fight. I went to see why. I found the men in the jungle, tired, hungry, dirty, jumpy, some of them wounded, sitting miserably about doing nothing. I looked for the CO – for any officer; none was to be seen. Then, as I rounded a bush, I realized why that battalion had failed. Collected under a tree were the officers, having a meal while the men went hungry. Those officers had forgotten the tradition of the Service that they look after their men's wants before their own. I was compelled to remind them. I hope they never again forgot the integrity and unselfishness that always permeates good leadership. I have never known men fail to respond to them.'

The principle is a simple one. If you give you will receive. Show care and solicitude for the individual and the individual will repay you a hundredfold by their service to the cause.

To establish an organization, however, which is oriented towards the individual in this way does depend on commanders who are leaders in the sense that they own and act upon *all* the three circles. In fact there is a long tradition in the British Army, as in others, that commanders are expected to be leaders. It is clear that even before the days of Nelson and Wellington officers were expected to be first and foremost leaders where it mattered most – on the field of battle. No coercion but the *willing* response of each individual is what counts.

The most obvious characteristic of a leader in this context is leading from the front, going first into battle. When a leader goes out in front others may follow him, but it is their choice – they are not *compelled* to do so. His example is like a magnet, however, drawing them on. As a leader is more likely to be killed in this position than those in the rank-and-file, the soldiers know that their leader faces a greater risk than they do and yet overcomes fear and advances at their head.

This expectation that leaders should lead from the front is deeply ingrained – not that all officers have responded to it. In the British Army it has always been a strong tradition. Cyril Fields's military anthology entitled *Old Times Under Arms* (1939) contained these observations by the famous lexographer in the eighteenth century:

Doctor Samuel Johnson considered that the special characteristic of the British soldier is a species of 'plebeian magnanimity'. His greatness of heart is exhibited not only in his bravery, but in the qualities he expects in his officers. He relies on them to lead them, and they, on their part are quite satisfied that they will follow him. It is not that the British soldier lacks initiative, but he considers his officer's leadership a tribute to his own loyalty and *esprit de corps*. 'In the case of other nations,' said Doctor Johnson, 'the officers do not lead their men, but follow behind to ensure that there is no skulking to the rear.'

Literally leading from the front is not part of the role of
a military strategic leader. He will usually have proved that
he can do it (Eisenhower was an exception) and he will be
in the zone of danger, so his personal courage is not in
question. The art of being a commander-in-chief involves
standing back and seeing the whole picture.

Napoleon always distinguished between the bravery that
a general must display and that required of a divisional
commander, and neither, he wrote, should be the same as
the bravery of a captain or grenadier. When General Slim
was visiting his men before the advance into Burma, a
sergeant anxious to ingratiate himself assured him that
'We'll all be behind you on the day, sir.'

'Make no mistake, Sergeant,' replied Slim. 'On the day
you'll be a long way in front of me.'

Leading from the front is obviously a *task* activity. Like
the parts of an iceberg below the surface of the water, the
team and *individual* circles are submerged and less visible.
As the stories above illustrate, however, effective military
strategic leaders are not only *team builders* but also always
show a direct and indirect (through the line of command)
concern for the welfare of the *individual*.

The individual circle encompasses not only material
needs for food and shelter, but the more intangible need to
feel a valued part of a great and worthwhile enterprise. It is
the diametric opposite to the sense of being merely a cog
in an impersonal machine, an engine part to be thrown on
the scrap heap when it is broken or worn out. Of course, in
organizational life we *are* replaceable parts, we *are* means to
corporate ends. None of us is indispensable, and we should
be lacking in elemental humility if we thought otherwise.
But we are not *merely* means to ends. We work best when
we are made to feel equals and partners, with an intrinsic

worth and dignity of our own which is not lost in the
organization and which we will take away with us when
we leave this service.

To a young reader the Second World War may seem an
age away, but six decades are just a drop in the bucket as
far as history is concerned. Computers, nuclear energy, and
jet engines are but three of the technological innovations
in that war which have transformed our lives. The much
slower revolution we also owe to it – the transformation of
management into business leadership – is only just beginning to gather momentum. But we have yet to address the
major challenge of transforming managers throughout the
world into leaders who achieve the *task*, build *teams* and
find time for each *individual*. Slim had a clear vision of the
essential difference between leadership and management, as
he explained to an Australian audience in Adelaide in 1957
in a lecture which has become a classic.

GENERAL SLIM ON
'LEADERSHIP IN MANAGEMENT'

The problems met at the top of any great organization,
whether military or civilian, are basically the same – questions
of organizations, transportation, equipment, resources, the
selection of men for jobs, the use of experts and, above all
and through all, human relations. Now, while the problems
are much alike, there are certain differences between the
military and the civil approach to them and in the climates in
which they have to be solved.

To begin with, we do not in the Army talk of 'management'
but of 'leadership'. This is significant. There is a difference

between leadership and management. The leader and the men who follow him represent one of the oldest, most natural and most effective of all human relationships. The manager and those he manages are the later product, with neither so romantic nor so inspiring a history. Leadership is of the spirit, compounded of personality and vision; its practice is an art. Management is of the mind, more a matter of accurate calculation, of statistics, of methods, timetables and routine; its practice is a science. Managers are necessary; leaders are essential. A good system will produce efficient managers, but more than that is needed. We must find managers who are not only skilled organizers but inspired and inspiring leaders, destined eventually to fill the highest ranks of control and direction. Such men will gather round them close-knit teams of subordinates like themselves and of technical experts, whose efficiency, enthusiasm and loyalty will be unbeatable. Increasingly this is recognized and the search for leadership is on.

What should we look for? Where are we likely to find it? When we have found it, how shall we develop and use it? Can the experience of the army be any help? Let us see.

In this matter of leadership we in the Fighting Services have, of course, certain very marked advantages over civil life:

- The principle of personal leadership is traditional and accepted.
- Besides, there is a strict legal code for the enforcement of obedience to lawful direction.
- Officers and men recognize that they are on the same side, fighting together against a common enemy.
- The commanders do not, in war at any rate, have to

pay so much regard to the financial effects of their action.

I can well understand a businessman saying, 'If we had all that, management would indeed be simple!' So, lest you should think that military management is too easy, I would remind you that:

- Personal leadership exists only as long as the officers demonstrate it by superior courage, wider knowledge, quicker initiative and a greater readiness to accept responsibility than those they lead.
- Again military command is not just a matter of bawling orders that will be obeyed for fear of punishment. Any commander's success comes more from being trusted than from being feared; from leading rather than driving.
- Officers and men feel themselves on the same side only as long as the officers, in all their dealings, show integrity and unselfishness and place the well-being of their men before their own.
- In war the general may not be haunted by finance, but his is the responsibility for good management and economy in matters more important than money – his men's lives.

These things, not stars and crowns or the director's Rolls-Royce, are the badges of leadership anywhere.

In industry you will never have to ask men to do the stark things demanded of soldiers, but the men you employ are the same men. Instead of rifles they handle tools; instead of guns they serve machines. They have changed their khaki and jungle-green for workshop overalls and civvie suits. But they are the same men and they will respond to leadership of the right kind as they have always done.

Infuse your management with leadership; then they will show their mettle in the workshop as they have on the battlefield. Like me, they would rather be led than managed. Wouldn't you?

WHO MAKES THE DIFFERENCE?

As a strategic leader you may hope that when your top team do achieve their goals and say to themselves in Lao Tzu's words, 'We did this ourselves', they will also look towards you and add, 'But *you* made a difference.'

Strategic leaders are frequently invited to identify their legacy – the difference or added value that should result from their tenure of office. To leave an organization with a large 'golden handshake', however it is termed, but to leave it no better than when you came, does not count as success in this book. It will be natural for you one day to look back in hindsight and say to yourself, 'I made a difference there in these specific ways . . .' Or, to put it slightly differently, 'Had I not been there such-and-such would not have happened.'

Actually, it doesn't matter too much if others recognize that difference, still less that it is acknowledged in public. Often you are the only person who knows the full story. What stays with you forever is the knowledge of how you did make a difference. It may or may not have led on to other things – who can follow all the threads of destiny? – but you played your part effectively and creatively.

But I don't want to leave you there. We are commanded to love others as we love ourselves. If making a difference matters so much to you, why not make it your business as a strategic leader *to see that each individual in your organization also has a sense of making a difference?* On the principle that everyone finds time for what they see and feel to be important, you will not find difficulty in focusing upon it and taking time to check that it is happening at other levels of leadership as well.

Human Resources is a much-used phrase these days, employed now as a substitute for the older (military) term *personnel*. It is a bit of management-speak really, for it appears to classify people as if they were economic resources, along with finance, machinery and energy. But it is a misuse of terms. For a human *resource* is not the available number of people to act as means at your disposal to achieve strategic ends. *Resource* indicates a *new* source of supply or support, one that may be hidden from view. The word itself comes from the Latin *resurgere*, to rise again. For example, you may not discover your resources until you are confronted with an unexpected or threatening crisis in your life. Organizations are not dissimilar. The phrase *human resource* really describes that inner or hidden reserve of energy, life or spirit that lies within the human individual. Crisis, opportunity or ideals are usually the three keys that unlock it, and leaders are no more than catalysts in the process.

SUMMARY OF KEY POINTS

- 'Our costliest expenditure is time,' said the Greek philosopher Theophrastus (c. 370–287 BC), and how right he was. The potential time bill for a strategic leader – 'inside the egg' and beyond the bounds of the organization – is an enormous one. Two things are necessary: (1) to avoid wasting time on what should not concern you, and (2) to establish some clear priorities and policies as to how you are going to spend it.

- The ten principles of effective time management should be observed. Apart from learning to say no – the chief time-saver of all – the principle of delegation is critically important. To a person of above-average common sense, the candidates for delegation are usually fairly obvious. Delegation saves you from becoming immersed in day-to-day administration or descending into too much detail. As a policy, if something can be delegated, delegate it.

- Don't just delegate the work that does not interest you. Delegating interesting and challenging work is a means of developing people. Remember, however, that delegation is not abdication, and you remain accountable: 'The buck stops here.'

- Apart from accountability (as contrasted with responsibility), you cannot delegate leadership. At strategic level that means spending your time on the seven functions of your role (see p. 95). Time to *think* is top of that list, as strategy – you will recall – is the *thinking* appropriate to a leader-in-chief.

- Apart from strategic direction and building teamwork, the third circle in the trinity which focuses on the *individual* invites your attention and time. It was not so much neglected by the top managers of yesteryear; it simply did not appear on their mental screen.

- You should develop a friendly but professional one-to-one relationship with each member of your top team, different in each case but equal in favour. Functions of *planning*, *reviewing* and *informing* are the main items on the standing agenda of this ongoing two-way communication. Take opportunities to help your colleagues to grow as operational and strategic leaders. At least one of them should be in the running as your successor.

- That every individual person in the organization should make a difference is strategically important these days. Make it your business to see it happens.
- Each individual person needs to know the plot, to understand clearly their part in the drama, to be encouraged to put their whole selves into it, and – when the curtain goes down – to have an enduring sense that their contribution has been worthwhile. That will not happen unless you and your leader-colleagues demonstrate in practical ways that each individual member matters to you.

> *The task of leadership is not to put greatness
> into humanity, but to elicit it, for the
> greatness is there already.*
>
> John Buchan

PART THREE

'I AM MYSELF MY OWN COMMANDER'

10

ON BEING YOUR OWN STRATEGIC LEADER

Ergomet sum mihi imperator.
(I am myself my own commander.)
Plautus (Roman playwright)

Imperator originally meant military strategic leader or commander. It was a title conferred by the salutation of Roman legionaries on a victorious general in the Republic. Later, it came to mean the head of the State, in whose name all victories were won. For, upon seizing power in Rome, a general like Augustus or Tiberius saw the importance of retaining for themselves the ultimate loyalty of the Roman army. So the old acclamation of the soldiers became their new title, commonly known to us as *emperor*, from the French form *empereur*. As a title of sovereignty it is considered superior to that of a king.

The Roman Empire, like others, was an aggregate of many states under the ultimate authority of one person. In our age there are many kinds of empire, such as industrial empires – large groups of companies controlled or owned by one company – or ecclesiastical empires, such as the Catholic Church. Within the organizational context itself we talk about some individuals as being 'empire-builders', someone who seeks to increase his or her authority or staff.

A CHIEF WITH NO INDIANS

Organizations, severally or in clusters, need effective strategic leadership – that has been the theme of Parts One and Two. But many people do not work in organizations, or certainly not for the whole of their working careers. There is no one above them, to provide any strategic leadership, so they have to find it within themselves. Many people working in organizations where there is a complete lack of strategic leadership may argue that they are in exactly the same boat!

Following the analogy, the 'empire' in each of us is our own life. It is the domain over which we gradually inherit an absolute sovereignty, a freedom from outside interference or domination which we guard jealously. You can think of yourself as the *monarch* of this territory, or an *emperor*, but those images sound rather grandiloquent. *Commander* sounds too militaristic, and *manager* too prosaic. So why not *strategic leader*?

The obvious objection is that *leader* implies others to lead. In its principal use that objection is sustained, but the concept of leadership is wider than that. We talk of individuals as being leaders in their field, those who show the way. The subject of Robert Browning's poem 'The Lost Leader' was his fellow poet William Wordsworth, who lived a solitary life amid the Cumbrian lakes and fells. Yet as a poet he was a pioneer, if not a revolutionary. When Browning, like other younger poets, felt that Wordsworth had abandoned the ideals that had inspired them he wrote:

> We that had loved him so, followed him, honoured him,
> Lived in his mild and magnificent ideal

> Learned his great language, caught his clear accents,
> Made him our pattern to live and die.

So you don't need a team or an organization to be a leader. If I may remind you, our own words *lead* and *leader* come from a North European root meaning a path, road, track or the course of a ship at sea. They are journey words. To lead is to go before, like a guide who knows the path and the dangers or difficulties ahead.

In fact we do talk about leading our lives, it is a common phrase. And *conduct* – the mode or standard of personal behaviour especially as reflecting moral values – derives from the Latin verb *ducere*, to lead. So conduct is one aspect of how you choose to lead your life. Another dimension is the career or livelihood you pursue. Both these words – one from the Roman word for a paved carriageway and the other from the Anglo-Saxon for a 'course of life' – also point to life as a journey or a way. You may have no followers but it is as if you are the leader. If so, how is the concept of *strategic* leadership relevant to you?

This book will, I hope, speak to you wherever you are on that vocational journey we call a career. You may be at or near the beginning, wondering if any sort of progressive path lies ahead in the fatter structures of today's organizations. Or you may be having the experience that Dante described so vividly:

> Midway upon the journey of our life
> I found myself within a forest dark
> For the straightforward path had been lost.

The dark wood is where your career trail seems to run out. You have lost sight of all signposts or markers and you can no longer see any path, let alone one that leads forward. It can be a place of anxiety and self-doubt.

THE NEED FOR STRATEGIC THINKING

One obvious way in which you can be your own strategic leader is by thinking strategically about your life. What do I mean by that?

It is easier to say what I do *not* mean. The received wisdom, especially in America, is that you should make a kind of *business plan* for your life, with a set of goals or long-term objectives – specific and time-bounded – that you should achieve. Winners are those who achieve these 'life goals'.

To my mind that model is far too restrictive. It induces a tunnel-vision. Nor does it encourage flexibility of mind. It is as if you are trying to command or order your life like a general, rather than to lead it like a strategic leader. There is something in it, but it falls short of the whole truth. The more specific your objective in the long term, the more likely you are to miss the mark.

At this point, let me review briefly what we now know about strategic thinking:

- Strategy is not a science – a well-organized body of knowledge – even in the fields of war or in any business. In earliest and most general use, it is the art of being a commander-in-chief or its civilian equivalent. More specifically, strategy is the *thinking* appropriate to such a person. Its scope is the whole nature and conduct of the Army organization, not merely its higher operations (in contrast to tactics) in battle or market-place.

- As strategic thinking is not a science, or art or skill, it cannot be taught as such. It is the product of *phronesis*, practical wisdom. Wisdom (from the Anglo-Saxon word for a leader) has three ingredients: intelligence, experience and goodness. Because of this chemical composition, wise people are learners − not least from their errors. So one can *learn* to be better at strategic thinking.

- Effective strategic thinkers are *independent* thinkers. Although they listen and consult, they *think* for themselves − as if from first principles, it seems to others. Humility preserves them against over-confidence or arrogance, but it does not rob them of confidence in their own intuition and judgement.

- Strategic thinking is essentially about *means-and-ends*. As compared to another form of fundamental thinking − *cause-and-effect* − it is always forward-looking and it concerns action. It is the kind of thinking that leads to choices or decisions on what course of action to pursue.

- What distinguishes strategic thinking from other forms of *means-and-ends* thinking is that it is concerned with the *important* rather than the trivial or mundane, and the *long-term* as opposed to the *short-term*.

- In a field such as war and business, there is a legacy of *strategic ideas* − things that more than one strategic leader has done with success. Those ideas can be useful guides, but you have to be able to think for yourself when it comes to applying them in a unique configuration of circumstances.

- With *ends* and *means* the horse doesn't necessarily have to go in front of the car. Creative strategic thinking starts with the means available − capabilities − and generates new ends.

- Magnitude and complexity at the strategic level of

thought and action are environmental factors which favour the selection of those with above-average *phronesis*. Some of its hallmarks, as abilities, include the faculties:

- to see the whole picture, entire and complete;
- to disentangle the essentials in a complex situation;
- to 'think' in order to match the scale of magnitude.

- Although these facets of practical wisdom are not all that common in those who occupy roles as strategic leaders, they are only forms of common sense. Therefore they are accessible to all of us. It is a grave error to limit practical wisdom to those who occupy positions or offices as leaders: we all have it, albeit in differing degrees.
- Strategic *thinking*, when the time is right, has to become strategic *planning*. Otherwise it becomes merely a form of daydreaming.

These ten principles are relevant to you, I submit, if you want to think strategically about your life. Nothing there invites you to fall into the trap of setting yourself an unrealistic framework of specific goals or objectives over the next forty years.

There does seem to be an analogy between strategic thinking in organizations and in an individual's life. In both cases, rather than a complicated plan full of objectives and times, what counts is having a broad vision and four or five equally broad strategic aims. Together, amid the changes and chances of life, they provide you with a sense of direction. You are able to sense or recognize what is *strategic* for you – that is, *important* and significant for the *long term* – as opposed to being merely tactical.

You will gather from the above philosophy of strategic

thinking that I have complete confidence that you can do it for yourself! For you have a *reasonable* level of *higher* common sense or practical wisdom, quite sufficient for the task in hand. And I have no doubt that you have imagination, a touch of creativity and a lack of arrogance as well, all the essential ingredients for an effective strategic leader.

Creativity is important. Free up your mind from preconceived notions. At this point books like this one often give you an 'instructor's manual' list of steps – (1) Identify your chief ends in life; (2) Write down your personal mission statement; (3) Enumerate your core values; (4) Determine your goals in career, family life, recreation, the community, and so on. But I have never found that approach works for me, and so I cannot recommend it to you. Not that I am against being systematic or marshalling your thoughts on paper and herding them into planning pens. Don't, however, do it too soon. You are never too old to daydream.

Imagine the rest of your life as a blank canvas. The foreground – the next period – is already sketched in and some colouring may have been done as well. But most of the canvas is white. Try taking a brush and splashing a colour – an idea that occurs to you – in the middle. It doesn't really matter what it is at this stage – 'I want to see Venice' or 'I want to become a potter.' If you think of strategic thinking as more like painting a picture than plotting a technical blueprint or writing a business plan, you will find that you have a lot more strategic ideas – and it's more fun.

Everyone's picture turns out to be very different, of course, though at sketching-in stage they may appear to be quite similar. Different, not better or worse.

As you work up the picture, not necessarily at one sitting, from rough sketched outlines to something with body, colour and form, it may seem to change direction as you paint. For it is a living process; new ideas join you like pilgrims on the way. The finished product, when unveiled in the exhibition, will most probably not be what you envisaged. Yet it may still, in some way, capture original vision. In other words, it will be a work of art.

'What is the difference between a skill or craft on the one hand and art on the other?' I once asked a philosopher friend.

'If you know how you did it, then it is a skill,' he replied. 'But if you don't know how you did it, then it's art.' (Compare what Ruskin says about great artists, see page 105.)

That vital difference, the x factor, which enables you to transcend limits, is called *inspiration*. In relation to one's life's work it is linked to the concept of vocation. One aspect of that is the idea that there is guidance and help available in the strategic leadership from God, or *as if* from a god if you would prefer it. As Shakespeare says, 'There is divinity which shapes our ends, rough hew them how we will.' I shall return to that theme of inspiration in Chapter 12 but here I want to pluck out and develop the concept of vocation as a *strategic idea* – something that you should know about even if you do not buy it for the self-picture that you are painting on that half-finished canvas. If you look the picture over when you have completed it you will see that it is also your self-portrait.

THE FRAMEWORK OF VOCATION

When I was twenty and contemplating my own blank canvas of the future, it seemed self-evidently *important* and *long-term* to find work where I could use what talents I had most effectively for the common good as well as earning my living. Not that I found it that easy to do. In *How to Find Your Vocation: A Guide to Discovering the Work you Love* (2000), I have shared my experience in that quest.

As a *strategic idea* I think the nub of the concept of vocation is that it points you to consider the personal *means* at your disposal as well as the *ends* which you propose for yourself. As I stood to inherit no money or property to speak of, the means in my case, as in so many others', consisted of my natural abilities, partly developed by education. If you consider your natural aptitudes, interests and temperament, I reasoned to myself, they should give you some clues as to the work which is meant for you. And so thinking could proceed both 'top down' – searching for the best purpose in life – and also 'bottom up' – considering what abilities you had to offer.

Thinking along these vocational lines – although I had no vocation to a religious profession – led me to formulate an overarching end in the important general field of work. Thus the vocational aim – the broad beam, I told myself, on which you need to align your life – is as follows (the actual words don't matter as opposed to the overall sense):

To identify, use and develop all my talents for the good of others.

Of course, you *can* use your talents simply to make money for yourself or others. That isn't necessarily unvocational. For some people have a talent, gift or even genius for making money in a complex economic system. Whether it is vocational or not, however, depends upon how the money is made and what it is used *for*. For vocation, I suggest, implies that a *good* end is served.

You will have noticed that I have already smuggled in the value of *good*, when it comes to thinking about ends, in my assumption that practical wisdom has three elements – intelligence, experience and goodness. And practical wisdom is the chief instrument in strategic leadership.

Of course I am not arguing that you or I may not be mistaken about what is *good*. We can fall into conceptual fallacies, only to discover that what we conceived of as being good is not really *good* after all. And so, as Keats said, by 'knowledge of good bought dear by knowing ill', we move on. Experience is also part of *phronesis*. Not that we shall ever know in full. For values such as *truth* or *beauty*, *good* or *love* are like two-sided coins: they are *givens* but they are also there to be endlessly explored – we never touch the bottom.

An end is the desired result. You should be able to establish some 'success criteria' in order to know whether or not you are achieving the result you had in mind. The success criteria of the vocational aim or end that I sketched above is not wealth, fame or even happiness. Thomas Wolfe captured the essence of vocational success in *You Can't Go Home Again* (1940):

> If a man has a talent and cannot use it, he has failed. If he has a talent and uses only half of it, he has partly failed. If he has a talent and learns somehow to use the whole of it, he has gloriously succeeded, and won a satisfaction and a triumph few men ever know.

The only measure or yardstick relates to making the fullest or most effective use you can of the attitudes, interests and temperament that are yours alone. It is an open-ended aim, for we always have something to offer even if it is only a kind word, a smile or even a thought.

For most of us vocation is not exclusively about work. For we have a natural calling to marriage and the procreation of children. You could almost call marriage another *strategic idea*, because it has both the key dimensions of strategy in abundant measure: it is *important* and it is *long-term*. If you are thinking strategically – or developing strategic leadership in your life – it is worth being patient and waiting until you meet the right person. Marriages fail at an alarming rate because one or both partners has a deficiency in *phronesis* or practical wisdom. They may lack enough experience of personal relationships with the opposite sex, or choose to ignore what their intelligence in its unconscious operations as intuition tells them. Or they may lack goodness, being unkind, devoid of integrity, selfish, malicious or even cruel.

Waiting for the right person, of course, is not to be confused with waiting for the perfect wife or husband. Common sense alone will tell you that you will wait for ever if that is your aim. You may know the story of a young man who did resolve to wait until he met the perfect woman to marry. After many years he finally did meet her. Unfortunately for him, however, she was looking for the perfect man! Perfection eludes us in this world, but excellence is within our grasp.

The other day I heard the novelist Elizabeth Jane Howard say in a radio interview, 'Women often think of themselves as people to whom things happen.' One common characteristic of poor strategic leaders is an over-passive attitude to their career. I am not suggesting that you transform yourself into a careerist of the worst sort, only that you should take on the ownership of your own career and full responsibility for its direction. The same, it has been said, is true of life. Life's real failures are those who blame their problems on others rather than assuming full responsibility for their situation.

It's so easy to find excuses for a career that is leaving you dissatisfied or unhappy. You can blame it on other people. You can blame it on fate. You can blame it on bad luck. But eventually you have to look in the mirror. Look objectively, look at yourself as a case study. Then you may come to see that there is some truth in those words of Cassius in Shakespeare's *Julius Caesar*:

> Men at some time are masters of their fates:
> The fault, dear Brutus, is not in our stars,
> But in ourselves that we are underlings.

Pause for a moment now and assess just how important your career is to you in the context of your whole life. To be blunt, is it a *career* – a path of progress – or is it more an *occupation*, a means of earning your family's bread?

In Tunisia I remember seeing a ruined Roman city called Bardia, on the edge of the desert. Walking down the main *carraria via* (the carriageway, you recall, that gives us our word *career*), I saw deep chariot-wheel ruts incised in the large paving-stones. So if your career has fallen into a rut, now is the time for a change of direction – however painful it is to extract yourself from that narrow, undeviating course of life. If you are in a rut your wheels are caught in a deep track. You have stopped thinking. The furrow is taking you forward in time but you are not in control. Work becomes monotonous. You experience it as increasingly dreary and tedious, and look to the day when you can take early retirement and regain control of your destiny.

THE CREATIVE SPIRIT

You may not be an author of books, but you are writing the book of your own life. For your life is not being dictated to you from a pre-recorded script. You can make at least some of it up as you go along. 'When the creative urge seizes one – at least, such is my experience – one becomes creative in all directions at once,' says Henry Miller.

If you decide to take a creative strategic approach to life it does change your perspective. You will seek out first some 'given' ideas about yourself. What are your distinctive strengths? These are not easy questions to answer. Self-discovery continues throughout life. Seek to identify what *you* are born to excel at, and make sure you are working in the right area.

Even when some conscious self-analysis and some imaginative thinking, supplemented by intuition, have given you some clues and insights or enabled you to make bold guesses about yourself, you still have to try to work out these ideas in a real life. That involves an element of trial and error, periods of frustration and despair, and moments of excitement and joy.

The fact that you are starting the journey with inadequate instructions, as it were, means that you are bound to feel bewildered, confused, even frustrated at times – often for quite long periods. You will be tempted to give up. But it is encouraging to know that many others go through this dark night of despair.

The author Hammond Innes tells us that he starts work on a novel with little more than a background and a theme, probably an opening scene, perhaps even some idea of the climax. 'But each book is different, something to be wrestled with, struggled over,' he says.

> And there is always the point, somewhere in the writing of it, when all seems hopeless and I am driven to desperation by the thought that I have lost my touch as a story-teller, will never be able to do it again. Blank despair is matched by excitement, the enormous satisfaction when suddenly it all falls into place, seemingly of its own accord, and the words begin the flow again, the whole thing fascinating, totally absorbing.

As Hammond Innes comments, the process sounds more like a battle – at least 50 per cent of his writing output goes in the waste-paper basket – than a recipe for success. 'Then why not an outline of the story first?' he is often asked. 'Surely that would be simpler?' He replies, 'Of course it would. But if I did that, then there would be no fun in writing it. And if the writer is bored, then the reader will be even more bored. The story must grow, naturally and of its own volition – a slow, haphazard, infuriating process, but the only one I know.' Just like a vocation!

For gradually the creative pattern of your life begins to emerge before your eyes on the loom of experience, with change and continuity as its warp and weft. At her eightieth birthday celebration the internationally famous weaver Theo Moorman had words to say that apply to our lives as well as our work:

> Set your sights high, otherwise the whole momentum collapses. Cherish your integrity and judgement. You can't work with one eye on the market, you have to stand for yourself. When I take my work off the loom, occasionally there's a

comeback feeling in one's guts that tells one it is good. It's a feeling to be prized above rubies.

Life should be an adventure. It is a usually interesting, occasionally exciting and sometimes painful journey forward into an unknown future. As you try to make something of it in a creative way – working things out as you go along, new ideas will come to you. Even in the desert stretches there are wells and springs of inspiration. But they are not to be had in advance.

We can all learn from creative thinkers to see life as essentially a series of beginnings. 'I love beginnings,' says novelist Christopher Leach. 'What I like about life is the potentiality of beginnings.' Perhaps our lives, like books, should never be finished, only abandoned to a receiver with as much trust as we can muster.

Even if your work in the narrow sense does not call for imagination, the art of creative thinking is still relevant to you. For our lives are unfinished creations. Shaping and transforming the raw materials of our lives and circumstances is endlessly interesting and often challenging.

The word *author*, incidentally, comes from the Latin verb *augere*, to grow. Forget about books, and think about *authoring* in the sense of growing and developing the unique business of your life's work: pruning here, applying some fertilizer there, planning extensions, and planting seeds for tomorrow.

The art is to set for yourself a broad strategic framework in life in which your abilities and gifts can unfold in a natural and creative way. That calls for some *strategic planning* – the wise sort.

THE ART OF STRATEGIC PLANNING

Strategy (in its narrow sense) has been defined as 'the art of devising plans and stratagems towards a goal'. Once you have identified what is *important* and *long-term* in an area that concerns you, then it is worth setting yourself a goal or two.

By 'area that concerns you' I do not mean just career. Marriage could be a goal. Or you may be deeply interested in a particular field, either professionally or as an amateur. Although you do not work for an organization in that field, you are contributing to its strategic direction. Not all directions of this nature have or need goals, but they are sometimes useful as markers or aiming points. You may not reach the goal, but like a lighthouse on a coast, it gives you a simple direction so that you don't have to be always checking your inner compass or the outline chart of your life you have drawn on the back of an envelope.

Sport is a good example of a field where it does make sense to set yourself a goal. A *goal*, to remind you, is a deliberately selected result towards which you choose to direct activity. A *goal* is different from an *objective* in that it can only be won with difficulty by dedicated effort and over a longer rather than a short period of time. Winning a gold medal at the Olympics or becoming heavyweight champion of the world are both goals that sportsmen or women, given the necessary aptitudes, could well set themselves. Although their aim may actually be an open-ended one – to achieve the highest standard possible in the chosen sport – it makes sense to turn it into a closed-ended one – concrete, specific and time-branded.

In order to think forward and make plans you need a vocabulary. For thinking is a discussion you have with yourself, usually to try to teach yourself something that others cannot tell you, and if the concepts you use are confused, so will your thinking be. It is not easy because the words which refer to the result towards which one chooses to think, plan and act – *purpose, aim, end, goal, object* and *objective* – overlap in meaning and are generally used merely as synonyms.

A framework for thinking about desired results that I have found useful as a means of clear thinking is based on a distinction between *purpose, aims, objectives* and *steps*, and explores their relationships. It is like the biblical ladder in Jacob's dream: stretching from heaven to earth, with angels descending and ascending.

You can now see that descending Jacob's ladder, from the *general* and abstract to the *particular* and concrete, you are answering the question *how?* This is my *purpose.* Yes, but *how* are you going to achieve it? By tackling these *aims* or *goals.*

Notice that *aims* are really no more than *purpose* broken down into manageable parts. It is like light being refracted into its primary colours. The same is true of the next stage in the descent. Take any one *aim.* How are you going to achieve it? Answer: by achieving these *objectives.* Now pick out any one of these *objectives* – *how* are you going to accomplish that? Answer: by taking these *steps.* Today.

Strategically, what matters in your career now is progress and not success. Progress means to go forward. It includes the Latin word *gradus,* a step. So to progress is to take steps onwards.

A step is the smallest measure of progress. A *journey,*

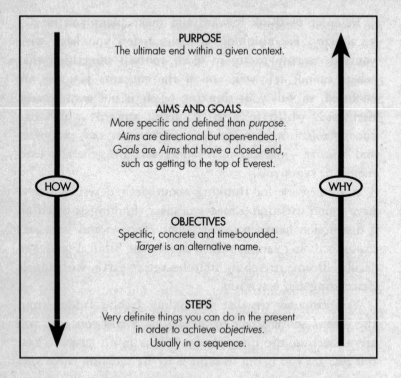

Figure 10.1 *Purpose, Aims, Objectives, Goals and Steps*

incidentally, used to mean the distance you could travel in one day. In many careers we can see clearly a course or track ahead, so we don't have to think much about our steps. At other times your progress in a forward direction appears to be blocked, and you may have to think laterally and take some sideways steps, on the principle that it is better to keep moving than to stand still. You may even have to take some backward steps, but always with the intention of resuming your progress at the earliest opportunity. A strategic withdrawal to prepared positions is not the same as a retreat. Sometimes, when visibility is poor and our legs weak, it's a matter of just taking the next step. A motto engraved over the mantelpiece on a sixteenth-century merchant's house in the Suffolk seaside town of Southwold reads: *Doe ye next thinge*. Longfellow wrote more poetically:

> Not enjoyment, and not sorrow
> Is our destined end or way;
> But to act that each tomorrow
> Finds us further than today.

Going *upward* rather than *downward*, you are then answering the *why* question. Why are you taking this step? In order to move in this general direction you have chosen an *aim* as part of a planned sequence towards achieving this *objective* or *goal*. Why this *objective* or *goal*? Why that *aim* or *goal*? In order to fulfil the overall *purpose*.

> This is the true joy in life, the being used for a purpose recognized by yourself as a mighty one; the being thoroughly worn out before you are thrown on the scrap heap; the being a force of Nature instead of a feverish selfish little clod of ailments and grievances complaining that the world will not devote itself to making you happy.
>
> George Bernard Shaw

Focusing more on *purpose* and *aims* rather than upon one specific *goal* has three major benefits for you. Being able to think easily upward and downward, like a pianist ranging a scale, brings you three advantages as a strategic thinker: flexibility, a sense of direction and a yardstick for progress.

Flexibility

The most obvious advantage is greater flexibility, that essential characteristic of any strategic planning. If you think in terms of *purpose* you can more easily alter your plans as circumstances arise. On the other hand, if you lock yourself into a *goal* like an intercontinental missile, then you are much more liable to be shot down and lose all. In times of change, you do have to be more general in your intention in order to give yourself maximum leeway – the off-course lateral movement of a ship under way, or, in other words, the allowable margin of freedom or variation. Remember that Columbus was sailing for India when he discovered America. Because his *aim* was to *explore*, we do not regard him as a failure.

A sense of direction

Having a *purpose* in life does develop you in a sense of direction. It serves as a Pole star in the sky in that respect. You may get to a destination, but you will never reach a star. The Pole star, incidentally, was also called a *lodestar*, which literally means the way-star – the star that shows you the way. Your *aims* – five or six of them – are like lesser stars. But in truth, the star which serves as the best metaphor for *purpose* in our lives is the nearest one of all – the sun. It gives us light, and that refracts into the colours of the rainbow which I call *aims*.

Purpose sounds static if it is expressed in philosophical language as the end of living, a kind of celestial mission statement. But think of the restless energy of the sun, a direct or indirect source of all the energy on earth. Purpose should act like a magnetic force that draws you in a certain direction. You may make navigational errors, but that magnetic influence constantly affects the compass of your spirit and – if you heed it – draws you back on course. 'Our plans miscarry because they have no aim,' wrote Seneca. 'When a man does not know what harbour he is making for, no wind is the right wind.' If you have *purpose* you will not lack *aims*, and if you have *aims*, they usually ask you to change them into the coinage of *goals, objectives* and *steps*. If you don't, they may look elsewhere.

A measure of progress

From time to time you may want to appraise yourself in terms of progress. If you think in terms of a specific *objective* or *goal*, it is relatively easy to know if you succeed or fail. I mean, either you did become President of the United States or you did not.

If, on the other hand, you are focused at wide angle on *purpose*, it follows that you will find it harder to experience success or failure – only successes or failures. The latter may be indicators of progress, but they are imperfect measuring instruments and you will need to develop a more holistic judgement. We should measure what we value, not value what we can easily measure in quantifiable ways.

In what direction are you moving? If you cannot answer that question you will find it hard to know whether or not a particular step is forward, backward, sideways or merely 'marking time'.

> I find the great thing in this world is not so much where we stand as in what direction we are moving. To reach the port of heaven, we must sail sometimes with the wind and sometimes against it – but we must sail, and not drift, or lie at anchor.
>
> Oliver Wendell Holmes

Is it the *right* decision? I cannot answer that question. For it all depends on your values, the stars by which you steer and the magnetic force which draws you in their direction. You will not succeed in touching them with your hands, but like the seafarers on the desert of waters you can choose them as guides, and following them make your personal progress. To *arrive* in Latin comes from *ad ripam*, to the banks of the river. Rivers were boundaries or limits, or perhaps just impassable obstacles. Don't camp on the banks: cross the river and press on to the next river or mountain beyond.

> When I turned seventy, I gathered all my children – four, which is not bad considering I am not a Catholic – and said to them, 'I've reached a certain age and I must, sooner or later, decide what I am going to do with my life.' There was a pause and my son said, 'Don't hurry!'
>
> Peter Ustinov

A NAVIGATION LESSON

Many years ago, I was holding the tiller of a small boat in the Aegean and listening to an old sailor telling me his story. I must have been quite absorbed, because he had to ask me to be more careful with my steering. 'But the following wind is favourable,' I said to him. The old man just smiled and said, 'It is for just that reason that the danger of going off course is so great.'

How right he was! How many times in my life, seeing people veer off course at the moment of success, I have remembered him!

C. A. Doxiaclis (Greek architect)

If you still want a strategic measure of success for your career as a whole, I have one suggestion. Digging around the roots of *success* I found one definition that concerns plants. They are described as succeeding when they are growing well or thriving. That seems to me to be a more promising line of thought for our times. Success isn't something that awaits us at the end of the journey, a commodity measured by such tangible yardsticks as riches and titles, honours and awards. Being successful in your career happens when you are planted in the right soil, fed by the right nutrients, growing, thriving, being productive and prospering. Success becomes almost a property of the journey, with all its ups and downs, not an ultimate destination or end to be gauged or measured by the kind of popular 'success criteria' mentioned above. Also, it's essential to enjoy the journey.

One advantage of following this line is that you can now look upon such things as wealth or promotion as *by-products* and not as *goals*. You will be aware of them, you may properly desire them, but they are not what you are aiming for. In one step you have acquired a holy freedom from trying to achieve success or struggling to avoid failure. In some lines from the most popular poem in the English language, Rudyard Kipling points to that freedom:

> If you can meet with triumph and disaster
> And treat those two impostors just the same . . .

SUMMARY OF KEY POINTS

- Each of us has our own 'kingdom' and we are responsible for our conduct – the way we lead our lives. Strategic leadership – 'I am myself my own commander' – implies developing a sense of direction or knowing where one is going.

- Reviewing the principles of strategic thinking and planning that have emerged in Parts One and Two confirms that they apply to those who are working in unstructured careers. In these kinds of occupation – as I know from personal experience – if any strategic thinking or planning is to be done, *you* have to do it.

- When it comes to strategic thinking and planning in your personal career and life as a whole, it is best to use your imagination and creativity at the outset. It is more like painting a picture than making the architectural plan of a house. Remain open to new ideas and inspirations as the picture unfolds.

- The frame around the picture is your vocation, your aptitudes, interests and temperament are the raw materials of your vocation in the occupational sense. Equal if not greater in significance, however, is your natural calling to marriage and family. There is an overarching purpose – the commonality of love – which holds the two together.

- It is useful to distinguish between *purpose, aims, goals* or *Objectives* and *Steps*. *Purpose* is what gives value, significance or worthwhileness to all else downstream of it. An *aim* is a general trend or tendency which confers direction. *Goal* (from the Anglo-Saxon boundary or limit) is a terminal point to which effort is directed, not reached without difficulty or dedication. *Objective* is also tangible but closer at hand, while *step* is any small movement forward.

- It is not necessary that you should be able to define a deep-seated, settled and significant end to your purpose, but, on the principle of thinking next level up, it is a means to a larger end – the purpose is the universe. Call it a *spiritual* end, for it transcends your own mortal life. You don't have to know this end; given your present level of intelligence, experience and goodness, your best guess is good enough.

We cannot direct the wind but we can adjust the sails.
                                                    Arab proverb

11

FIVE STRATEGIES THAT WORK WITH PEOPLE

Trust being lost, all the social intercourse of men is brought to naught.

Livy (Roman historian)

Leadership is about people as well as direction. It means taking people with you on a journey – usually by literally leading them from the front. If you are not in a team, operational or strategic leadership role in the organized forms of work we call organizations, you may be tempted to conclude that the people aspect of leadership doesn't apply to you. You have only yourself to lead, you might say. But is this the case?

No work appears more solitary than writing a book. You sit for weeks on your own, and the finished product has your name on the cover as if you did it all yourself. But considerable teamwork – publisher, editor, proof-reader, printer, sales and marketing team, distribution, bookshops, reviewers – goes into the book in your hand at this moment. Moreover, think of the number of individuals who, directly or indirectly, have contributed to these pages! It may be possible to write a novel without the company of such helpers, but certainly not a book like this one.

If you are working for yourself or leading a career that

lies outside conventional employment by an organization or a sequence of them, it is worth reflecting on how you may best get on with people. Even if you work in an organization and do not fall into one of those three clear roles of leadership I have defined, you may still exercise leadership as if from a marginal position. How effective you are in doing so will depend on whether or not you have thought out what strategic approach you will take in your personal and professional relationships.

Here I am using *strategic* initially in contrast to *tactical*. There are lots of books on what might be called the tactics of human relationships, ranging from the 'games-people-play' type of book to my own *Effective Teambuilding* (1986). Some of the former contain advice on the *stratagems* – tricks, ruses, artifices, ploys – you can employ to get others to do what you want them to do without them being fully aware of it. This is tactical manoeuvring of the 'one upmanship' variety – actions taken to secure some short-term advantage.

Both manoeuvring and manipulating have the root image of *manus*, the Latin word for hand. Our concept of *management* shares the same generic sense of handling something or someone. To manipulate can mean to manage or utilize skilfully or it may signify to manage people by (especially unfair) dextrous contrivance or influence. A manipulator is one who controls or plays upon others by artful, insidious or unfair means, especially to their own advantage. This intention to deceive is reflected in the military metaphors *stratagem* and *manoeuvre*, carefully plotted offensive or defensive tactics. Both imply conscious, calculated planning.

CASE STUDY: NICCOLO MACHIAVELLI

The adjective *Machiavellian* is often applied to the kinds of tactics or manoeuvres that are characterized by cunning, duplicity or bad faith. In fact Niccolo Machiavelli, who died in 1529, was a strategic thinker about *end* and *means*. He elevated the idea of one's own advantage to the sole political end: it is to attain and retain power for oneself. The ruler, with this end in mind, has to free himself from any moral scruples about the means he employs.

Machiavelli did not deny Christianity; he merely saw it as irrelevant to the work of governing people. A ruler should free himself from its restraints, however privately he might regret the necessity for doing so. He should not, of course, practise the wanton cruelty of Nero, but nothing must stay his hand from the actions that must be taken to achieve his task. Necessity, not morality, should be his sole guide. 'A prince who wants to hold his own', he wrote, 'must know how to do wrong when necessary.'

Machiavelli taught that princes or governors need not actually possess the qualities or virtues associated with leadership, as long as they seem to have them. 'It is unnecessary for a prince to have all the virtues, but very necessary to appear to have them.' But humility was one virtue that a prince need not even simulate, because it had no place in statecraft. For rulers Machiavelli advocated a return to the values of Greece and Rome. As he wrote in his *Discourses on Livy*:

> The old religion did not beatify men unless they were full of worldly glory: army commanders, for instance, and rulers of republics. Our religion has glorified humble and contempla-

tive men, rather than men of action. It has assigned as man's highest good humility, abnegation and contempt for worldly things, whereas the other identified it with magnanimity, bodily strength and everything else that tends to make men very bold.

The 'old religion', then, was best for the preservation of the state and the encouragement of the many facets of virtue as Machiavelli conceived it – strength, will-power, valour, high spirit, technique and efficiency. Its morality was political and secular, not personal and Christian.

The *end* that Machiavelli proposed for a prince was power: how to attain it and how to hold it. By power he meant the subjection of people to the will of the ruler. Machiavelli subscribed to the ancient Roman saying: 'Let them hate as long as they fear.' Seneca had denounced that proverb as a vile, detestable, deadly sentiment. The English tradition sided with Seneca; Machiavelli did not. 'It is far better to be feared than loved,' he wrote. 'The bond of love is one which men, wretched creatures that they are, break when it is to their advantage to do so; but fear is strengthened by the dread of punishment which is always effective.'

Machiavellianism, then, is the view that politics is amoral and that any means, however unscrupulous, can justifiably be used to the end of achieving and holding power. In broader terms, it suggests a view that makes one's personal advantage, however defined, the end, and uses others, willingly or not, as means to that end. What a political ruler needs is intelligence, experience and will-power or strength of character, but goodness is not required – merely the semblance of it if it serves some purpose in a given set of circumstances.

Paradoxically, Machiavelli wrote his treatise with a good end in view. Although, as a citizen of the Florentine Republic, he did not in theory regard absolute monarchy as the best form of government, in practice he did. His historical situation – an Italy riven by internecine warfare and dominated by its powerful neighbours – largely explains his desire for a strong, masterful dictator, one who would bring unity, peace and prosperity.

TOWARDS A FRAMEWORK OF PRINCIPLES OF CONDUCT

Experience of Machiavellian dictators – Mussolini in Italy, Hitler in Germany, Stalin in Russia – has long since taught us that *goodness* cannot be left out of the political equation. It is true that politicians in constitutional democracies often act as though achieving and retaining what they call 'power' is the sole end of party politics, and that any means – lying, cheating, intimidation – is justifiable to that end. But all that does is to make politicians even more unpopular with the public.

Moreover, Machiavellianism in the wider sense – making your own advantage the supreme end and treating others principally as means to that end (though you may *deceive* them into thinking you look on them as friends) – is equally self defeating. The main problem for someone who adopts this strategy is the perceptiveness of other people. It is extremely difficult to fool others, even though you may regard yourself as a master in the craft. We tend to see through people eventually. We are more transparent than we imagine. Is there an alternative?

Below I suggest what amounts to an alternative strategy

to this popular Machiavellianism. Like the legendary Seven Pillars of Wisdom, the seven strategies comprise a holistic strategic approach. I call them *strategies* because, taken by itself, any one of these virtues may appear to be counter-productive in the *short term*, but singly or together they make sense and work over the long-haul journey of life. In other words, they are both *important* and *longer-term* in the frame of reference.

I am making the assumption that you will apply these principles of conduct with *phronesis*, the prudence or judgement frequently mentioned above. The principles apply within organizations, of course, but in this chapter I am thinking more of your relations with the whole network of people who impinge upon your professional and personal life. Take the principles to be no more than strategies or ways of revealing yourself in your behaviour, reflections of your own values. For your conduct shows the extent of your power to control, direct or lead yourself. If you are a strategic leader, you should be an *independent thinker* in terms of conduct as much as strategic direction, as if working from first principles and not merely following others.

Here, then, are my suggestions. They are no more than that, so alter and adapt them to fit in with your own philosophy of life.

BE PREPARED TO TRUST OTHERS

'If you trust boys they will let you down,' a veteran head teacher told me once, 'but if you don't trust them they will do you down.'

Most of us have had experiences where we have trusted

others and have been let down. It is tempting to say to oneself, 'Never again.' But in the long term the benefits of trusting others far outweighs the tactical reverses which constitute such experiences.

Of course, some individuals are less trustworthy than others, and it would fly in the face of *phronesis* to trust them without safeguards. 'It is a vice to trust all,' wrote Seneca in a letter to a friend, 'and equally a vice to trust none.'

To trust is to have an assured reliance on the character, ability, strength or truth of someone. It is having the feeling that a person will not fail in any situation which calls for dependability, discretion or fairness. Such trust may be justified or misguided, so why commend trusting people as a general policy?

My argument is largely a subjective one. I know that I respond positively if another person trusts me and negatively if they seem to regard me as trustless. In fact in my case the differences of attitude and response can be dramatic. What grounds have I for believing that others are different in this respect to me? The principle of 'doing to others as you would have them do to you' clearly applies.

'Those who trust us educate us,' said George Eliot. To educate, related to the Latin verb *educere*, to lead out and to educe means to draw out something hidden, latent or reserved. Trust does elicit our inner human resource. 'Trust men and they will be true to you,' declared Emerson. 'Treat them greatly and they will show themselves great.'

'LOVE ALL'

Love all, trust a few
Do wrong to none: be able for thine enemy

Rather in power than use, and keep thy friend
Under thine own life's key: be check'd for silence
But never tax'd for speech.

This mother's advice to her son in Shakespeare's *All's Well That Ends Well* rightly reserves complete trust for the few. Confidence of that kind is a plant of slow growth. 'First try, then trust', says the proverb. Although, as I have just suggested, it is a wise policy to push out the boat and to trust where there are no rational grounds for mistrust, even if it means accepting as a cost some let-downs, trust in substance does only develop slowly. It is the main ingredient of friendship.

Love carries overtones of strong if not overwhelming positive emotion about someone or something, but there are kinds and degrees of love. 'Do wrong to none' is one basic principle of love. Paradoxically, you can love someone without liking him or her as an individual. If refraining from doing them wrong – much harder when a wrong has been done to you – is the basement of love, then the first floor is everyday sympathy and kindness.

No one can be a really good leader who does not love members of their team or organization in that sense, just as no one can be described as a good parent who does wrong to their child or withholds human warmth, sympathy and kindness. But the principle applies to all those with whom we work, whether in less structured ways in self-employed work, in involvement in community and political life as citizens.

Men think there are circumstances when they may treat their fellow beings without love, but no such circumstances exist. Inanimate objects may be dealt with without love . . . but human beings cannot be treated without love . . . If you feel no love for men – leave them alone. Occupy yourself with things, with your own self, with anything you please, but not with men.

Leo Tolstoy, *The Resurrection*

ACT WITH INTEGRITY

Acting with integrity means that you are giving others grounds to trust you: you do not lie, cheat or deceive. Mistrust, once there, is like an axe to the tree of relationship. 'Trust, like the soul,' said the Roman author Catullus, 'once gone is gone forever.'

Integrity, in the sense of plain speaking and above-the-board dealing, is a key quality for all leaders. Shakespeare captured its essence in *Hamlet*:

> This above all: to thine own self be true,
> And it must follow, as the night to day,
> Thou canst not then be false to any man.

Leaders who resort to cunning or crafty methods of manipulating people to their will may gain short-term advantages, but in the long run they forfeit trust. 'Subtlety may deceive you,' wrote Cromwell in a letter to Robert Barnard in January 1642, 'integrity never will.' For integrity implies adherence to moral standards – especially truth and goodness – that lie outside oneself.

Integrity will always be tested, not least if money is involved. 'Few men have virtue to withstand the highest bidder,' observed George Washington. Yet if you permit someone to take away your honour, you permit them to remove your life. Integrity is the last keep of the mind, worth defending to the last when the outlying bastions and ramparts have fallen. Don't forget who you are, because you see what others can be like.

Literally meaning soundness or wholeness, integrity to me is rather like a suit of armour. On the one hand it is a policy of being simple and straightforward in your dealings with others. On the other hand, integrity has a protective or defensive function, especially when life is probing you for your weaknesses. If well-tempered, the armour baffles those who come at you with tricks and duplicity. As the seventeenth-century Sir Henry Wotton, writes:

> How happy is he born and taught,
> That serveth not another's will,
> Whose armour is his honest thought,
> And single trust his utmost skill.

BE COURTEOUS

Courtesy is graceful politeness. It was a virtue possessed, along with integrity, by Chaucer's 'very perfect, gentle knight':

> He loved chivalry,
> Truth and honour, freedom and courtesy.

Being respectful and considerate in your language and behaviour towards others always signals that you have a sense of the personal dignity of that person by virtue of being a person.

Courtesy is more than being merely civil – the bare

minimum of fulfilment of requirements of common manners and forbearance from roughness or unpleasantness. It transcends politeness, which often suggests a lack of cordiality. Thoughtful politeness, a dash of warm regard for feelings or dignity of others, and there you have courtesy revealed.

A policy of 'humble and familiar courtesy', as Shakespeare called it in *Richard II*, is defensible in itself, but in my view it also does pay off in the practical affairs of life on the principle of the proverb *Honey catches more flies than vinegar*. Good manners is the art of making other people easy with whom we converse, and that helps good communication in business as much as in private matters. Courtesy is a business asset. Big organizations may struggle with 'customer service' but never let that be your problem – you cannot afford any lack of courtesy to your customers, suppliers, colleagues or associates. Courtesy is a habit, and one which is fortunately almost impossible to get rid of once you have acquired it. Encounters with discourtesy in others only serves to reinforce it. Without 'small sweet courtesies' to smooth the way, the road of life would be a lot more rough and stony.

BE GENEROUS

A generous person is one who gives freely and unstintingly. It is not the largeness in the thing or amount given which constitutes generosity, but the warm-hearted readiness to give more. Originally generosity meant to be high-born, of noble birth, now it only means to be characterized by a noble or forbearing spirit. This spirit is open-handed and liberal in giving on the one hand, and magnanimous or willing to forgive on the other.

A generous person will be unstintingly helpful by habit. Often human generosity does look for an equal return – we give in order to receive. But a truly generous spirit lacks this note of self-concern. It is unselfish or self-effacing, intent on the interests of the other without thought of any form of reward.

Generosity, it is said, gives help rather than advice, but you can be generous with all sorts of things. 'True generosity gives recognition,' said Goethe. You do not have to be rich to be generous. Indeed, lavishness is not generosity, nor is being prodigal with your assets.

'Cast your bread upon the waters: for you shall find it after many days,' wrote the author of *Ecclesiastes*. If, within reason, you are open-handed to others with help, giving freely and generously of your time, you usually find that you receive more than you give. The law of reciprocity – that giving evokes giving – ensues from that fact. For all sorts of reasons you may not be the recipient of the 'returns' that your giving evokes, but others will be down the line. It is a delayed payment, undirected to self, that you can accept when you reflect upon how much you benefited (and still may benefit) from the generosity of others who have helped you with no prospect of a return.

> One other thing stirs me when I look back at my youthful days, the fact that so many people gave to me something or were something to me without knowing it.
>
> Albert Schweitzer

THE PHILOSOPHICAL FRAMEWORK
FOR THE FIVE PRINCIPLES

'We should love people and use things, but we love things and use people,' it has been said. Whether or not you agree, it is worth reflecting on the philosophy that underlies the five principles outlined above.

Strategic thinking is essentially thinking about ends – the important or long-term ones – and the means. Deliberation, decision and action are the three acts in its drama. The means at your disposal include your own assets of talent, time and treasure. You may use some of the latter to hire others to work for you. They then become part of the means you are employing to achieve your ends.

It is easy to slide into thinking of other people, whether you directly employ them or not, as *only* means to an end. In many cases, but by no means all, that means their value is assessed in terms of their degree of usefulness to your own advantage.

But an individual person, by virtue of possessing personhood or personeity, is always an end in himself or herself. From that principle comes a simple moral imperative. The philosopher Immanuel Kant (1725–1804), defined it thus in his *Critique of Practical Reason*:

So act as to treat humanity, whether in your own person or in that of any other, in every case as an end withal, never as means only.

Note that key word *only*. Of course we do have to treat others as means, for we all use other people to our own ends, just as they use us. Nothing wrong with that. We also make ourselves means to secure desired results, be they ones that advantage us only or ones that serve the common good. Yet we know we are ends-in-ourselves, and we respond better to those who acknowledge the fact.

There is a balance, then, in dealing with people as means to ends and dealing with them as ends-in-themselves. It is not a question of one or the other, for both are important. For strategic leadership to work in your own life and career, it is really essential to get the balance right. In the longer term your success and happiness depend upon the quality of your relationships with others. They should be productive but also personal.

By *personal*, to repeat the point, I do not mean that you should treat everyone in your wider 'team' as if they were personal friends. You can be friendly even to those individuals you naturally like less than others.

In working relationships there is always an *impersonal* relation that has to be right. 'Justice is love in impersonal relations' is a sentence that sticks in my mind. It is fulfilling the contractual obligations, such as paying your fare on the train. Equivalence or justice in your dealings with others – so that giving and receiving are in equitable balance – is the necessary foundation on which trust is built. If the impersonal foundation gives way, the edifice of working partnership soon comes tumbling down.

Therefore *personal* doesn't mean friendly or unfriendly, it is simply the recognition of the other as an end and not only a means. You don't have to say it, but it informs your whole strategy of human relationships.

To prevent this chapter ending on a philosophical and abstract note, let me leave you with a negative example. A year or two ago I was in Zimbabwe and read an article in the press entitled 'Circle of Fear'. An employer had been compelled by trade union action in the law courts to re-employ a man who had been wrongly dismissed. 'Right,' he said to the man, 'I have to pay you for eight hours a day. This is how you will earn your wages.' He took him out to the car park where he had drawn a circle in chalk on the sweltering tarmac. 'Now stand in that for your money,' he ordered. And the African sun grew even hotter as the hours went by.

SUMMARY OF KEY POINTS

- It makes sense to think of others as partners, colleagues and – in some respects – members of your team. And so even in your work as an independent contributor the skills of leadership and communication are equally important for you if you want to realize your personal vision.
- The 'self-made' success story is a myth. We all depend on others, as they do on us. The individual (like an organiz-ation) swims in the sea of society. In managing your own 'organization–society interface' you have a potential advan-tage. You can command yourself – you don't have to get others to toe the same line.
- The difference between strategy and tactics in dealing with people. Trust is a good example. In the short term it may seem foolish or ineffective, but in the longer term it is essential. 'Trust being lost, all social intercourse comes to nought' (Tacitus).
- Being your own strategic leader involves working relations with groups and individuals where you have no formal authority or position. Advice abounds on the tactics to employ to get people to do what you want them to do –

how to be persuasive or assertive, for example. But, in the spirit of this book, you should think strategically about the human relations which are so vital to your success and happiness.

- Machiavellian philosophy suggests that you define your own end – your own advantage, your acquisition of power, your accumulation of wealth – and use whatever means at hand to achieve it. Lying, duplicity and deceit are all allowed, on the principle that the end justifies the means.

- As goodness is left out of the equation of *phronesis* – intelligence, experience *and goodness* – the Machiavellian is deficient in practical wisdom. Consequently, as history repeatedly confirms – we are slow learners – Machiavellian strategies are self-defeating. For you cannot work against the grain of human nature for long.

- There are five principles or habits that work positively *over the long term* in human nature. They are trust, love, integrity, courtesy and generosity.

- What are the behaviours that create trust? The importance of truthfulness or honesty, e.g. doing what you say you will do.

- These principles, habits, strategies or policies, call them what you will, do actually confer tactical advantage. 'All doors open to courtesy,' said the seventeenth-century critic Thomas Fuller, and that is but one example. But, paradoxically, they only work because they reflect a set of values where others are regarded as ends, and not as means only. It is called being a person.

- 'Character is long-standing habit,' wrote Plutarch. Character is no less important to one who is their own strategic leader as it is to the general of an army, the chief executive of a business or the bishop in a diocese. Like integrity which is its soul, character is easier to keep than recover when lost.

*It is not possible to be true to yourself without
also expanding your capacity to create, to serve,
and to produce results.*

Dag Hammarskjöld

12

DISCOVERING WELLS
OF INSPIRATION

I may not hope from outward forms to win
The passion and the life whose fountains are within.
Samuel Taylor Coleridge

As well as providing direction and building teamwork, leadership is about inspiring people. But who inspires the leader? And if you are your own strategic leader, who inspires *you*?

Let me say at the outset that I regard inspiration as a mystery. 'God alone can inspire,' said Dame Flora Robson. Just as the sun is the ultimate source of all physical energy, so there may be some unitive source for all the inspirations which gives us spiritual energy. Be that as it may, I cannot tell you where inspiration comes from. All that I can do is offer you some examples and suggestions on how you can refresh your spirit on your personal journey as a strategic leader.

What I think may be the case – I could be completely wrong – is that below the depths of our personality there is an even deeper level. It is the water-table of the spirit. We can draw on it, but it is not like a private well. The water-table is common to us all. So others, living closer to the fountain-heads than you or me, may say or write things which resonate with that deeply buried reservoir within us. They stir the waters, and we feel the influences rising like a fresh breeze into our conscious minds.

That is only a mental model. We are all different. What matters, if I am remotely right, is that each of us discovers the wells of inspiration that lie alongside the long, dusty and often uphill journey through life. To die of spiritual thirst when there is a well of inspiration within reach is tragic.

CASE STUDY: PROFESSOR TERRY HAMBLIN, CANCER SPECIALIST

The following example is drawn from an article by Cheryl Buggy in *Professional Manager* (September 2000):

Whilst travelling in London by train recently, I became engrossed in a story that leapt off the pages of the newspaper I was reading. Amongst the usual endless columns of negativity was a story about the potential breakthrough in a cure for cancer and a photograph of the doctor responsible, one Professor Terry Hamblin.

Looking up, I noticed a great deal of similarity between the man in the photograph and the man sitting next to me on the train and as it transpired they were one and the same person.

Professor Hamblin was on his way to give a presentation in London and our ensuing conversation has become the subject of this article. It's not about being open to and seizing opportunities when they come your way in life, even on a train, although that does form part of it . . .

Professor Hamblin clearly remembers how at the age of three he decided to become a doctor because he admired the local GP so much. Then his grandfather died of cancer when he was thirteen and that served to further clarify his mission in life – to find a cure for cancer.

Such grand ambition at such a young age has been tempered by experience and time. And yet he is as purposeful as ever after some twenty-five years of research. So what, beyond having a vision, has kept him on course over the years when there must have been many times when he felt like quitting?

'I certainly had no idea of the enormity of the journey towards a cure for cancer that I had set out on,' says the professor, who now heads up a hospital department in Bournemouth with a budget of £5 million, a staff of over 200 and a patient base of 6,000.

'Meetings, working with and reading about the inspirational work of others keeps things in perspective and helps keep me on purpose,' he says.

'Recently I was looking at the life of Edward Jenner. He became an apprentice surgeon at the age of thirteen and had a strong sense of vocation. He wanted to find a cure for smallpox at a time when it was killing huge numbers – around 10 per cent of the population.

'Jenner spent his entire life working on a cure but realized that he was just a cog in the machinery for that breakthrough. In fact it took another 200 years before the disease was defeated.

'I realize now I probably will not be around when the cure for cancer is finally found but I will continue to value my role as a cog in the machinery of that cure and that keeps me going,' he explains.

'Another strategy that has helped me in my journey is

summed up in the saying "Seize the day". Always be aware of possibilities, seek and search and be enterprising.

'Let me give you an example. Some time ago there was a laundry strike at the hospital that resulted in some spare funds. I laid claim to the money and used it to buy a specific piece of equipment needed in the department.

'The thing was, I could only use the money in £1,000 chunks, so I had to have the equipment delivered in parts, each with a separate invoice. That piece of equipment has become instrumental in the treatment of bone marrow disease world-wide,' he says.

'I feel very privileged in my work and that is a great motivator. However, there are times when a sense of despair can set in. The patients I work with may often be with me for a very long time and you get close to them. If they die it hits you very hard and there was a time when I just seemed to see death all around me.

'One day one of my patients asked me what I believed in and I had no answer. The patient in question was a Christian and when I attended his memorial service some six months later I suddenly touched the spiritual dimension of myself. I faced my own mortality and in doing so was able to accept the inevitability of death and the existence of God. I do feel that the current idea of an individual "renting" themselves out professionally creates an inner feeling of spiritual unrest,' says Professor Hamblin.

Many people would empathize with this view, that the workplace can be a spiritual desert where short-term results are the only focus. His long-term perspective is very much sustained by the spiritual dimension and it is interesting to note that one of the qualities often present in successful and inspiring individuals is a belief in some greater force.

'I have had some wonderful moments and every time they

happen, or I remember them, it refreshes my spirit,' says Professor Hamblin.

THE SOURCES OF INNER CONVICTION

A sense of calling to serve a purpose which has value, one that transcends self and the limits of one's lifetime, is clearly one well of inspiration for Terry Hamblin. As Ordway Tead wrote in *The Art of Leadership* (1935):

A good leader has faith. There is unfortunately no other word which might be less objectionable to some readers to convey what is here meant. But it should be possible to suggest a precise usage for the word despite the fact that vague meanings have conventionally been attached to it.

Faith has been well conceived, as 'the giving substance to things hoped for and as the conviction of things not seen'. As the word here is used, it connotes an active effort to bring good to pass based on the confirming experience that such activity is and does good. It is not a mere fatuous trust in something nor the mere wish for something. It is a corroboration, which the individual finds through his efforts, of his sense that worth is being achieved . . .

Fundamentally, deeper kind of faith seems also invaluable if not essential. It may be called a spiritual faith.

The words are not popular today because they are so often used as a cloak for lazy thinking and as implying an indiscriminately optimistic feeling about life – one which is grounded in no deep experience or justified by no tested convictions. There is, nevertheless, a permissible even if non-rational belief, by whatever name it is called, that the enterprise of living has a meaning and values which are precious, permanent and not at odds with the larger processes of the universe.

Futilitarianism – the philosophy that all human striving is futile – is no philosophy for a strategic leader. For the leader is essentially the affirmer, the doer, the creator. He or she pre-eminently believes that purposes can be realized, that experience can be directed and controlled, that events can be moulded nearer to the heart's desire. The contagion of power cannot spring from a sense of futility or profound pessimism. No one lavishes energy and creative effort on any project for long unless they believe the task worth doing.

Of course there are degrees of importance in the tasks undertaken. But every leadership situation involves an attitude in both leader and followers which tacitly agrees that the task has value, is more or less attainable, and has some relation of significance to other activities of life. You need these elements in your own 'empire' if you intend to lead your life rather than merely muddle through it.

Remember, too, that the greatest leaders have been sustained by a belief that they were in some way instruments of destiny, that they tapped hidden reserves of power, that they truly lived as they tried to live in harmony with some greater, more universal purpose or intention in the world.

Again, the experience of great leaders suggests a further element too vital to be ignored. No accounting for the strength of their inner resources can fail to appreciate the part that suffering has played in their development. They have seemed in many instances to discover their faith and power in meeting and overcoming opposition of one sort or another, in surmounting seemingly insurmountable obstacles, in refusing to admit defeat, in sacrificing to the limit of their cause. In a word, they have suffered in the depths of their being as one of the prices paid for the superb confidence and courage they were gradually able to manifest.

A spiritual faith of this kind has always been realized by those leaders we call great or the greatest. It is a peculiar demand in our own times upon all team, operational and strategic leaders. It is a demand even in enterprises where the immediate aims and objectives may seem completely material. Without it you or I will not get very far as strategic leaders in our own lives.

INSPIRING COMPANIONS

'Meetings, working with and reading the inspirational work of others keeps things in perspective and helps keep me on purpose,' says Terry Hamblin. Again, I can only agree. The enthusiasm and dedication of colleagues or others in the same field are contagious; they stir the embers in your own heart so it bursts into flames. For *passion is catching*.

In Shakespeare's *Julius Caesar* there is a scene where Mark Antony stands alone by Caesar's murdered body plotting his revenge on the assassins. A Roman soldier enters and turns away with tears in his eyes. Mark Antony says to him: 'Thy heart is big, get thee apart and weep. Passion, I can see, is catching, for mine eyes, seeing those beads of sorrow stand in thine, begin to water.' Passion is catching! That is exactly how you or I catch a common cold or a viral infection. It is why, as humans, we tend to cry or laugh or yawn when with another who is crying or laughing or yawning. If strong emotions or passions are contagious, so is inspiration.

Admiral Lord St Vincent once wrote a letter to Horatio Nelson in which he said: 'I never saw a man in our profession . . . who possessed the magic art of infusing the same spirit into others which inspired their own actions . . . all agree there is but one Nelson.' I doubt if Nelson ever consciously tried to inspire others. But those around him caught inspiration from him, so that in course of time his very presence was a source of inspiration. For others may find inspiration in your work without your being even aware that it is there. William Blake once commented on a beautiful drawing of an avenue of fir trees, 'Why, this is not drawing but *inspiration*.' John Constable replied, 'I never knew it before; I meant it for drawing.'

To some extent inspiration can be bottled, either in concentrate as a poem or in a book. 'A good book is the precious life-blood of a master spirit, embalmed and treas-ured up on purpose to a life beyond life,' wrote John Milton. The written word – stories, sayings, proverbs – can be as inspirational as hearing someone with the gift of oratory.

The media – television, radio, journals, magazines, news-papers – may be laden with bad news about human nature, but they also bring the gold and silver threads of inspiring examples too. What is extraordinary is how ordinary people reveal a nobility of spirit an adversity which humbles and inspires those around them and sometimes those afar. There are buckets of inspiration in the lives of others, and you only need a few drops each day to help you keep things in perspective, renew the vital interests, and to stay on purpose.

It's no good trying to shine if you don't take time to fill your
lamp.

Robert Browning

Borrow from many sources the oil you need to keep your
lamp burning brightly. There are wells of it, hidden
reserves, beneath the soil of human nature – enough to last
as long as the sun. You will run into deserts on your
journey in this world, desolate places where others often
abandon hope. Yet there is always a well of inspiration
ahead if you persevere.

In the deserts of the heart
Let the healing fountain start.

W. H. Auden

Morale – our basic attitude to the task in hand – has to
have *spiritual* foundations if it is to endure all the vicissi-
tudes of life. As a strategic leader in your own life, you
need to check those foundations are in place as much as a
general in command of an army. You are in command of
yourself, remember, and so you too need to reflect on the
same agenda if your own morale is to remain high.

CASE STUDY: GENERAL SIR WILLIAM SLIM

In this case study drawn from his *Defeat into Victory* (1956)
Slim describes how he analysed his responsibilities as a
leader in a given situation, and then carried them out. Of
particular interest is the way in which his appreciation and
action cover comprehensively the task, team maintenance

and individual needs of a great army. General Slim saw from the outset that it was necessary for the leader to explain not only 'how' the aim is to be achieved, but also 'why', and this he did by relating objectives to larger purposes. The passage illustrates most clearly the inter-relation of the three areas, and how the leader went about providing the necessary functions effectively.

So when I took command, I sat quietly down to work out this business of morale. I came to certain conclusions, based not on any theory that I had studied, but on some experience and a good deal of hard thinking. It was on these conclusions that I set out consciously to raise the fighting spirit of my army.

Morale is a state of mind. It is the intangible force which will move a whole group of men to give their last ounce to achieve something, without counting the cost to themselves; that makes them feel they are part of something greater than themselves. If they are to feel that, their morale must, if it is to endure – and the essence of morale is that it should endure – have certain foundations. These foundations are spiritual, intellectual and material, and that is the order of their import-ance. Spiritual first, because only spiritual foundations can stand real strain. Next intellectual, because men are swayed by reason as well as feeling. Material last – important, but last – because the very highest kinds of morale are often met when material conditions are lowest.

I remember sitting in my office and tabulating these foun-dations of morale something like this:

Spiritual
- There must be a great and noble object.
- Its achievement must be vital.
- The method of achievement must be active, aggressive.

- The man must feel that what he is and what he does matters directly towards the attainment of the object.

Intellectual

- He must be convinced that the object can be obtained; that it is not out of reach.
- He must see, too, that the organization to which he belongs and which is striving to attain the object is an efficient one.
- He must have confidence in his leaders and know that whatever dangers and hardships he is called upon to suffer, his life will not be lightly flung away.

Material

- The man must feel that he will get a fair deal from his commanders and from the army generally.
- He must, as far as humanly possible, be given the best weapons and equipment for his task.
- His living and working conditions must be made as good as they can be.

It was one thing thus neatly to marshal my principles but quite another to develop them, apply them, and get them recognized by the whole army.

At any rate, our spiritual foundation was a firm one. I use the word spiritual, not in its strictly religious meaning, but as belief in a cause . . .

We had this; and we had the advantage over our enemies that ours was based on real, not false, spiritual values. If ever an army fought in a just cause we did. We coveted no man's country; we wished to impose no form of government on any nation. We fought for the clean, the decent, the free things of life, for the right to live our lives in our own way as others could live theirs, to worship God in what faith we chose, to be free in body and mind, and for our children to be free. We fought only because the powers of evil had attacked these things. No matter what the religion or race of any man in the Fourteenth Army, he *must* feel this, feel that he had indeed a worthy cause, and that if he did not defend it life would not be worth living for him or for his children. Nor was it enough to have a worthy cause. It must be positive, aggressive, not a mere passive, defensive, anti-something feeling. So our object became not to defend India, to stop the Japanese advance, or even to occupy Burma, but to destroy the Japanese Army, to smash it as an evil thing.

THINKING UPWARDS

Vision, purpose, belief in a cause – both Professor Hamblin and General Slim could set their work in the context of a much broader cause that had spiritual value. Most of us are not battling in our daily lives against a self-evident evil such as cancer or Japanese militarism. How can we discover a sense of spiritual purpose in our lives?

Without traversing again the ground I have covered in *How to Find Your Vocation* (2000), it is worth reflecting on the two great metaphors of spiritual life. One is to do with *depth*, the idea of looking deeper inside ourselves or human nature. The main images I have used in this chapter – wells, fountains, springs, water-tables, hidden reserves of water or oil – all depend on this more fundamental metaphor of depth. We all know what people mean if they tell us that they love someone *deeply* or have a *deep* interest in a subject.

The other great metaphor is *height*, to rise above or

ascend to a higher plane. To some extent it is natural to do that, for ends at one level of thought prove to be means at the next level up. For example, as we have seen, war turns out to be a means to a political end. For, paradoxically, it is a means (not usually very effective and certainly most unpleasant) to a 'better peace'. Justifiable only if it really is the least worse course of action open.

Equally, I have suggested that business may be an end or set of ends in itself at one level of thought and practice, but when you take the helicopter view and stand back and reflect upon it, business serves society. Personally I would attach spiritual value to *society* as a whole as much as I do either to an *individual person* or to the *natural environment* that is our physical *milieu* in this universe. Therefore someone engaged in producing or distributing goods and services, be they members of an organization – team or self-employed, has the entitlement to see their work as a contribution, to lift it up into the realm of service to society. Service to society may not be quite so rewarding as service to individuals – there is no one to smile and say thank you – but it is none-the-less service. The entitlement is there, but whether or not you want to take it up is entirely up to you. Spiritually, however, you have a choice.

PRESERVE YOUR IDEALS

Adults are only too partial to the sorry task of warning youth that some day they will view most of the things that now inspire their hearts and minds as mere illusions, but those who have a deeper experience of life take another tone. They exhort youth to try to preserve throughout their lives the ideas that inspire them. In youthful idealism man perceives the truth. In youthful idealism he

> possesses riches that should not be bartered for anything on earth.
>
> Those who vow to do good should not expect people to clear the stones from their path on this account. They must expect the contrary: such others will roll great boulders down upon them. Such obstacles can be overcome only by the kind of strength gained in the very struggle. Those who merely resent obstacles will waste whatever force they have.
>
> Albert Schweitzer, *My Life and Thought* (1933)

Society has no mechanism for recognizing your contributions, at least none that is remotely efficient. How do you work for ends where there is no visible reward and often not much encouragement? That is where discovering your own wells of inspiration is so important. We are told that we need to drink eight glasses of water a day to prevent dehydration. The good news is that a few drops of inspiration will hydrate your spirit for a week.

But don't expect it to last forever. The Israelites fed on manna in the wilderness, but they were only given enough for the day. 'Perpetual inspiration is as necessary to the life of goodness, holiness and happiness as perpetual respiration is necessary to animal life,' wrote William Law.

As patients can inspire a doctor, common soldiers a general, or team members a business leader, so – if you open yourself to all others – inspiration may come from every quarter. You may not know it as such at the time. 'True inspiration always steals on a person,' said Samuel Butler, 'its importance not being fully recognized at the time.' In my experience, that is equally true about a sense of purpose: if you seek it in life it has a habit of creeping up on you from behind and surprising you with its presence.

We are amphibious creatures. We are best when submerged in practical action of one kind or another, but occasionally we need to come up to the surface and take some spiritual breaths before immersing ourselves in this troubled but absorbing life of ours.

In Greek, Latin and Hebrew, *spirit* originally meant wind or breath. To inspire literally means to breathe in. Breath is life. Metaphorically it is the animating or vital principle that influences a person. To be inspired is not just to have a noble or exalted feeling, but to be infused with confidence or resolution, to be fired with enthusiasm. It is a prompting towards action, creative action.

It may be that the example or words of another provides this oxygen of the human spirit. Or perhaps, in the hour of solitude, you may be – in Robert Browning's words – 'stung by the splendour of a sudden thought'. Such moments of truth renew our spirits and put us back into the front line. As William Wordsworth wrote:

> Dust as we are, the immortal spirits grow
> Like Harmony in music; there is a dark
> Inscrutable workmanship that reconciles
> Discordant elements, makes them cling together
> In one society.

MENTORS AND SPONSORS

Fortunately for you, he is wrong. In any personal journey of a vocational nature, you will find unexpected helpers on the journey. With hindsight the appearance and role of these helpers seem quite unpredictable and rather mysterious, an odd argument for the existence of providence – that 'destiny which shapes our ends, rough hew them how we will'.

Using an ancient metaphor, these helpers are now commonly called *mentors* and their function is as much to inspire us as to guide our path.

Vocational guidance often comes through inspired people. Mentor, for example, was a Greek elder on the island of Ithaca in Homer's *Odyssey* who was the means through whom the goddess Athene – the daughter of Zeus – was able to educate and guide Telemachus, the son of Odysseus, to resist the suitors of his mother Penelope who had occupied their home and oppressed them. Mentor, inspired by Athene, later guided the young man to go in search of his father and eventually to work with him in order to recover Ithaca. For, as the poet Aeschylus wrote in another context, 'Never shall at any time the scheme of mortals evade the harmonious system of Zeus.'

You may not draw upon your mentors with great frequency, but it is good to know that they are there and you can consult them whenever need or occasion arises.

A sponsor is not quite the same as a mentor. A sponsor actually assumes some responsibility for you at a particular juncture. He or she enters your life, it seems, for a specific purpose and for a given period of time. He or she may recommend you for a job, for example, and show much more confidence in you than you have in yourself or than other less intuitive people have shown. But the distinction is a fine one. The purpose or aim in both such relationships is to inspire and to develop the capability of a younger and more inexperienced person.

A good example of such a sponsor in my own career was Peter Young. Without telling the story in detail, I met him first when I was a Scots Guards second lieutenant on leave in Jerusalem and he commanded the Arab Legion garrison regiment. He sponsored me to join the Arab Legion and made me the Adjutant of the 9th Bedouin Regiment. Six years later, by then Reader in Military History at Sandhurst, he invited me to join his new department and again acted as sponsor. He also sponsored me as a first-time author, and even came up with the right subject – the Parliamentarian general Sir William Waller – for my doctoral research and second book. Nor was I the only person whom he helped in this way. We sometimes mused together about these three crucial interventions, but oddly enough, we were not close personal friends. Perhaps a difference of age militated against that, but Peter stands high on my list of personal benefactors – those who literally do you good.

No one sponsor will do it all for you. Peter Young, for example, was a natural military leader. As a Commando leader in the Second World War, he won a Distinguished Service Order and three Military Crosses and became a brigadier at twenty-six. 'Leadership is done from the front,' he told me, and that was that. He showed little or no interest in my emerging work in the field of leadership training. It fell to another mentor, Canon Harold Wilson, the Church of England's Adult Education Officer, to introduce me to the group-centred approach to adult education that was to become so central to my career.

Personally, I rather doubt if mentoring, as it is called, can ever be organized or taught. But you can encourage people like myself – who have received help beyond price – to extend it to other less inexperienced people as they appear over the horizon. How else, apart from with enduring gratitude, can we pay our debts?

SUMMARY OF KEY POINTS

- Spirit is a quality that enables you to hold your own and keep up your morale when opposed or threatened. Your own spirit, however, is an indefinable immaterial entity distinguishable from and superior to the body.

- For its quality, movement and activity our spirits need 'perpetual inspiration', as William Law called it. Leadership is about the spirit, and so if you are going to be your own strategic leader you do need to find wells of inspiration within yourself and along the way.

- 'No man was ever great without some portion of divine inspiration,' said Cicero. In all traditions there is a deeper tradition, that all inspiration flows from God, named or nameless, just as the sun is the ultimate source of all energy in nature.

- The ancients believed that every river, stream or fountain was inhabited by a god. Does the human spirit in each of us have such a denizen in its depths? 'There is God within us,' said Ovid, 'and we glow when he stirs us.'

- Another person's spirit, sometimes without them being aware of it, can touch and stir our own. Music, art and literature are all bottled products of the human spirit, 'embalmed and treasured upon purpose to a life beyond life'. Never complain about lack of inspiration. There are buckets of it around.

- To strike the oil of inspiration you can, as it were, prospect within yourself, searching *deeper* than your everyday values. Or you can elevate your mind. By that I mean thinking on the next *higher* level. Take your ends – the desired results of your strategic thinking – and see them as means to a higher and more exalted end. Become a servant to *that* larger purpose, one which transcends you in importance and longevity, and merits your dedication and love.

- 'There is no money in poetry,' said Robert Frost, 'but then there is no poetry in money either.' Money and material things (unless they have beauty) are essentially means to ends, not ends in themselves, though we often have to treat them as if they were ends. Our deeds are our words, and we need inspiration as much as a poet, artist or composer.
- Mentors and sponsors are the godfathers and godmothers in our vocational stories.

> Look well into yourself; there is a source which
> will always spring up if you will search there.
> Marcus Aurelius (second century AD)

IN CONCLUSION: THE WAY AHEAD

The author Graham Greene was once asked if he considered himself to be a great novelist. 'Not great,' he replied, 'but one of the best.'

If this book has aroused in you the desire to be 'one of the best' as a strategic leader – whether in the 'proper' sense of leading an organisation or the 'improper' sense of being your own strategic leader – my pen will rest. If, moreover, you have found some practical ideas and suggestions that will take you on your way, I shall be delighted.

Beyond that I hope that somewhere you may have heard the music of leadership. Competencies, functions, models, checklists, action plans – all have their place in helping you to form a framework for effective strategic leadership, buttressed by the examples of those ahead of you on the journey. As leadership is now seen to match management in importance, if not have a head in front, it is natural that textbooks of the 'how-to-do-it' variety will appear. I have written some of them myself.

Yet the tendency of purely managerial writers to reduce leadership to lists of competencies and to invent new jargon, so as to make leadership seem like a well-organized body of knowledge, if not actually a science, is doomed from the start. As General Slim said, 'Leadership is about the spirit.' Therefore it will always remain an art and not a science.

How far you can progress in that art depends upon your natural ability, your opportunities and your willingness to learn. Why is continuous learning so important? Because it develops your *capability*. Two thousand years ago, Cicero said the same thing. He admitted the power of natural talent, but went on to say, 'When the method and discipline of knowledge are added to talent, the result is usually altogether outstanding.'

By developing your capability you are adding to your resources: the stock or reserve which you can draw on when necessary. Your ability to meet and handle situations is enhanced. In a word, you are becoming a more resourceful person.

Never complain about lack of opportunity. Capability attracts opportunity, like iron to a magnet.

One night I dreamed that I saw my own tombstone, and on it beneath my name and dates I saw engraved in Roman letters: 'He foolishly believed he could teach leadership.'

I know that is impossible, at least beyond introducing others to the basics of the subject. 'You cannot teach leadership, it can only be learned,' it has been more wisely said. True, but it takes *continuous* learning throughout your career if you are to become 'one of the best'.

My last word to you in this book, as we come to the end of our journey together, is – never give up.

> *There must be a beginning in any great matter,*
> *but the continuing unto the end until it be*
> *thoroughly finished yields the true glory.*
> Sir Francis Drake

INDEX

JOHN ADAIR

Effective Communication

PAN BOOKS £6.99

Communication skills are arguably becoming the most important management tools. The four basic communication skills are speaking, listening, writing and reading but many managers may think they have them already. Do they? Do you?

Do you use words to their maximum effectiveness, to persuade and really be heard? Listening is perhaps the most elusive of the communication skills. Do you hear what people are really saying? You can write, but do your letters and reports get across what you want and need to say? And could you improve your absorption and comprehension of the thousands of words you have to read every day?

Professor John Adair not only helps you to improve your natural capacities, he also goes beyond these basics looking at such derivations as presentations, the use of visual aids, interviews, appraisals, giving and receiving criticism, conducting and participating in meetings, communication between departments, and much more.

JOHN ADAIR

Effective Teambuilding

PAN BOOKS £6.99

Most tasks in modern business are carried out by teams, so the ability to build and lead them is a vital management attribute.

John Adair has written *Effective Teambuilding* to show how productive working groups can be forged by:

- selecting the right people
- working together
- sustaining group morale
- raising standards of performance

Effective Teambuilding is enriched by a potent blend of examples, anecdotes, case studies and action checklists, all designed to improve team performance.

JOHN ADAIR

Effective Motivation

PAN BOOKS £6.99

Understand what motivates you and your staff and become aware of how you can increase energy and motivation to achieve your goals.

People are the most important asset in any business today. Great results come from great people. Every manager needs to be able to motivate or draw out the best from others, which is not easy in times of corporate change and personal uncertainty.

Effective Motivation is a practical guide to this key leadership skill. Based on a careful evaluation of the research into motivation, John Adair presents a set of strategies for motivating high-performance teams.

JOHN ADAIR

Effective Decision Making

PAN BOOKS £6.99

Few managers devote enough time to the thinking processes they should apply to their jobs. Yet long hours at work are wasted if business decisions are not logical, clear and correct.

Effective Decision Making is the definitive guide to the crucial management skill of creative thinking. John Adair draws on examples and case studies from business, recent history, sport and entertainment to show:

- how to approach problems
- imaginative thinking
- sixth sense
- how to argue your case
- how to develop your thinking skills

JOHN ADAIR

Effective Time Management

PAN BOOKS £6.99

Time is a precious resource, both irreplaceable and irreversible. But how can you learn to save time and spend it wisely? *Effective Time Management* will help you make the most of every hour. In this unique guide John Adair focuses on managing time using a wide range of examples and case studies. These will help you to:

- identify long-term goals and middle-term plans
- plan the day and make the best use of your time
- learn to delegate and acquire time effectiveness in the office and at meetings

Effective Time Management will show you how to eliminate time-wasting activities, leaving you with more time for your real priorities.

JOHN ADAIR

Effective Innovation

PAN BOOKS £6.99

Innovation – the process of taking new ideas through to satisfied customers – is the lifeblood of any organization today. Nothing stultifies a company and the individuals working in it more than a lack of interest in positive change. You cannot stand still: you either go backwards or move forwards.

In *Effective Innovation*, John Adair looks at both creativity and innovation, generating new ideas and bringing them to market. His 'seven habits of successful creative thinkers' provide a compelling framework for developing your own productive-thinking skills. This readable book also covers leadership of creative teams and discusses how to build an innovative climate in organizations.

OTHER PAN BOOKS

AVAILABLE FROM PAN MACMILLAN

JOHN ADAIR

EFFECTIVE COMMUNICATION	0 330 34786 1	£6.99
EFFECTIVE TEAMBUILDING	0 330 29809 7	£6.99
EFFECTIVE MOTIVATION	0 330 34476 5	£6.99
EFFECTIVE DECISION MAKING	0 330 28748 6	£6.99
EFFECTIVE TIME MANAGEMENT	0 330 30229 9	£6.99
EFFECTIVE LEADERSHIP	0 330 30230 2	£6.99
EFFECTIVE INNOVATION	0 330 34475 7	£6.99

All Pan Macmillan titles can be ordered from our website,
www.panmacmillan.com, or from your local bookshop
and are also available by post from:

Bookpost, PO Box 29, Douglas, Isle of Man IM99 1BQ
Credit cards accepted. For details:
Telephone: 01624 677237
Fax: 01624 670923
E-mail: bookshop@enterprise.net
www.bookpost.co.uk

Free postage and packing in the United Kingdom

Prices shown above were correct at the time of going to press.
Pan Macmillan reserve the right to show new retail prices on covers
which may differ from those previously advertised in the text
or elsewhere.